# MEMORIZE THE STOICS!

KEVIN VOST

# MEMORIZE
# THE STOICS!

*The Ancient Art of Memory*
*Meets*
*The Timeless Art of Living*

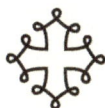

Angelico Press

For information, address:
Angelico Press, Ltd.
169 Monitor St.
Brooklyn, NY 11222
www.angelicopress.com

ppr   978-1-62138-829-6
cloth   978-1-62138-830-2
ebook   978-1-62138-831-9

Book and cover design
by Michael Schrauzer

# DEDICATION

To
James Bradley (Jamie) Vost

*"I believe that each one of us ought to try to leave broth-
ers rather than money to our children to give them
greater chances of blessings."*
Musonius Rufus (*Lecture 15*)


*and to*
Henry Dean Vost & Colin Fahy Vost

*"But it is a beautiful thing for a grandfather to be
conducted by the hands of his grandchildren, and to
be considered by them as deserving of every other
attention."*
Hierocles (from Stobaeus's *Florilegium*)

# CONTENTS

**INTRODUCTION:**
Keeping Stoic Lessons Ready at Hand and Ever in Mind . . . . . 1

**PART I:** How to Think like Epictetus
(and Memorize His *Handbook*) . . . . . . . . . . . . . . . . . . . .17
    Pillars of Stoic Freedom (1–10) . . . . . . . . . . . . . . . .19
    From Devastation to Invincibility (11–20) . . . . . . . . . .41
    From Death to Duties (21–30) . . . . . . . . . . . . . . . .57
    On Building One's Character—
        From Piety to Modesty (31–40) . . . . . . . . . . . . . .73
    Tending the Temple of the Body and Mind (41–50) . . . .85
    The Time to Begin Living Well
        is Now, by Zeus! (51–53) . . . . . . . . . . . . . . . . .99

**PART II:** Memorize Seneca's *Letters!* . . . . . . . . . . . . . 109
    Gaius Lucilius Junior, "You've got mail!" (1–10) . . . . . . 111
    From Rosy Cheeks to Consistent Hobgoblins (11–20) . . . 125
    From Selene to Socrates (21–30) . . . . . . . . . . . . . . 137
    From Sirens to Cicero (31–40) . . . . . . . . . . . . . . . 147
    From Succoring the Sacred Spirit to
        Suffering the Fool Within (41–50) . . . . . . . . . . . 157

**PART III:** Memorize Marcus's *Meditations!* . . . . . . . . . 173
    The Magnificent Seven Maxims of
        Emperor Marcus Aurelius . . . . . . . . . . . . . . . . 175

**PART IV:** How to Live Like a Stoic
in Heart, Mind, and Soul . . . . . . . . . . . . . . . . . . . . . 191
    How to Learn Stoic Sayings by Heart . . . . . . . . . . . 193
    How to Keep Key Stoic Concepts in Mind . . . . . . . . 201
    How to Feed Our Souls upon Stoic Tables . . . . . . . . 207
    Out from the Porch and into the World . . . . . . . . . 215

# KEEPING STOIC LESSONS READY AT HAND AND EVER IN MIND

*"Remember..."*
Epictetus[1]

*"And now for something completely different..."*
Monty Python

## FROM READY AT HAND TO EVER IN MIND

RRIAN OF NICOMEDIA (AD 89–160), THE ACCOM-plished student of the great Stoic Epictetus (AD 50–135), compiled the condensed *Enchiridion* (*Manual* or *Handbook*) from Epictetus's *Discourses* so that readers could have easy access to many of Epictetus's fundamental Stoic insights, keeping them always ready at hand when needed.[2] In the short 10th chapter of that *Handbook* Epictetus explains that whatever difficult life situations we face we need to ask ourselves what capacities we have developed to deal with them, calling into play our *self-control* when confronted with a beautiful body, our *endurance* to deal with hardship, or our *patience* if someone insults or abuses us. The lessons of that very *Handbook*, if studied, mastered, and internalized, can help us develop and display those and a host of other capacities or virtues.

In that same chapter, Epictetus instructs us to *remember* to turn to ourselves to activate these capacities and to habituate ourselves, to get used to doing this. Indeed, by my count, Epictetus uses words

---

1  Epictetus, *The Handbook (The Encheiridion)*, Nicholas P. White, trans. (Indianapolis, IN: Hackett, 1983), *Handbook* chapters 1, 2, 3, 10, 15, 17, 20, 32, 33, 36, 42, 46.

2  Indeed, in the size of a book that would easily fit in one's hand, or within a modern-day pocket. The aforementioned White translation is all of 35 pages with a shipping weight of 2.01 ounces!

1

translated into English as "remember," or "keep in mind," at least a dozen times in the 53 brief chapters of the *Handbook*.

In his *Discourses*, Epictetus reminds his students that sheep do not vomit up grass to show their shepherds how much they have eaten, but they chew and digest that grass and then produce wool and milk of their own. It is through *remembering* fundamental Stoic principles, and becoming habituated to using them in our own daily lives that we will produce the wool and milk of lives lived well, with a good flow, fulfilling through virtuous thoughts and deeds our capacities as rational and social human beings.

Within these pages, I will propose the use of a simple and effective memory method that can help us follow Epictetus's repeated exhortations to literally "remember," indeed, to *memorize* essential Stoic principles, and not only those of Epictetus. We will examine, employ, practice, and *master* ancient Greco-Roman memory techniques that help us can keep ancient Greco-Roman Stoic principles not only *ready at hand*, but *ever in mind.*

And bear well in mind, though the memory techniques and the Stoic principles are ancient indeed, they are every bit as practical, powerful, and useful in our time and place as they were in the days of the Greek agora and the Roman forum.

## A BOOK OF A VERY PARTICULAR SORT

THIS BOOK YOU HOLD IN YOUR HANDS IS OF A VERY PAR-ticular sort. The text and illustrations have been structured in such a way, that if you read slowly and carefully, look at the pictures, and follow the instructions, by the time you finish you will be able to name the key themes and lessons of seven golden maxims culled from the *Meditations* of Marcus Aurelius, all 53 chapters of Epictetus's *Handbook*, the first 50 of Seneca's *Letters to Lucilius* (and indeed all 124 of them for the stalwart souls who would care to go the extra mile). *And all of these in order, literally both forward and backward!* (For example, not only will you be able to recite the key idea of each *Handbook* chapter from 1 to 53 in order, you could recite them backward from 53 back down to 1, if for some reason you wanted to. These methods place everything you remember in its precisely proper place.)

You will also be shown how to use specialized memory skills to recall the exact wording of some inspiring Stoic quotations well worth remembering verbatim, to learn and recall the pronunciations and meanings of over twenty Greek and Latin terms essential to Stoic thought, and to comprehend and recall some key Stoic processes and schemata, from Epictetus's three disciplines (and philosopher Pierre Hadot's nine concepts that flow from them), to the ABC model of cognitive psychotherapy Albert Ellis built upon Stoic foundations.

*Now, how is it possible that you will come to remember so much so thoroughly?* The cornerstone in the construction of this book is a mnemonic (memory-aiding) system built into its very foundation, floors, walls, ceilings, and interior decoration. (You'll see in Chapter 1 why I use the architectural metaphor.)

To make a long story short, in 1990 I completed a Master's thesis in Psychology entitled "Memory Strategy Instruction and the Internalization of Higher Psychological Processes in Adolescence." (That I can recall that title from memory should lend credence to the power of these memory techniques.)

Therein I studied the popular, ancient, and scientific literature on memory strategies as employed with children, adolescents, college students (perennial research guinea pig favorites) and adults of all ages. Such techniques were often most effective. Indeed, in one study 1st and 2nd graders taught the techniques could recall new material like vocabulary words better than 5th and 6th grade control subjects who were not taught the techniques. In another study, middle school students who were taught the methods outperformed high school juniors and seniors who were not. For students of the same age, those taught the memory methods often recalled 100% more material than their peers who were not.

Now, if I might be allowed to toss out a few anecdotes upon a pile of experimental studies, in the late 1970s at a library book sale I chanced upon a little book published in 1958. No one was reading it anymore so the library was discarding it.[3] I can certainly say it was the most profitable quarter I ever spent! I found the book's simple techniques worked amazingly well for me, making memorization for college courses a joy and a breeze and even aiding me decades later in 1997 when taking the Examination for Practice of Professional Psychology (EPPP), to obtain the highest score in the state that year and to set my own school's all-time record.

---

3   O. W. "Bill Hayes," *Your Memory: Speedway to Success in Earning, Learning, and Living* (New York, NY: Exposition Press, 1958).

Not only did these memory techniques lead to my Master's thesis as already mentioned, I also employed them successfully during my Doctoral training in Clinical Neuropsychology at the Southern Illinois University Center for Alzheimer's Research and Treatment, Memory and Aging Network in the mid-1990s. One memorable man with whom I worked had undergone surgery for uncontrollable seizures in which tissue from his left hippocampus was surgically removed. Though he had worked as an attorney and was a bright man who still had an IQ of 125 (top 5% of the population) when I tested him, his verbal memory capacities were so severely impaired that he was disabled from full-time employment.

In one simple test of memory involving a list of 15 words we would repeat a full eight times to patients and research subjects, most people without brain damage or dementia would recall at least 8 or 9 of those words when asked about them without forewarning half an hour after the test. He recalled a full *zero*.[4]

In most people (even left-handers) the left hemisphere of the brain is dominant for processing of verbal material while the right side is dominant for visual-spatial material. This man's right cerebral hemisphere, including the right hippocampus, was completely intact. In tests of visual memory, for things like different shapes and colors, he was completely normal, in fact, above normal, in that his visual memory was commensurate with his high IQ.

Now, my neuropsychology mentor knew of my work in mnemonics and suggested I test them with this patient, since one thing these techniques do is encode and store *verbal* information in *visual* form through the use of visual imagery. Perhaps this man's visual memory strength could be used to compensate for his verbal memory weakness. So, how did it go?

Well, when I trained him for one session using the main method of this book he said he was getting tired so we practiced only *three* times with the memory method as opposed to the *eight* trials that are part of the standard test. Still, he recalled not *zero*, but *nine* words half an hour later. My psychology mentor presented this intervention at a conference on rehabilitation of brain damage in Washington, DC. Alas, the patient grew displeased with his

---

4  This was the *second* worst performance I ever encountered. How so? At least he remembered we had done the word test. Another man, a victim of a severe electrical shock, reported he did not recall having repeated any words!

neurologist, switched medical centers, and we were unable to work with him any further.

Later, in 2006, I wrote *Memorize the Faith!*, a book that applied these same memory methods to Catholic catechetical material, such as how to memorize the 10 Commandments or the names of all 73 books of the Bible. It was received so well that *Memorize the Reasons!* on apologetics, *Memorize the Mass!*, and *Memorize the Latin Mass!* followed in years to come. Personal emails and electronic bookseller reader reviews confirmed that these memory methods *work* (and indeed, that many people find them *fun* as well).

Now, part of the reason I first applied these materials to Catholic subject matter was that St. Thomas Aquinas, the Church's premier theologian, and St. Albert the Great, his brilliant mentor, had actually studied, written about, used, and strongly endorsed these ancient memory methods invented by ancient Greeks and preserved for the Western world through the Latin works of Marcus Tullius Cicero (106–43 BC) and others. Oddly enough, I had never seen the methods used in modern Catholic works.

The situation is somewhat similar for the world of Stoicism. I had not seen the ancient memory methods explicitly applied to Stoic teaching, so when *Memorize the Faith!* was published in 2006 I began taking notes for *Memorize Epictetus!* I got busy with other projects and never wrote it—until now. Of course, now we will memorize Epictetus—and more!

There are also some interesting Stoic connections to the memory methods as well. For example, one of our greatest external sources on the Stoics is Cicero, the same man from whom medieval philosophers and theologians learned about the ancient art of memory. Furthermore, Seneca's own father was described as a prodigy of memorization, and our own Stoic Seneca the Younger is cited multiple times in modern texts on the history of these memory techniques. (I'll provide some details in our Part II on Seneca.)

To conclude this section, please know that this is a book of a very particular sort because *it is a fully-guided and illustrated tutorial, showing you exactly how to apply these memory methods to fundamental Stoic texts.* I'll leave it up to you to let me know how it works out for you, but before we get down to business, let's look at these methods from the perspective of Stoic *spiritual exercises* and dig just a bit deeper into their intriguing origins.

## SOMETHING DIFFERENT:
## MEMORY TRAINING AS SPIRITUAL EXERCISE
## (AND A PART OF PRUDENCE)

MENTAL OR SPIRITUAL EXERCISES HAVE LONG BEEN ESSEN-
tial to Stoicism, to not merely understand it as a philosophical system, but to employ it as an art of living. Marcus Aurelius's *Meditations*
have been a prime example of Stoic spiritual exercises practiced
through *writing* notes to oneself. Many of Aurelius's exercises involve
powerfully focused use of one's memory and imagination, from seeing things from a historical perspective and recalling how emperors
from the distant past and all the people who lived in their time
are no more, to mentally viewing the whole of the earth from a
perspective of one high above it.

Now, the memory method I will describe is also heavily dependent upon the power of imagination, and in ancient texts, it is
called an "inner writing." This method is certainly nothing new,
usually being attributed, as it was by Cicero, to a discovery and
invention by Simonides of Ceos (c. 556–468 BC). Many readers have
probably encountered it as the "method of loci" or "memory palace"
technique, and some may see it as a gimmick of sorts to produce
ostensibly impressive memory feats of questionable utility. Some
experts, for example, have used the method to recall the digits of
*pi*, with a current world record of 100,000 digits. Further, some
modern writers seem to give the impression that they invented
the techniques themselves, rather than letting the at least *2,500-
year-old* cat of its origins out of the bag.

As to the "completely different" aspect of this ages-old method,
I don't ever recall seeing it suggested or applied as a form of Stoic
spiritual exercise, whereby one can take Epictetus's advice quite
literally and train oneself to systematically *remember* key Stoic
principles, not merely to echo them back like a parrot, but to
hold them in mind so as to digest them like a lamb and eventually
produce some grade A milk and wool.

Musonius Rufus (AD c. 25–c. 100), Epictetus's great teacher and
mentor, strongly emphasized (along with many other Stoics) the
four cardinal virtues of *sophrosyne, andreia, phronesis,* and *dikaio-
syne* (or temperance, courage, prudence, and justice). Interestingly,
thinkers including Cicero in the 1st century BC, and Saints Albert

the Great and Thomas Aquinas in the 13th century AD, have argued that *memory itself* is an essential "part" of the virtue of *phronesis* or prudence, the practical wisdom we use to make the best choices in the acts of our daily lives.

How so? Cicero described three essential "parts" or allied capacities of prudence as *memory, understanding,* and *foresight,* for to conceive of and achieve virtuous goals in the *future* (requiring *foresight*), we must act in the *present* (applying our powers of *understanding* to current situations), guided by the lessons we have learned in the *past* (retained through *memory*).

Furthermore, Cicero and St. Albert considered *memory* the *most important part* of prudence. Why? According to St. Albert: "We say that of all those things that point toward ethical wisdom, the most necessary is a trained memory, because from past events we are guided in the present and the future, and not from the converse."[5] Note too that Albert refers to a "trained" memory, and he also states elsewhere that the method described by "Tully" (Cicero) is the best. This is the age-old method of *loci* or locations that involves the use of visual imagery in a systematic order.

The oldest extant book on the subject, the *Rhetorica ad Herennium,* dates from the mid-80s BC and was long attributed to Cicero. Though modern scholars do not believe Cicero wrote it, its method is also discussed in Cicero's authentic *De Inventione,* which includes the fascinating story of how Simonides of Ceos (c. 556–468 BC) came to invent it. Though a few different versions have come down to us, here is the gist of the story.

## THE HONEY-TONGUED GREEK ORATOR
## GIVES BIRTH TO THE ART OF MEMORY

A WEALTHY MAN OF THESSALY NAMED SCOPAS INVITED Simonides (sometimes called Simonides Melicus or "honey-tongued" due to his melodious voice) to give an oration at a banquet one evening. Simonides acknowledged his thanks to Scopas and during the recitation of a poem honoring a boxer he also expressed thanks to the twin gods Castor and Pollux who were popularly considered

---

5   From *De Bono (On the Good),* cited in Mary Carruthers, *The Book of Memory: A Study of Memory in Medieval Culture* (New York, NY: Cambridge University Press, 1990), 275.

7

patrons of athletes. Well, during a break, the ungracious Scopas told Simonides that since he thanked him *and* Castor and Pollux as well, he would pay him only *half* his fee and that he could collect the other half from Castor and Pollux!

A short while later, Simonides was told that two young men had come to a door and said he was needed for an emergency. As Simonides left the building, he saw the young men far down the street and ran after them. He never could catch them and eventually returned to the building, after what amount to an extended wild goose chase. While he was away, however, the roof of the building had collapsed. So complete was the destruction that the bodies of the diners were crushed beyond recognition. Simonides discovered, to his surprise, that from his perspective as orator he could recall the visual image of where every person reclined and could identify them all. As the story goes, who were those two young men? Bingo! Castor and Pollux! And they paid him not only by saving his life but by leading to his invention of the methods of "artificial memory."

Simonides discovered through this incident the power of *visual impressions* and of *orderly arrangement* as aids to the natural memory. Further, he soon came to realize that we do not need to actually *see* orderly arrangements of visual information to enhance our memory powers. Indeed, we need merely *imagine* them. This systematic use of visual images and a series of locations became the gist of "artificial memory," or "the art of memory," which employs our powers of imaginative visualization, reason, and language capacities to perfect our natural, non-strategic memory capacities. Indeed, viewed from a Stoic perspective, such memory methods could entail a revised impression of our own memory capacities, moving them from what we might have considered outside of our control to something within our control, for some to a surprising extent.

## THE MEDIEVAL SCHOLASTIC PHILOSOPHER
## BOILS IT DOWN TO FOUR KEY POINTS

OVER 1,700 YEARS LATER, THOMAS AQUINAS (A PHILOSOPHER who cites Seneca dozens of times in his masterwork, the *Summa Theologica*) summarized the gist of this method into four essential elements, which are the following:

1. *visual images,*
2. a system of *orderly arrangement,*
3. focused *concentration,* and
4. rehearsal or *repetition.*[6]

We already know the power of the 3rd and 4th elements since they are essential to most tasks employing natural memory, and they continue to play an important role when employing the art of memory. Thomas also explained (borrowing much of his cognitive psychology from Aristotle) that *visual* images should be used because all of our knowledge begins with information that comes in from our senses and visual images tend to be most powerful and memorable for most people. Further, he pointed out that even abstract or "spiritual" information is best held in memory when it is represented by a concrete, "corporeal" image that is easily pictured in the mind's eye. Indeed, he also noted that we should make such memory images strange and unusual since we encounter so much information every day that we tend to forget what is mundane or routine.

As for orderly arrangement, among the possible ordered location systems mentioned in the ancient *Ad Herennium* itself, our most ancient book on the art of memory, the first one mentioned is that of a *house.* You will encounter such a memory house in our very next section. Further, as you make yourself at home in its rooms throughout the course of this book, you will encounter, remember, ponder, and prepare to *live* a treasure house of Stoic wisdom within its walls.

So, rather than just *talk about* this memory method, let's get in a quick preview, and *do it* together, right now.

## WELCOME TO THE HOUSE OF MEMORY

PLEASE NOTE THAT IN EACH OF OUR CHAPTERS WE WILL first *memorize* a series of locations and their associated images and then I'll explain what they *mean.* This will enhance the dramatic effect, make the memory exercise a little more fun, and hopefully arouse your interest to find out what serious lessons for life the mnemonic shenanigans are helping us lock in our minds. So, please set your powers of imagination and concentration on maximum

---

6   Condensed from the *Summa Theologica,* IIa-IIae, 49, 1, "Whether Memory is a Part of Prudence?"

and I'll guide you through the entrance way both to our house of memory and to Epictetus's *Handbook*.

I invite you to imagine you've arrived at my home, a rather sprawling ranch style house nestled between mature maples and oaks. You ring the bell, the *front door* opens, and what do you see but a modern jet fighter's cockpit, complete with two very daunting looking control panels.

You decide to step into the cockpit in the entrance way, since there is a welcoming little *door mat* right inside the door, but as you step in, a little man in a white suit tugs on your shirt, points to a crowned king right next to him, and calls out with an accent at the top of his lungs "Dee Sire!"

Pondering your possible exit, you look out a *glass panel* next to the front door and spy in the front yard a little child crying over a broken mug. (You hope to yourself that he or someone else does not step on the jagged shards.)

Looking back into the foyer, you notice a *picture on the wall* on the other side of the door. It's a scene from a Roman bath, and believe it or not, watery bubbles are oozing from it down the wall.

On the adjacent wall, oddly enough, you observe a locked *gun rack*, and before it stands old Socrates himself, plucking out not guns, but leaves with large letter "B's" on them.

Smack dab in the *center of the foyer* you are shocked to see a thoroughbred horse trampling on a broken mirror.

As you glance up toward a *chandelier* overhead, you notice it has a ship's wheel at its front and a salty sea captain behind it, sailing his way through the entranceway.

Turning to the right wall you spy a mounted *mirror,* but you see not your own reflection, but a birthday cake brimming over with candles.

Below the mirror on a small *cushioned bench* sits Yoda of Star Wars fame. He points to a hirsute professional athlete seated next to him, and proclaims to you, "Pro hairy, he is!"

Finally, you spy a little *drawer in the bench*, and when you pull it open, out pops the cartoon superhero He-Man. He raises his sword aloft and calls out to you (as he is wont to do), "I have the power!"

So, regarding our first little memory tour, I surmise you might be wondering, if I might recall a favorite line of my own no nonsense, farm-raised mother, "What's that got to do with the price of beans?"

That's a fair enough question. Just what did our little memory excursion have to do with memorizing the lessons of Epictetus's *Handbook*?

Well, I know I have some explaining to do, so let's get down to business. First, let's review that scene again. Can you picture the foyer in your imagination? Here are the locations: ❶ the front door, ❷ the doormat, ❸ the glass panel next to the door, ❹ the picture on the wall, ❺ the gun rack, ❻ the center of the foyer, ❼ the chandelier overhead, ❽ the mirror on the wall, ❾ the bench under the mirror, and ❿ the drawers in the bench.

Next, let's look at the strange visual images associated with those locations. When you open the door you see a *cockpit full of controls*. The mat under your feet contains a small man pointing to a king and calling out *"Dee Sire!"* Peering through the glass panel you see *the child crying over a broken mug*. Next, how strange that the picture of the *Roman bubble bath* is dripping down the wall! On the wall adjacent to that picture was a gun rack, and how nice it was to see *Socrates* plucking out *"B leaves,"* rather than guns. In the center of the foyer was that *horse trampling on a mirror*. Right over our heads, in the chandelier, was a *sea captain* sailing through the foyer. In the mirror on the wall we saw the image of that *birthday cake with candles*. Upon the cushioned bench a sat a hairy athlete and *Yoda* proclaimed, *"Pro hairy, he is!"* Finally, out from the drawer in the bench popped *He-Man* himself, boldly declaring, *"I have the power!"* Let's lay this out:

| LOCATION | IMAGE |
|---|---|
| ❶ FRONT DOOR | *Jet fighter control panel* |
| ❷ DOOR MAT | *"Dee sire!"* |
| ❸ GLASS PANEL | *Child crying over broken jug* |
| ❹ PORTRAIT ON BACK WALL | *Roman bubble bath* |
| ❺ GUN RACK | *Socrates with "B" leaves* |
| ❻ CENTER OF FOYER | *Horse tramples mirror* |
| ❼ CHANDELIER | *Sea captain* |
| ❽ MIRROR ON WALL | *Birthday cake with candles* |
| ❾ CUSHIONED BENCH | *Yoda:"Pro hairy, he is!"* |
| ❿ DRAWER IN BENCH | *He-Man:"I have the power!"* |

So far, so good? If you now know these ten locations and their associated images, that's great! If not, repeat them a few times until you have them, until you can *picture them vividly in your mind's eye*. Got them? Good. If you do, you're very close to knowing and retaining one fundamental lesson from each of the first 10 chapters of Epictetus's *Handbook*, in order. Let's see how close we are.

Let's recall from our introduction how Thomas Aquinas said we should memorize even *spiritual principles* by using *concrete visual images* and that we will be more likely to recall our images if they are *strange or unusual*. This is precisely what we have just done together. Each of those strange visual images was used to represent and remind us of one of the lessons in the first ten chapters of Epictetus's *Handbook*.

The jet fighter's *control* panel represents the famous Stoic principle of the *"dichotomy of control"* presented in the *Handbook*'s first chapter. (And indeed, there is a specific reason I choose a fighter jet, as you will see when we examine each of Epictetus's chapters one-by-one in this book's next chapter.) The small man calling out *"Dee Sire!"* will serve to remind us of the *"discipline of desire"* addressed in the *Handbook*, no. 2. You see, our visual images can be based on something as simple as a homonym or a word or words that sound reasonably similar to whatever we want to remember. (Readers old enough to recall the "Fantasy Island" TV show from the 1970s will know exactly what inspired this image for me!) The *child crying over the broken mug* will remind us that in the third chapter Epictetus teaches us a lesson about *remembering the nature of things* starting with the example of *a broken mug*.

Here's a quick preview of the rest of the chapter's images—and lessons, in the form of a summary chart:

| HANDBOOK CHAPTER/LOCATION | MNEMONIC IMAGE | HANDBOOK LESSON |
|---|---|---|
| ❶ FRONT DOOR | *Jet fighter control panel* | Dichotomy of control |
| ❷ DOOR MAT | *"Dee Sire!"* | Discipline of desire |
| ❸ GLASS PANEL | *Child crying over broken pot* | Remember the nature of things |
| ❹ PORTRAIT ON BACK WALL | *Roman bubble bath* | *Premeditatio malorum* |

| **5** GUN RACK | *Socrates with "B" leaves* | Beliefs mediate emotions |
|---|---|---|
| **6** CENTER OF FOYER | *Horse tramples mirror* | Horse sense over vanity |
| **7** CHANDELIER | *Sea captain* | The shortness of life |
| **8** MIRROR ON WALL | *Birthday cake candles* | How to fulfill your wishes |
| **9** CUSHIONED BENCH | *Yoda:"Pro hairy, he is!"* | Prohairesis rules! |
| **10** DRAWER IN BENCH | *He Man: "I have the power!"* | We have many powers |

Every silly image we'll employ throughout this book will serve to help us remember a serious Stoic lesson. As we progress through our commentary sections (the heart and the bulk of the text) I will make these connections crystal clear so you will both understand and remember them.

Oh, and here is one more thing worth remembering before we dip into the *Handbook* itself. The *location* systems we use serve as a mental *notepad* or word processing *template* if you will, while the *images* serve as our *ink* or our *keystrokes* to write down in our memories whatever we desire. Once you have learned a particular location system, like this foyer and the four other rooms in the chapters to come you can use them again and again and again for all kinds of new information. You could use them for something as mundane as your grocery list.

Okay, so you open the front door and are greeted by a giant banana. You trip over a sack of potatoes sitting on the doormat, and so on. Oh, but your list is different every week? No problem. Recall that *repetition* is one of the four things (along with images, and ordering system, and concentration) we employ to perfect our memory powers. In fact, some ancient Latin speakers used to like to say *"repetitio mater memoriae,"* "repetition is the mother of memory." Lists that we do not rehearse, like last week's grocery list, will fade away on their own, while things worth repeating, like profound Stoic lessons, will become more deeply engraved in our hearts the more we repeat and practice them.

I'll sprinkle in more information on just how these memory methods work and on how they can be adapted for other uses as we move throughout the book. Now is the time, however, to preview just what we are going to *memorize, contemplate,* and *put into practice* in the pages that follow.

## STOIC LESSONS HOUSED IN THIS BOOK

IN PART I WE WILL LEARN HOW TO MEMORIZE AT LEAST ONE key theme and lesson from all 53 of the brief chapters of Epictetus's *Handbook*. Indeed, when we have finished, you will know them literally backwards and forwards. Here is the general tripartite game plan within each of our six chapters.

1. First, we will take a guided *memory tour*, usually for ten of his chapters.
2. Next, we will go through each of his chapters and with a *summary* of his own words.
3. Finally, after each chapter's summary we will *contemplate* the chapter's lessons, at times examining how it compares to lessons in Epictetus's *Discourses*, to lessons from other Stoics or philosophers of other schools, to pertinent passages in the Bible, to the lessons of prominent thinkers, leaders, and theologians since Epictetus's time, with a special emphasis on how this Stoic sage's timeless lessons for humanity have predated and inspired many major modern theories of general human psychology, psychiatry, and the most effective of current philosophical and psychological therapies.

The goal of our tripartite scheme will be to come to know, understand, and remember these lessons so well that they will become housed in our own souls and displayed in our own thoughts, words, and deeds.

Part II houses the first 50 of Seneca's remarkable 124 *Letters to Lucilius*. We will apply our same tripartite scheme to remember, ponder, and strive to apply 50 gems of Senecan Stoic wisdom, from an incredible writer as polished and elegant as Epictetus is blunt and to the point! Oh yes, and you will also be given instructions on how to remember the gist of *all 124* letters with additional assistance, should you be inclined to do so.

In Part III our gaze turns to the timeless musings of Emperor Marcus Aurelius. To give our memory muscles a bit of a rest we will lock in our memories a mere seven "golden maxims" from his *Meditations*. You'll have to wait until Part III to see which maxims I mean (unless you are inclined to skip ahead). Furthermore, to add to your artistry in the art of memory, we will forgo the memory house for this part and I'll introduce a new memory system. While you might think at first that I'm horsing around, I think that you will find that the method works just as well (as it should, since it's fit for a king).

In Part IV we'll tie up some loose mnemonic and Stoic ends. In its first chapter we'll learn how to memorize verbatim a few important and most memorable sayings from two prominent Stoics. The Stoics said some things so well that it is well worth remembering every single word!

Realizing the some of the most fundamental concepts of the ancient Stoics may be all Greek (or Latin) to you, next we will examine a list of 20 key concepts as first presented in the original Greek or Latin, along with an English translation. But recall, if you will, that this book is about the art of memory too, so we will also introduce you to the "keyword method" of memory, a technique designed to help people remember both the *pronunciation* and the *meaning* of foreign vocabulary words. Indeed, in my aforementioned master's thesis on memory, most of the studies employed just this method. I think you will find it most *chrisimos* and *utilis!*[7]

Some ancient memory masters also stressed the benefits of memorizing materials as they appear in the pages of books. Perhaps this is why the medieval scribes so carefully and artfully "illuminated" sacred books like the gorgeous "Book of Kells" of the Gospels housed at the Trinity College Library in Dublin. While this book in your hands is not "illuminated" in living colors, it is indeed illustrated. In our last chapter though, I will provide in the form of *tables* a few important Stoic concepts and schemes, like Epictetus's and Aurelius's "three disciplines" and Albert Ellis's ABC model of emotions.

So, it is time to depart from this introduction and to re-enter a modern house of memory, full to the rafters with ancient Stoic wisdom! I will meet you again at the front door at the beginning of chapter 1.

---

7   *Chrisimos* is one of the Greek words for "useful," "practical," or "helpful." Want to remember that? Just picture a *Christmas tree* with a large *O* decoration on top *helping* you wrap a present. Christmas sounds a lot like *chrisimos* and the O on top is to you remind you that it ends with an "o" sound, not "a." The fact that the tree is *helping* you locks in the meaning of helpful or useful. As for *utilis*, the Latin word for "useful" is pretty simple to remember because it forms the base of our English words utility and utilize, and a bit more remotely, of "useful" itself. If you want a mnemonic aid, imagine our "chrisimos" tree also pointing to the singer Mel Tillis and declaring "You Tillis!" These are previews of the keyword method, by the way. Stay tuned for Chapter 14 for all the details.

# PART I

# How to Think
# like Epictetus
# (and Memorize
# His Handbook)

*"It is easy, indeed, to observe that Plato is found only in the hands of those who profess to be literary men; while Epictetus is admired by persons of ordinary capacity, who have a desire to be benefited, and who perceive the improvement which may be derived from his writings."*
Origen, *Contra Celsum*, VI, 2

*"He was a man who relied wholly upon himself and God, but not on Fortune. In origin low and servile, in body lame and feeble, and in mind most exalted, and brilliant among the lights of every age.... There is no one who better influences and shapes a good mind. I never read that old man without a stirring of my soul within me, and, as with Homer, I think more of him each time I re-read him, for he seems always new; and even after I have returned to him I feel that I ought to return to him once more."*
Justus Lipsius on Epictetus[1]

---

1   16th-century Flemish author of *On Constancy in Times of Public Evil* (cited in Oldfather, v. 1, xxix).

# CHAPTER 1

# PILLARS OF STOIC FREEDOM
### (Handbook *Chapters 1-10*)

*"What upsets people is not things themselves, but their judgments about things."*

Handbook Ch. 5

## MEMORY TOUR:
### *HANDBOOK* CHAPTERS 1–10

O
UR INTRODUCTION ALREADY PROVIDED A MEM-
ory tour of the foyer housing the first ten chapters of the
*Handbook.* You will recall as well that *repetition* was one of
the four things said to be needed to perfect our memories (along
with *visual images,* an *ordering system,* and good old *concentration*).
Indeed, we saw that ancient and medieval Latin memory masters
were often fond of declaring that *"repetitio mater memoriae"* ("repetition is the mother of memory"). Therefore, I'm going to repeat
that memory tour one more time, albeit much more briefly.

Since you are probably new to this memory method (at least for
its use in memorizing Stoic lessons), I presented our first memory
tour in the introduction in a leisurely, multi-step fashion over the
course of several pages. Now that you pretty much know what
we're up to, the memory tours in this and in subsequent chapters
will cut to the chase and take up no more than one page of text
and one more for the summary chart. Let's go!

### SECOND REHEARSE, BRIEFER THAN THE FIRST

YOU RANG THE BELL, THE FRONT DOOR (LOCATION ❶)
opened, and what did you see but a modern jet fighter's cockpit,
complete with two *control panels.* You decided to step into the cockpit in the entrance way, since there was a welcoming little door
mat ❷ right inside the door, but as you stepped in a little man

19

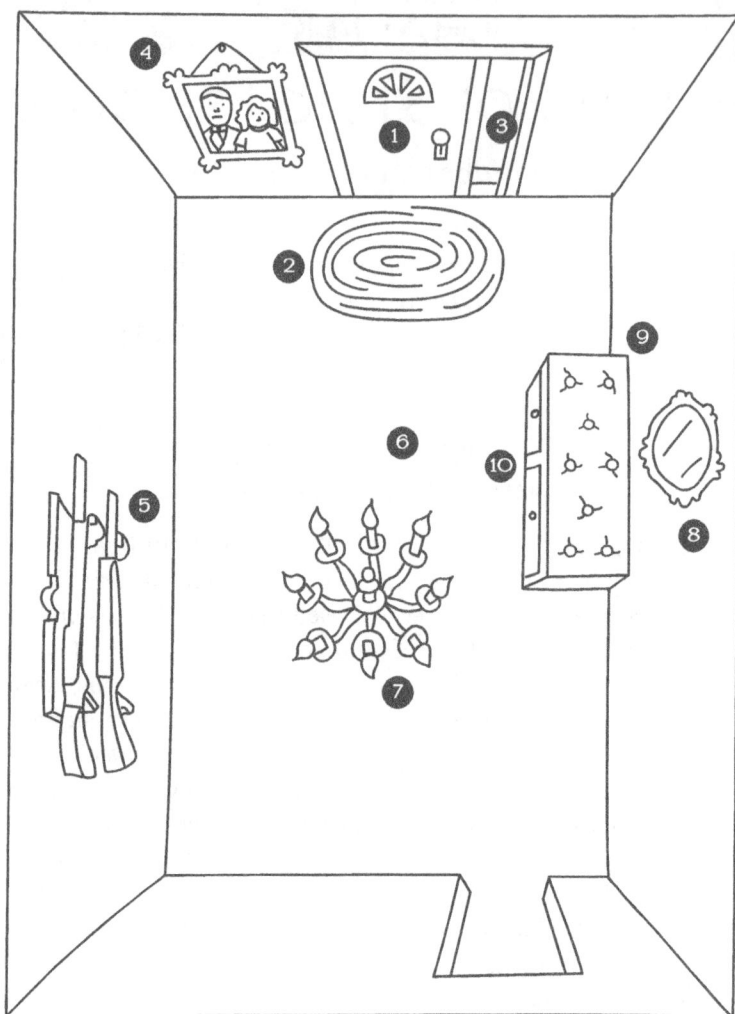

in a white suit pointed to a crowned king right next to him, and called out *"Dee Sire!"* Pondering your possible exit, you looked out a glass panel ❸ next to the front door and spied in the front yard a little *child crying over a broken mug.* Looking back into the foyer, you noticed a picture on the wall ❹ on the other side of the door. It was a scene from a *Roman bath* with sudsy *bubbles* oozing down the wall. On the adjacent wall, you observed a locked gun rack ❺, and before it stood old *Socrates* himself, plucking out not guns, but *leaves* with large letter *"B's"* on them.

Smack dab in the center of the foyer ❻ you were shocked to see a thoroughbred *horse* trampling on a *broken mirror*. As you glanced up toward a chandelier ❼ overhead, you noticed a salty *sea captain* sailing his way through the entranceway. Turning to the right wall ❽ you spied a mounted mirror, and saw not your own reflection, but a *birthday cake* brimming over with *candles*. Below the mirror on a small cushioned ❾ bench sat *Yoda* pointed to a hairy *pro athlete* as he called out to you, *"Pro hairy, he is!"* Finally, you spotted a little drawer in the bench ❿, and out popped *He-Man*, raising his sword aloft and calling out to you, *"I have the power!"*

So, there we went again. Do you have all ten locations and images down now? (Below is the chart one more time.) If you do, thank you for your diligence. If you don't, don't forget *"repetitio mater memoriae."* Now, let's get down to business to find out why we worked our left and right hippocampi so hard!

| HANDBOOK CHAPTER/LOCATION | MNEMONIC IMAGE | HANDBOOK LESSON |
|---|---|---|
| ❶ FRONT DOOR | *Jet fighter control panel* | Dichotomy of control |
| ❷ DOOR MAT | *"Dee Sire!"* | Discipline of desire |
| ❸ GLASS PANEL | *Child crying over broken pot* | Remember the nature of things |
| ❹ PORTRAIT ON BACK WALL | *Roman bubble bath* | Premeditatio malorum |
| ❺ GUN RACK | *Socrates with "B" leaves* | Beliefs mediate emotions |
| ❻ CENTER OF FOYER | *Horse tramples mirror* | Horse sense over vanity |
| ❼ CHANDELIER | *Sea captain* | The shortness of life |
| ❽ MIRROR ON WALL | *Birthday cake candles* | How to fulfill your wishes |
| ❾ CUSHIONED BENCH | *Yoda: "Pro hairy, he is!"* | Prohairesis rules! |
| ❿ DRAWER IN BENCH | *He Man: "I have the power!"* | We have many powers |

## THE LESSONS BEHIND THE IMAGES:
## PILLARS OF STOIC FREEDOM
## (*HANDBOOK* SUMMARIES CHAPTERS 1–10)

**①** *"Some things are under our control, while other things are not under our control."* [1] We can control things like our beliefs, choices, desires, and aversions which are of our own doing. We cannot control things like our own bodies, possessions, reputation, and political power which are not completely within our own powers. If you treat things that are up to others as if they are up to you, you make yourself a slave to them. You'll whimper and whine, blaming both gods and men when things don't turn out how you'd like. If you always remember what you can control and what you cannot, and set your sights on what you can control, no one will be able to coerce you or hinder you, you will blame no one, accuse no one, and do nothing against your will. You will be raised above harm because you will always recognize that those inner things that you can control cannot be taken from you. So then, if you encounter what appears to be an evil event say to it that it is merely an impression, which you will examine according to our rule. If it concerns something that is not under your control, tell it that it is nothing to you! Ω [2]

THE VERY FIRST LESSON IN EPICTETUS'S *HANDBOOK* IS often referred to as "the dichotomy of control," the recognition of the strict distinction between what is *"eph' hêmin,"* "up to us," and *"ouk eph' hêmin,"* "not up to us." *The first key to freedom of the soul is to train oneself to know the difference.*

Epictetus's Greek is sometimes translated as "in our power," and "not in our power," or as "in our control," and "not in our control." I went with the "control" translation to help us remember the dichotomy of control concept. Further, the memory image of the *control* panel within a jet fighter's cockpit is in honor of James Bond Stockdale, a famous modern Stoic who used the lessons of

---

1 W. A. Oldfather (trans.), *Epictetus: Discourses Books III-IV, The Encheiridion* (Cambridge, MA: Harvard University Press, 2000), 483. Italics added for emphasis. (First published in 1928. Volume One includes introductory material and Books I–II of the *Encheiridion*. Further references to the set will specify Oldfather, v. 1. or v. 2.)

2 *Handbook* chapter summaries, written primarily in my own words based on the Greek and on multiple English translations, will conclude with the Greek symbol for omega, Ω, "the end," so you can tell where the summary ends and where my commentary begins.

Epictetus to preserve his dignity and sanity during almost eight years in a North Vietnamese prison camp.[3]

So what exactly *is* under our control? The things of our intellects and wills, things like our opinions, thoughts, beliefs, judgments, and the choices we make, including the pursuit of what is good and the avoidance of what is bad.[4] What is *not* under our control? Epictetus includes things like possessions (which might be stolen or taxed away), reputation (we can't control what others think of us), and political offices (we can't force a person to vote for us or appoint us to a position).

The *first* thing he mentions, however, is the thing closest to each us, that of our very *bodies*. James Stockdale experienced this truth in a way that hopefully few of us ever will. As a prisoner of war he could not control where he took his body, what he ate, or even whether or not he could preserve it from torture.

Still, some readers might object to a strict dichotomy that places our bodies outside our control. After all, if the motor strips in my left and right cerebral cortexes were not under my voluntary control, I would not be typing these words, and if you could not control your eye saccades, you would not be reading them.

Further, a lifelong bodybuilder or fitness enthusiast with decades of intense training and closely monitored dietary practices might bristle at the idea that he or she had no more control over his or her hard-won physique than the typical overweight couch potato! Clearly, we need to examine this idea a little more closely.

Consider that people who try to properly care for their bodies *desire* health and fitness, invest time in *learning* and *thinking* about proper exercise and nutrition, make *choices,* and *practice behaviors* most likely conducive to robust fitness. Those kinds of thoughts,

---

3 After his jet fighter was hit by enemy fire, and as he parachuted down to earth in 1965, Stockdale whispered to himself: "Five years down there, at least. I'm leaving the world of technology and entering the world of Epictetus." If it was within his power to embrace the world of Epictetus in a prisoner of war camp, it should be well within our power to embrace it regardless of our station in life. The quotation is from Jim Stockdale, *Thoughts of a Philosophical Fighter Pilot* (Stanford, CA: Hoover Institution Press, 1995), 189.

4 Aversions to things like excessive disturbing emotions or vice—our own immoral, vicious behaviors, are under our control. Further, as we will examine in due course, while our *intentions* to obtain good things and avoid evil things are in our control, whether or not we *actually obtain them* may well depend on events outside of our control.

choices, and behaviors are indeed within their control, yet their bodies themselves and the *outcomes* of those activities are certainly not completely within their powers. The healthiest person in the world can be run over by a truck or develop a cancer or neurological disease due to genetic or environmental factors completely contrary to her will and outside of her control.

As an aspiring Mr. Universe wannabe in my teens, I learned this hard but true lesson from a philosophical bodybuilder named Mike Mentzer, the first man to win the Mr. Universe contest with a perfect score. My workout buddy and I drove down to St. Louis to attend one of his seminars back in 1978.[5] In a most memorable moment Mentzer asked if the audience wanted to know the secret to becoming a world class bodybuilder. (We salivated like Pavlov's dogs, most willing to work out for eight hours per day or even drink quarts of motor oil, if that's what it took!) What a great disappointment ensued when he revealed the secret: "If you want to be a word class bodybuilder, you've got to choose the right parents!" *Choose the right parents!* Now how were we going to do that?

Mentzer was correct, of course. Any healthy person can improve their muscularity and physical appearance through proper exercise and nutrition, but to be among the best in the world, factors like the width of the bones of one's clavicles (the wider the better) and the width of the bones of one's hips (best to be narrow to produce the famous V-shaped torso) are inherited traits that cannot be altered by training. The same goes for the length of one's muscle bellies. Some people have very long biceps muscles, for example, that attach to the tendons right at the crook of the elbow, while other people have shorter muscle bellies that attach to the tendons further up the arm producing an unbridgeable gap. We can improve whatever genetic potentials we might have, but only within the limits of the individual genetics we have inherited.

Our bodies are not entirely within our own control the way that our *thoughts* and our *choices* are. If we are to strive to think like a Stoic, to live a happier, more tranquil, more productive life, while building the kind of character best suited to serve our fellow man (which includes our fellow woman, of course!), Epictetus tells us

---

5   Indeed, I would find decades later in *High-Intensity Training the Mike Mentzer Way* by Mentzer with John Little (2003) that my buddy Joe and I can be seen near the lower bottom edge of a photo from that seminar on page 204!

*we must direct our thoughts and actions to those things that are truly within our control.* More than one commentator has noted that his advice anticipates the famous "serenity prayer": "God grant me the serenity to accept the things I cannot change (i.e., what is *'ouk eph' hêmin'*), the courage to change the things I can (i.e., what is *'eph' hêmin'*), and the wisdom to know the difference."

This is not to say that we cannot value or pursue things outside of our control, be it a fit body or an occupation that matches our inclinations and capacities. Some Stoics call such things "preferred indifferents," things we would rather have than not, but which are not essential to our happiness or well-being. Epictetus himself makes this clear in regards to the things of the body in a passage from his *Discourses:*

> Epictetus will not be better than Socrates; but if only I am not worse, that suffices me. For I shall not be a Milo, either, and yet I do not neglect my body; nor a Croesus, and yet I do not neglect my property; nor, in a word, is there any other field in which we give up the appropriate discipline merely from despair of attaining the highest.[6]

Milo of Croton (6th-century BC) was credited in legend as the Father of Weightlifting. The story went that when Milo was a young boy he lifted a young calf every day, and as the calf gradually grew into a bull, so too did Milo grow into a bull of a man, indeed, into a veritable Herakles, undefeated in wrestling for decades in the original Olympic Games. Epictetus, who sometimes referred to himself as "a lame old man," says that while he knows he cannot completely control his body and can never be anything close to a Milo, it does not mean that he will not take proper care of the body he has been given. The same goes for his efforts in philosophy and in his personal finances. He will attend to them in due measure, but his ultimate concern is for what is under his control, his thoughts and his moral character.

I have tried to follow Epictetus's lead here whenever possible. Even though Mentzer revealed that I could not control my body to the extent that I thought I could, that I would never be Mr. Universe, it did not dampen my enthusiasm to properly care for my body to become the best Mr. Me I could be. Though you can

---

6   Oldfather v.1, 25 (*Discourses* I.2).

surely tell by now that I'm no Socrates or Epictetus, I do enjoy contemplating their ideas, sharing them with readers, and striving to heed their advice. Though I'm no threat to match the riches of old King Croesus, so far I've stayed out of the poorhouse. I imagine you can think of ways in which you have successfully applied this principle in your own life, but perhaps, if you are like me, there may be some areas of concern in your life where you could still stand to profit by thinking and living more like a Stoic.

Preferred indifferents aside, Epictetus tells us that a laser-like concern with *what is under our control* makes us truly *free,* so that even if we should lose our possessions, or job, or reputation, or even our physical health, we will not look for someone to blame, or for someone to hear our whining, since we will realize we can still live happy, fulfilling, and dignified lives. Those who would use their minds to think like a Stoic will not use their tongues to blame or demonize others, to whine or complain to any who will hear, or to proclaim to the world (perhaps with their keyboards, through social media) their entitlement or their victimhood.

Epictetus concludes this section with a bit of concrete advice to that effect. When something we would typically consider to be bad has happened to us (perhaps some loss, injury, or insult), we should assess it with our measuring stick of the *dichotomy of control.*[7] We should ask it if it was within our control, or not, and *if not,* declare: "Big deal! You are nothing to me!"

> **2**   As for *desires* and *aversions,* when you fail to get what you desire, that is *un*fortunate and when some bad thing happens that you hoped to avoid, that is a case of *mis*fortune. You will avoid misfortune if you are only averse to things that are within your control and that are contrary to nature. But if you are averse to illness and death and other things beyond our control, you will eventually meet misfortune. For those starting in philosophy, don't even think about desires at first, because you will end up unfortunate, since you have not trained yourself yet in how to desire

---

7   For a recent, well-reasoned, and nuanced analysis of the dichotomy of control, complete with arguments for preferring the translation "up to us," rather than "under our control," see Michael Tremblay's *Modern Stoicism* article of 01/30/2021, "What Many People Misunderstand about the Stoic Dichotomy of Control." https://modernstoicism.com/what-many-people-misunderstand-about-the-stoic-dichotomy-of-control-by-michael-tremblay/.

> and acquire what is truly good. Use only *impulse* and *repulsion*, though even these lightly, and without straining. Ω

OUR LITTLE MAN ON THE MAT POINTING OUT "DEE SIRE!" will help us recall chapter 2's theme, "the discipline of *desire*."[8] To summarize the theme with a popular maxim, "Be careful what you wish for!" Having established the importance of distinguishing what is in our control and what is not, Epictetus tells us that only if we desire or are averse to things *within our control* will we avoid distress. If we follow the common course of desiring things not up to us (winning the lottery, obtaining our ideal mate, the ideal job, etc.) and being averse to things not up to us (financial setbacks, rejection from others, a recession, etc.) we often will not get want we want and will often get what we don't want. That's why so many people are unhappy.

Simplicius of Cilicia, the 6th-century Neoplatonist commentator on Epictetus's *Handbook,* makes some notable and noble comments on this point: "Note how Socratic this argument is, and how accommodating, since it leads us from the very things we are eager for, on up to nobler things." Vicious people "judge the objects of their desire by pleasure rather than what is beneficial." Virtuous people, to the contrary, "desire the beneficial things which are really and purely the goods proper to us, and avoid the really harmful and bad things, because what judges them is reason..."[9]

Epictetus would indeed guide us to desire nobler, more rational, more virtuous things, and yet he tells those starting to pursue wisdom to *set aside desires*, even noble ones, at the beginning. So, what is he up to here? Simplicius graphically suggests: "Perhaps it is because people beginning to transition from a vicious way of life to a better one must first of all vomit out the poison of their bad style of life, and then only nourish themselves with the goods of a good life."[10] (Feel free to add the mnemonic image of

---

8  In his *Discourses* 3.2, Epictetus lays out three *topoi* or areas of study, commonly referred to as the discipline of *desire*, the discipline of *assent* or *judgment*, and the discipline of *actions* or *impulses*. We will encounter each of these many times in these pages, and in our Chapter 15 we will memorize a helpful table that sheds further light on all three.

9  Charles Brittain & Tad Brennan, trans., *Simplicius: On Epictetus Handbook 1–26* (New York, NY: Bloomsbury, 2014), 61.

10  Ibid., 64.

the little man vomiting on the doormat if you'd care to remember Simplicius's insight—and if it won't unsettle your stomach.)

This parallels some Christian depictions of growth in the spiritual life which starts with rejection of sin, then moves toward the development of virtue, and finally strives for unity with and enjoyment of God. Indeed, St. Thomas Aquinas provided a vivid image depicting how those pursuing virtue must still be on guard to fight off sin, like those who built the walls of Jerusalem while fighting off their enemies, who "with one hand labored on the work, and with the other, held up his weapon" (Neh. 4:17).

If I might be permitted a Star Trek analogy, Epictetus warns us at the end of this chapter not to pursue a life of wisdom at warp speed, but to slow down at first to merely *impulse* power.

He seems to mean that before we have acquired enough wisdom to know what is truly good and have trained ourselves to rein in inappropriate desires, we should not get too fired up by noble goals we are not yet in a position to attain. We are advised in Scripture: "Seek not what is too difficult for you" (Sir. 3:21), and "Do not lift a weight beyond your strength" (Sir. 13:2). It appears Epictetus would agree. Yet, as every weightlifter knows, a weight that is beyond your strength as you begin training may become mere child's play and hardly even a warm-up weight after months or years of training.

So too if we are to think like Stoics, we must progressively train our philosophical "muscles" and give them time to adapt and grow. We must, for a time, move at "impulse power," seeking simple things that are obviously good to meet our basic needs, before we try to act as if we were already as wise and self-disciplined as Socrates.

Epictetus, our learned trainer, also leaves us with some practical training advice. We are not to desire even good things too vehemently at first, but should do so with *hupexhairesis* (reservation). Modern Stoics often call this the "reserve clause." In other words, we should seek to *act* in a virtuous way (which is in our power), while realizing that the *outcome* of our actions may be impeded by things outside our control.

Cicero provided the analogy of an archer who does everything right to hit the target, while realizing that external forces, like a sudden gust of wind, might lead to a miss. Seneca said "the safest policy is to rarely tempt (Fortune), though to keep her always in mind and trust to her nothing. Thus: 'I shall sail, unless something happens,' and 'I shall be praetor, unless something prevents me.'"[11] St. James expressed a quite similar idea for Christians: "Instead you ought to say, 'If the Lord wills, we shall live and we shall do this or that'" (Jas. 4:15). (If you'd care to add this concept to your chapter 2 mnemonic, one option would be to place a small table between the little man and the king with a "RESERVED" placard on top.)

> ❸ We should remember to ask of everything we find attractive or useful, or of which we are fond, *"What is your nature?"* If you say to yourself, "I am fond of a jug!" you will not be disappointed when it breaks, since you will remember that fragility is part of its nature. Now, consider too the nature of your child or your wife, and when you kiss them remind yourself that you kiss a fragile, mortal human being, so that if they should die, you will not be devastated. ♎

DO YOU REMEMBER LOOKING OUT THE *GLASS PANEL* NEXT to the front door and seeing a *child crying over a broken mug?* Its mnemonic purpose is pretty straightforward, since Epictetus talks about broken mugs and children in chapter 3. Continuing on with his fundamental lessons, we are called to "remember" that everything has a nature, and everything's nature is outside of our control.

Here in his simple, earthy brilliance, Epictetus starts with the example of a mere mug. It is childish to cry over a mug (even if it was our very favorite) because as mature adults, we know that ceramic or earthenware mugs are certainly not indestructible. Fragility is indeed a part of its nature. (I wonder if there are many readers who have never broken a mug or a glass?)

So far, so easy, we might say, but Epictetus then suddenly asks us to take a quantum leap. Do not the very people we love most dearly, like our spouse or our child, also have a nature, a mortal nature that can be quite fragile? Why then should we not also remember, even while kissing them, that we kiss a being who might die at any time? If we do so we will not be devastated like a crying child, should we suddenly lose them.

Now, this may seem to some a very hard lesson, suggesting that perhaps Epictetus lives up to the stereotype of the Stoics as harsh,

---

11 Seneca, *On Tranquility of Mind,* 13, 1, in *Seneca: Moral Essays,* vol. II, trans. John W. Basore (Cambridge, MA: Harvard University Press, 2001), 267.

stone-like, uncaring human beings. Personally, as a husband and a father, I think this clearly misses his point. To remember that those whom we love are *mortal* (and indeed, that we are as well), will remind us that our time on earth with them is limited, and we do not know when it might end. This should inspire us to cherish and love them all the more with the time that we do have with them in this life.

I find this lesson most poignant and powerful in regard to the people we love, but it also has important ramifications for our attachments to every external thing we possess. Ever see a shiny new sports car parked diagonally taking up at least two spaces in a crowded parking lot? How easily we may be traumatized if some prized object should become damaged.

I recall such an incident that involved a brand-new car, a beloved young son, and a beloved wife. How proud he was to show his mother and father how he had pulled his toy fire engine out from the back of the garage all by himself! How surprised we were to see that the little fire engine's metal ladder hook had scratched the new car's paint all the way from bumper to bumper! Fortunately, we realized both the nature of cars and of little children. We were able to look at the scratch, determine it was outside our control, and say, to paraphrase Epictetus: "You are nothing to me!" (And then we called the insurance agent.)

❹ When you are about to begin any undertaking, remind yourself what sort of action it is. You are heading out to the public baths today? Remind yourself that people are going to splash you, jostle you, and maybe even insult you or steal your clothing. Say to yourself from the start that you want to take a bath, but you also want to keep your choices, indeed your very moral purpose, in accord with reason and nature. Then, if you are splashed, jostled, insulted, or robbed, you will remind yourself that you wanted to bathe, but you also wanted to act in harmony with nature, and therefore you will choose not to be annoyed at those less important things beyond your control.[12] Ω

IT'S OBVIOUS NOW WHY WE DEPICTED A BUBBLY ROMAN (or Greek) bath at our fourth location. Not only should we consider the nature of any human being we love or any *material thing* that we own, we should also consider the nature of any *activity* we are

---

12  Perhaps a worthwhile practice for every time we buckle up and take our cars out on the road!

about to pursue. What elements are under our control and what elements are not? *Indeed, every one of our daily undertakings provides opportunity to practice the principle of freeing the soul by recognizing what is within our control and what isn't.*

Public baths were very popular in Epictetus's day, but not so much in our own. A commensurate activity today could be going to the gym. We might seek an enjoyable workout, but would do well to keep in mind that we might encounter what my old workout buddy and I would call the "Murphy's Law of the Gym," that is, regardless of how empty it is, someone is likely to be sitting on the very piece of equipment you want to use. Further, it is possible that people might jostle you, or at least jostle your nerves by loud grunting or other boisterous behavior. Someone might ask you to spot them and you end up doing most of the work. Somebody else might have forgotten their deodorant or left a bench covered in sweat. When it's all over, maybe someone will have stolen your clothes from the locker room—or you may find you forgot to pack fresh underwear before heading back to work. And of course, we might encounter even more annoying behaviors on our way to or from the gym, be it the tailgater or a person with "road rage."

I've suggested for this chapter's lesson the Latin phrase *"premeditatio malorum."* It means thinking ahead about bad things that might happen and is a classic Stoic exercise to help us endure undesired external events without becoming unduly distressed. In modern psychological terminology, this can be referred to as "negative visualization" when we vividly imagination an undesired event and practice our capacity to cope with it. It is also referred to as "stress inoculation," when, like a vaccine, we give to ourselves a small dose of a toxin to build up our power to ward off large doses.

Indeed, I used it myself years ago to help a shy person (me) overcome fears of public speaking. I repeatedly imagined that people would see how nervous I was when speaking, and said to myself "So what!" and to paraphrase psychologist Albert Ellis (strongly influenced by Epictetus), "Somebody's got to be the world's worst public speaker, so it might as well be me!" Then, in a mandatory talk in college I openly acknowledged my sweaty palms, flushed cheeks, and pounding heart at the beginning, and then just got on with my purpose of giving the talk. Since then, I have never been unduly nervous when teaching college courses, giving public talks, or speaking on the radio, podcasts, or television. (Thank you Epictetus and Dr. Albert Ellis!)

Certainly, there are particular activities in your life that would prove much more bearable and less irritating if you remind yourself of their nature in advance and do your best despite external circumstances outside of your control.

Epictetus also briefly addresses a theme even more important than the *premeditatio malorum* when he advises us to recall our desire to keep our moral purpose *(prohairesis)* in accord with nature. We'll dig into this more deeply when we meet up again with *Yoda on the bench.*

⑤   *What upsets people is not things themselves, but their judgments about the things.* Death itself is not fearful, otherwise wise Socrates would have faced it with dread, but he faced it calmly. Whenever we let the fear of death, let alone a myriad of other lesser events distress us, we have only ourselves to blame. Epictetus ends with a pithy lesson well worth pondering, memorizing, and applying. People uneducated in Stoic philosophy blame *others* when things go wrong; those who have started such education blame *themselves;* those whose education is complete blame *no one* at all. Ω

HERE EPICTETUS UNVEILS ANOTHER KEY PILLAR, A PILLAR which would go on to become the acknowledged cornerstone of 20th-century cognitive psychotherapy. *"People are disturbed not by things, but by the views they take of things,"* is another common rendering of Epictetus's Greek. This implies that we can *choose not to upset ourselves* by changing the ways we look at things. Here Epictetus starts with no simple jug or pot, but with the thing humans fear most, death itself. Further, he proves that even death in itself need not provoke fear, by pointing to Socrates, one of the great precursors and heroes of the Stoics, a man with unusual capacity and inclination to control his own emotions through exceptionally rigorous thinking. He calmly accepted his death by poison, concluding it worked for the greater good. But what about the rest of us and all of the lesser problems we face every day before the day we die?

Let's jump ahead nearly twenty centuries to the theories and lessons of modern psychiatry and psychology. Early in the 20th century, Sigmund Freud's psychoanalytic theories held sway in psychiatry with their great emphasis upon childhood conflicts and traumas as the source of emotional distress. If you are chronically emotionally disturbed today, Freud and the Freudians espoused, it must be because of some traumatic experience you suffered in your childhood.

Around the same time in the field of academic and clinical psychology, behaviorism reigned as psychologists focused on outside sources of stimulation and seemingly automatic direct behavioral responses in what was first called S-R, stimulus-response psychology, extending the findings on the famous salivating dogs of the Russian physiologist Ivan Pavlov and the hungry pigeons of B. F. Skinner to realms of human behaviors far exceeding those of salivation and pecking! If you are emotionally disturbed today, it is because of some distressing external event or events now or at any point in your past (including, in Skinner's version, how your own past behaviors have been rewarded or punished by others).

If you are emotionally distressed, both the psychoanalytic and strictly behavioristic theories essentially declare, contra Epictetus, that some external stimulus or event has caused your disturbance. In essence: *"You are disturbed by things!"*

Epictetus would clearly have disagreed, recognizing that if someone is upset by some event that happened long ago, it is clearly because the judgments they are making, the things they are telling themselves about that event *today*. This insight is so crucial that we'll look at it again and again in the pages ahead, especially those on Epictetus and Marcus Aurelius. I'll let you know in advance that near this book's end, in chapter 15, I'll go into great depth about how modern cognitive psychotherapists have taken this particular Epictetian insight and run with it, fleshed it out, and even made it literally as easy as "ABC" to understand and remember. For now, though, on we go to that ornery horse in the middle of our foyer!

**6** Do not to be elated with joy over any excellence that is not our own. If a horse itself were to exclaim with joy, "Look at me, I'm beautiful!" we could put up with that, but for you to brag joyfully about your beautiful horse, bear in mind you are joyful not about *your own* good, but about the good of the horse. *Why not then be joyful about that which is truly your own—your ability to choose how you will deal with impressions or appearances?* If you do so in harmony with nature, enjoy away, for your joy is truly joy for a good of your own! Ω

33

IT IS TIME TO RECALL OUR THOROUGHBRED *HORSE* THOR-
oughly trampling a *mirror* in the center of the foyer. Epictetus
explicitly mentioned a horse, and what better time to say "Look at
me, I'm beautiful!" than right after gazing into a mirror, seeking,
perhaps, the fairest of them all.

Here our great Stoic warns us to stamp out a vice that Catholic
theologians would later describe as the sin of *vainglory*. It appears
that Catholic theologian St. Frances de Sales was no stranger to Epictetian wisdom. In counseling against the sin of vainglory he writes:

> Vainglory is the glory that we give ourselves; either
> for what is not really in us, or for what is in fact in us
> but not owing to anything we did, or for what is in us
> and owing to us but which does not deserve to be the
> cause of a boast.... There are those who are proud
> and haughty because they ride a magnificent horse or
> because their hat sports a fancy feather, or because they
> are wearing some fashionable clothing. Who does not
> see the folly here? If there is glory due, it belongs to
> the horse, the bird or the tailor! And what a pitiable
> heart is his who expects esteem because of a horse, a
> feather or some lace![13]

In our day, we might be more tempted to brag about our car
than our horse, but the principle applies to our possession of anything outside of our control. True joy should come from crafting
a beautiful, noble moral character. Deep down, as we'll see, when
we get to Yoda's lesson, our *prohairesis* is what is best in us!

> **7** Next Epictetus takes us on a sea voyage and has us imagine
> that our boat has anchored. Go ahead, he says, and snatch up some
> fresh water and a shellfish and vegetable while you are at it, but
> always stay mindful of the boat so that you'll *be ready when the Cap-*
> *tain calls*. If he calls you must be ready to drop those other things
> if need be, to get back to the boat on time. Life is such a voyage. If
> you are blessed with a wife and a child instead of a vegetable and a
> shellfish, they are no hindrance to you, but if the Captain calls, you
> cannot take those things with you. You must be prepared to leave

---

13  *Introduction to the Devout Life: A Popular Abridgment*, abridged by Madame
Yvonne Stephan (Rockford, IL: TAN Books, 1990), 126.

them behind. Indeed, if you are very old, never go far from the boat, so you won't be left behind. ⊠

HENCE OUR *SEA CAPTAIN* UP IN THE *CHANDELIER*, SAILING his way through the foyer. Of course, by the Captain, Epictetus means God. Simplicius interpreted it this way: "We must make everything dependent on our turning back to God, the Pilot of the universe; and we must engage with other things according to their rank, holding fast to God."[14] Those other things include our own bodies, which require nourishment, and our families, who require our care, attention, and love.

In the *Handbook's* third chapter Epictetus advised us to recall the fact that our loved ones are mortal, and we never know when we might lose them. Here, he reminds us to remember that *we* too are mortal and we never know when *they* might lose *us*. Here is yet another reason to cherish life with our loved ones every day we've been given to share together. Still, we must remember God foremost, and recall that we do not know when he might call us. We should be ready to go when he calls for us so we won't be left behind or be hauled away kicking and screaming.

❽ Here is chapter 8, in its entirety: *Do not seek to have everything that happens happen as you wish, but wish for everything to happen as it actually does happen, and your life will be serene.*[15] ⊠

HOPEFULLY IT IS CLEAR NOW THAT WE IMAGINED IN THE *mirror* a *birthday cake brimming with candles*, because in the one sentence of chapter 8, Epictetus, like some kind of genie on steroids, has shown us how *all* of our wishes can be granted! Of course, harking back to our lesson on the discipline of desire, we must

---

14  Please note that Epictetus and the other ancient Stoics were not Christians and wrote little to evidence any great familiarity with Christianity, yet their reason led many of them to some kind of pantheistic or theistic conception of God. Some write interchangeably of "gods" and "God" in the singular, and Epictetus sometimes wrote of Zeus, not simply as one of a group of Olympians, but as an eternal Father. Of all the Stoics, Epictetus writes of God in the most personal and endearing terms. For those who would care to dig a little deeper into Stoic conceptions of and arguments for God, please consider my *The Porch and the Cross: Ancient Stoic Wisdom for Modern Christian Living* (Angelico Press, 2016).
15  Oldfather, v. 2, 490.

wish for the right things. In essence, we must wish that everything that happens, happens!

I should note that Epictetus is not encouraging or condoning any kind of physical or moral laziness or complacency, failing to strive to make the world a better place. As we will see in our very next chapter, we are to strive mightily with great moral purpose to achieve things virtuous and good. Our lesson here is that even when our strivings do not yield the results we had expected, or when arduous external circumstances come our way, no external event should be able to shatter our internal peace. Perhaps we find a concordant lesson in the writings of St. James: "Count it all joy, my brethren, when you meet various trials . . ." (Jas. 1:2).

> **❾** Disease harms our bodies, but not our moral purpose, unless we let it. Lameness impedes our leg, not our moral purpose. So, say this to each event that happens to you and you will find that it interferes with something else, not with *you*. Ω

AT LAST WE COME TO *YODA*, WHO EXCLAIMS IN REGARD TO the hirsute *pro athlete* at his side on the *cushioned bench*, "Pro hairy, he is!" Yes, it is time to dig deeper into Epictetus's foundational concept, that of *"prohairesis."*

Modern scholar of Stoicism A. A. Long notes rightly that *"prohairesis"* is a favorite and frequently used concept for Epictetus,[16] indeed, "the most noteworthy feature of his entire philosophy."[17] In the original Greek, *pro* means "what comes before and leads to" and *hairesis,* "choice." Aristotle used the concept and Epictetus made his take on it central to his approach to philosophy and to life. Long translates *prohairesis* as "volition," but indicates it can be also be translated by "will." Keith Seddon, another modern master of Epictetus's thought, goes so far as to provide a table showing his and seventeen other English translators' choice of words of words for *prohairesis.* His own preferred translation is "moral character," and others include "choice," "choices," "faculty of choice," "moral choice," "sphere of choice," "will," "freedom of choice,"

---

16   Scholars have tabulated uses of *prohaireis, prohairetic,* and *apohairetic* 168 times in Epictetus's works. R. Dobbin, *"Prohairesis* in Epictetus," in *Ancient Philosophy,* XI, 111–35 (1991).

17   A. A. Long, *Epictetus: A Stoic and Socratic Guide to Life* (New York: Oxford University Press, 2004), 28.

"moral nature," "moral personality," "volition," and "purpose."[18]

For the practical, moral purposes of this book (as was the case when I wrote *The Porch and the Cross*), when summarizing Epictetus's lessons of the *Enchiridion* I primarily use (and hopefully quite fittingly) *"moral purpose"* unless I use *"prohairesis"* itself. "Moral purpose" is used in the translation of W. A. Oldfather, originally published in 1928 by the Loeb Classical Library, through which I first came to know Epictetus. To my ears, the phrase is also more inspiring and ennobling than merely "volition," "will," or "purpose" unadorned with the "moral" adjective. "Moral *character*" and "moral *personality*" are also well-suited to the goals in this book, but I like the more active, dynamic, and future-looking connotations of moral *purpose*. Time and time and time again, Epictetus will exhort us to remember and live by our "moral purpose" (i.e., *prohairesis*) as our highest good, our greatest gift from God.

Regardless of one's choice of translation, for Epictetus, *prohairesis* is what distinguishes human beings from the animals. It is what, beyond our physical bodies, makes humans what we are in terms of all of our mental faculties, abilities, thoughts, choices, character, values, goals, and self-reflective consciousness. It is what enables us to be free, to determine what is up to us and to act accordingly. It corresponds to our innermost self. To make progress in philosophy is to work toward the perfection of our *prohairesis*. As Marcus Aurelius would often write to himself, it is a spark of divinity within us.

In this particular *Handbook* chapter, of course, Epictetus contrasts the proper use of our *prohairesis* with undue concern over our bodily health and integrity, which are not completely up to us. Epictetus speaks from experience. He frequently calls himself a "lame old man," and a story often repeated in ancient writings relates that an owner once intentionally twisted and broke Epictetus's leg. According to the tale, Epictetus calmly told his owner in classic Stoic fashion that if he kept doing what he was doing, his leg would break, and then, indeed it did.

Some scholars have questioned the story, noting that one ancient source, Suidas,[19] mentions that his leg grew lame from

---

18  Keith Seddon, *Epictetus' Handbook and the Tablet of Cebes: Guides to Stoic Living* (New York: Routledge, 2005), 209.
19  The tenth-century author, possibly a Christian cleric at Constantinople, of a

rheumatism. The story that a master broke it is preserved in the Christian writings of Origen and St. Gregory of Nazianzus. Simplicius simply notes that Epictetus's leg was lame from a very young age. The 20th-century classicist W. A. Oldfather has weighed in that while the cause of his lameness is not known, Epictetus clearly uses far more examples of bearing up to physical abuses from others than bearing up to natural illnesses.

In either case, the lesson is clear that keeping our moral purpose intact is of greater importance than even physical health. Therefore, if we should suffer illness or injury, it need not defeat us.

> **⑩** *Whenever something happens to you, remember to ask yourself what powers you have for dealing with it. If you see a beautiful body, call forth your self-control. If hardship comes your way, get out your endurance. If you are insulted, find your patience. If you train yourself in this every day, appearances will not carry you away.* Ω

WHEN MY OLDEST SON WAS LITTLE WE ENJOYED WATCHing the "He-Man" cartoon on TV together. In virtually every episode Prince Adam, when faced with a crisis, would hold his sword aloft, proclaiming aloud in an echoing voice: "By the power of Grayskull, I have the power!" as lightning struck his sword and he transformed into the herculean He-Man. He was my choice of the visual image for chapter 10, wherein Epictetus essentially proclaims to each one of us, "Within not Grayskull, but *your own skull*, you have the powers!"

Epictetus again asks us to *remember*, this time to remember the various *"powers"* within us. Some English editions use "capacities," or "faculties," which are also legitimate translations of Epictetus's Greek word *"dunamis,"* from which we derive English words like "dynamo," "dynamic," and "dynamite." This passage on particular powers is particularly interesting because Epictetus is so known for discussing what we could call our power with a Capital P, that of our *Prohairesis* (as we just saw in his chapter 9). *Prohairesis,* our capacity for rational, moral, self-directed thoughts, emotions, and behaviors is the "big P" Power from which all of our "little p" powers flow, things like self-control, endurance, and patience.

Now, *virtues* themselves are *perfections of our powers.* Some Stoics, like Epictetus's own revered teacher, Musonius Rufus, frequently

---

very influential lexicon or encyclopedia of ancient and medieval Greek learning.

espoused the Stoic principle that only virtue is truly good. One of his favorite themes was the cultivation of virtue. The Greeks called virtue *arête*, or *excellence*. Musonius preached virtue in general, as opposed to vice, and he also championed the four classic cardinal virtues of *temperance* (moderation or self-control), *fortitude* (courage), *prudence* (practical wisdom), and *justice*.[20]

This chapter is one of the few times in the *Handbook* that Epictetus emphasizes the value of particular virtues like self-control,[21] endurance, and patience. So how do we cultivate and perfect them? Well, Epictetus tells us that we must first *remember* that we have powers lying in wait to be put into use in response to whatever particular obstacles or hardships should come our way. Second, he says we must *train ourselves* (some translations show "habituate" for his *ethizô*) to put these powers into action.

Aristotle rightly said we become builders by building and harpists by playing the harp. Epictetus chimes in that we become self-controlled by repeatedly controlling ourselves when tempted, patient by practicing patience when insulted,[22] and enduring by persevering in the face of hardships. Indeed, we can even change our outlook on such temptations or difficulties by welcoming them as opportunities to develop our powers. As St. Catherine of Siena would declare centuries later: "a man proves his patience on his neighbor, when he receives injuries from him."[23]

THAT WRAPS UP OUR MEMORY TOUR, SUMMARIES, AND commentaries for the first ten *Handbook* chapters. Can you reel off all ten images and chapter themes now in order, indeed, even

---

20  *Sophrosyne, andreia, phronesis,* and *diakaiosyne* in the Greek.
21  Simplicius, working from a Platonic/Aristotelian framework, concludes that Epictetus uses not *sophrosyne* here for temperance, but *enkrateia* for self-control "because this advice is directed to those who are still being educated" (v. 1., 92), that is, the *prokoptôn* whose reason must still wage battle with the emotional parts of the soul. There is a parallel in St. Thomas Aquinas's treatment of these virtues, following Aristotle, wherein the virtue of *continence* entails the successful struggle of rational over irrational urges, whereas the full-blown cardinal virtue of *temperance* is found in those who have progressed to the point that they no longer feel the pull of irrational desires. The repeated exercise of *enkrateia/ continence* is the path that leads to *sophrosyne*/temperance.
22  Stay tuned for our analysis of *Handbook* chapter 33 where Epictetus provides some delightful advice on just how to patiently respond to insults.
23  Algar Thorold, trans., *The Dialogue of St. Catherine of Siena* (Charlotte, NC: St. Benedict Press, 2006), 17.

forward and backward? If not, and for future refreshers, please note that the entire memory system for all 53 *Handbook* chapters is presented at the end of Part I. I also invite you to sometime read or reread the first ten chapters of the *Handbook* itself at your leisure.

It's time now to move from our foyer into our living room where we will find out why a store's "returns counter" is sitting right in its center.

# CHAPTER 2

# FROM DEVASTATION TO INVINCIBILITY

### (Handbook *Chapters 11–20*)

*"If you would be invincible, enter no contest that you cannot win."*

Handbook Ch. 19

## MEMORY TOUR:
### *HANDBOOK* CHAPTERS 11–20

INVITE YOU NOW TO STEP FORTH FROM THE foyer to enjoy the sights and the lessons of our living room. It seems that some kind of business is operating from this home, for in the living room's center (location ⓫) you spy a little booth with a sign reading *"Returns Counter"* above it. You peer out the picture window ⓬ into the back yard and there you see a *slave* (you can tell by the ankle shackle) running away with your favorite *bottle of wine with a big dollar sign ($) sign on it* (and you realize that you are not at all upset). Back in the living room, sitting on a sofa ⓭, how nice to see old *Socrates* again. How odd that he's wearing a *dunce cap*, though he doesn't seem to mind. Upon a large coffee table ⓮ you find yourself sitting in shackles. You feel the need to sit down on the *swivel chair* to the *right* of the window ⓯, but you see that an entire *feast* has been laid out upon its cushion.

You have no more luck sitting down on the left swivel chair ⓰ because its already occupied by a *person dressed in black* loudly *mourning*. You place a gentle hand on her shoulder. You are pleasantly surprised when you spy a piano ⓱ across the room with your own *favorite movie actor* smiling at you as he hammers away at the keys. You hear an odd *croaking* noise coming from the fireplace ⓲ and you strain your eyes to see a pitch-black *crow* covered in

41

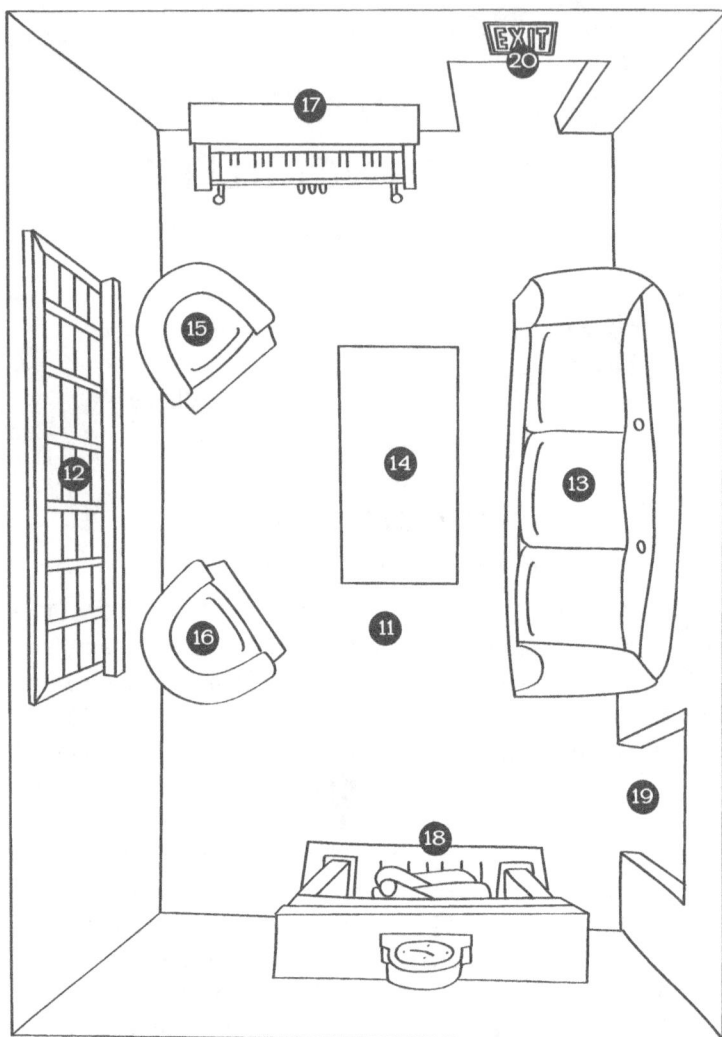

pitch-black soot. Next to the fireplace is the doorway into of the living room **19**, and it's almost filled up by a *gigantic first place trophy* for you. Finally, trophy or no trophy, you decide you've had enough of the contents of this strange living room, and apparently someone else felt just the same way, for the exit sign **20** above the doorway out has just been pelted by a big, juicy, red *tomato!*

Let's lay this all out succinctly, and with a bit more practice, we'll see if you've got the locations and images down:

| LOCATION/<br>*HANDBOOK* CHAPTER | IMAGE | LESSON |
|---|---|---|
| ⓫ CENTER OF<br>LIVING ROOM | *Store "Returns" counter* | How to handle loss |
| ⓬ PICTURE WINDOW | *Slave with wine bottle* | Freedom is not free |
| ⓭ SOFA | *Socrates in a dunce cap* | Focus on what<br>really matters |
| ⓮ COFFEE TABLE | *You sit on it in shackles* | How not to<br>enslave yourself |
| ⓯ RIGHT SWIVEL<br>CHAIR | *Banquet feast on cushion* | Etiquette for<br>dinner & life |
| ⓰ LEFT SWIVEL CHAIR | *Bereaved person moaning* | Don't moan on the inside |
| ⓱ PIANO | *Your favorite actor* | Play your role well |
| ⓲ FIREPLACE | *Croaking crow* | It's all good |
| ⓳ LIVING-ROOM<br>DOORWAY | *Giant 1st place trophy* | How to be invincible |
| ⓴ EXIT SIGN<br>DOORWAY OUT | *Heckler throws tomato* | How to deflect<br>all insults |

If you have them, that's great. If not, please wait before you throw any tomatoes! Let's recall two things about these memory methods. First, "repetition is the mother of memory." If you don't have these ten all down pat, please rehearse them another time or two. Second, recall that these methods are designed to help you learn materials *literally forward and backward.* So, combining both things, why not try to rehearse them all in *backward* order? Can you move from the tomato-splattered exit sign, down to the trophy underneath, over to the crow in the fireplace, your favorite actor at the piano, the mourner in the left chair, the feast laid out in the right, you in shackles upon the coffee table, Socrates with dunce cap sitting on the couch, the slave with the wine seen out the picture window, all the way back to our returns counter in the living room's center? When you can, you will indeed have mastered our mnemonic tour backwards and forwards.

Oh yes, and one more note on the mnemonics before we dig into Epictetus's own lessons. If you have numbers 11–20 from our living room down pat now, it might be a good time for a quick review of the foyer's 10 locations and images. If you've still got them too, you are more than a third of the way through the entire *Handbook* memory tour!

## THE LESSONS BEHIND THE IMAGES:
### *HANDBOOK* CHAPTERS 11–20

⑪  Whenever something or someone you had is gone, don't say, "I lost it," but rather, say, *"I have given it back."* If your wife or your child dies, then they were given back. If your farm is taken, it too was given back. If it was taken by a scoundrel, it is not your concern how the Giver asked for it back. Treat whatever you are given as something not your own, like travelers while staying at an inn. Ω

SO THIS WAS WHY THAT *RETURNS COUNTER* WAS IN THE center of the living room. It we remember that external things are not under our control, we will realize that one day we may well be required to return them, and will not be devastated by it. Again, though this is no easy teaching, it need not imply that one be completely unmoved by the loss of something so dear as a spouse, a child, one's inheritance or source of income. Rather, its lesson holds that one need not be devastated, crushed, or immobilized by the loss of anything outside of our control.

Let's recall that in our first *Handbook* chapter, Epictetus told us that if we recognize what is not truly our own, we will not be harmed by such losses, and we will not *blame* anyone, gods or men, including the "Giver" himself. To put this in the familiar words of Job: "Naked I came from my mother's womb, and naked shall I return; the LORD gave, and the LORD has taken away; blessed be the name of the Lord" (Job 1:26).

Though few of us may have the patience of Job, Epictetus would have us cultivate this capacity for our own emotional good. Indeed, a common feature of clinical depression, a state we should hope to avoid, if possible, is a profound sense of irrevocable *loss.*

⑫  *There is a price to pay for tranquility.* If you want to make progress in wisdom, give up all worries that if you neglect your business you'll have nothing to live on, or if you don't punish your slave boy, he'll turn out bad. It's better to die of hunger without distress than to live in plenty with a troubled mind. So too is it better that your slave boy be bad than for you to make yourself unhappy over it. Start with the small things. If your oil or wine gets stolen, tell yourself this is simply the price of tranquility, the price of not being upset.

Nothing comes for free. When you call to your slave boy, it's up to him whether he pays attention or chooses to do what you ask, but it is not up to him whether or not you are disturbed. Ω

HOPEFULLY YOU'LL RECALL LOOKING THROUGH THE PIC-ture window into the back yard where a shackled *slave boy* ran off with your favorite and most expensive *bottle of wine*, and yet, you were not disturbed! Well, first off, we can be thankful, that in our time, we, unlike Epictetus, who had been a slave boy once himself, will not really see shackled slaves running around. Second, this chapter's lesson calls to my mind two common, and common sense sayings: 1) "Don't cry over spilled milk (or oil, or wine)," and 2) "Don't sweat the small stuff (or even the big stuff)."

Remember our child crying over the broken mug in *Handbook* chapter 3? We must ask ourselves of anything we value, "What is its nature?" (Is its nature under our control or not?) Epictetus revisits that lesson with some additional twists.

Simplicius states that this lesson "is addressed to people whose education is still underway, and are not yet in the sort of condition that would allow them to be concerned simultaneously with what belongs to them and with external things without suffering harm."[1] Indeed, in the Stoic *prokopton* "the irrational is still throbbing"[2] in its desire of external things, so Epictetus provides advice to still the throbbing to foster the kind of tranquility that can cope calmly with losses of external things or the undesirable behaviors of others.

When he says it is better to die of hunger than to live upset in the midst of plenty, he counsels us to train ourselves to be content with little, as Epictetus himself did. In the *Discourses* (1.18.15–16 & 1.29.21) he relates the story of the time a thief stole his iron lamp. He said it was a pity that the thief would sell his dignity and render himself beast-like for the price of a lamp, and as for Epictetus himself, he did have need for lamp, so he simply bought a more homely earthenware one to replace it, one he would be content with, and one not too likely to inspire another thief's covetousness.

There is a price we pay for tranquility and for dignity, and hopefully we'll come to realize that it's worth far more than a bottle of wine or even the finest of iron lamps!

---

1   Simplicius, v. 2, 95.
2   Ibid., 96.

⑬    *If you want to make progress in wisdom, let people think you are a hopeless fool when it comes to the kind of external things they care about. If you acquire a reputation about being learned about such non-essential things, take a hard look at yourself. It is no easy thing to focus both on your moral purpose and external things, and a person who devotes his attention to one of these things will end up neglecting the other.* Ω

REMEMBER *SOCRATES* SITTING ON THE COUCH WITH A *dunce cap*? Well, he didn't mind it a bit!

Ancient philosophers (like modern ones) had a reputation among non-philosophical folk for being impractical and having their heads in the clouds. I can't help but think of the story of Thales (6th c. BC), the first of the great philosophers, natural scientists, and sages of ancient Greece. The story is told that after repeated chiding over the impracticality of his speculation into the workings of nature, Thales used his knowledge of weather patterns and agricultural principles to predict a bumper crop of olives one year. He then hired out all the olive presses. When the bumper crop arrived, the supposedly impractical philosopher with his head in the clouds was immersed in money up to his eyeballs!

A century or so later, the great playwright Aristophanes made Socrates and his students the butt of his jokes, so to speak. In *The Clouds*, when a visitor to Socrates' school finds his students on their knees with their heads to the ground, he is told that one end is studying what's under the earth while the other end is studying astronomy! (And it gets far sillier than this.) Socrates, unlike Thales, was far more interested in ethics and virtue than natural science, and his response to ridicule was quite a bit different. He felt he had nothing to prove and was not disturbed in the slightest.

More than 2,000 years later, of the myriad of external things that disturb people untrained in philosophy, *what other people think about us* often remains high on the list. Note well though that Epictetus does not advise us to *act* foolishly and not care what others think, but not to care if we *appear* to be foolish to others when we are truly pursuing wisdom. People who spend their lives striving for external things think people who pursue internal things like wisdom and moral character are fools who don't know how to get the good things in life. Let them think away (or at least let them think they are thinking, we might say).

Further, the pursuit of philosophy should be true to its name, deriving from one's *philia* (love) of *sophia* (wisdom), and not one's desire to show the world how smart or learned one is. Again, we might hark back to Epictetus's great hero Socrates, who realized that a true sign of wisdom is being aware of how little one knows.

> **14**    How foolish you are if you desire that your children and your wife live forever, since you are treating things outside of your control as if they were inside it, and things that are not yours as if they were. It is equally stupid to expect your vicious slave boy to do no wrong, since you are expecting badness not to do badness, but something else. You are capable, however, of not failing to get what you desire, if you desire only what is within your power. A master has the power to give or take away what a slave desires. *If you would be free, don't desire things within another's power or you'll render yourself a slave.* Ω

SURELY *YOU* WILL RECALL SITTING ON OUR COFFEE TABLE in *shackles!* This is because Epictetus is going to explain to you and me how we can keep from enslaving ourselves and instead achieve true freedom. He reiterates the themes of recognizing the nature of even the dearest of things, our loved ones, how they are mortal, and how their life span is outside our control. Indeed, he believes we should have progressed far enough along now that he can outright call us *hêlithios* (foolish, stupid, idiotic) if we persist in yearning for things outside our control.

Epictetus then provides a much simpler example, that of expecting a flawed slave boy to act as if he was a sage—and becoming upset if he doesn't. Though slave boys, thank God, are a thing of the past, this simple lesson has *very* extensive implications and applications for every one of us today.

Are there any persons in your life who fly off the handle over the smallest thing, who easily break into a rage cursing the bedpost that dared stub their toe, or who shiver with fear and seek out reassurance when the most trivial things go wrong? (I imagine that any readers with friends or family members, or who work with the public, might be able to think of someone like that. And heaven forbid, if such a person is *you*, don't despair since this lesson is about how we can set ourselves free.) So, if we encounter such a person in a stressful situation are we not being stupid if we expect a chronic hothead, a belligerent, or perhaps a timid and fearful person to act as if he or she were Epictetus? Must we let *their* irrationality disturb *us*, especially if we darn well should have seen it coming?

We must not allow the behaviors of others to disturb or shackle us. No, if we are to be masters of our own thoughts, feelings, and actions, we must not hand over such leverage to people or events outside our control.

> **⑮** *Remember that life is like a banquet and you should always act accordingly.* If something is passed to you, reach out and take a reasonable portion. If the plate passes by you, don't hold it back. If it hasn't made it to you yet, don't stretch out your arm and go reaching for it. Mind your manners! Don't stretch out your desires. Be patient and wait. Behave the same way toward your wife and family, toward your job, toward wealth, and you will render yourself worthy to share a banquet with the gods. If you should come to disregard even delicacies when they are set before you, you will not only dine with the gods, but rule with them. This is how people like Diogenes and Heraclitus acted and why they were rightly called gods.[3] ⧉

WHEN WE CAME TO THE SWIVEL CHAIR ON THE RIGHT WE did not sit down since a veritable *feast* covered its cushion. This was to remind us of Epictetus's banquet of life. Such feasts may be full of delicious preferred indifferents! Even a Stoic in training may go ahead, reach out, and snag one if a preferred goody is passed their way. He or she will do so mildly and calmly, on *impulse* power as we described it before. But while budding Stoics will stretch out their *arms,* they will *not* overstretch their *desires.* Indeed, Simplicius has described *desire* itself as "a stretching of the soul towards the object of desire."[4]

We may gladly partake in the necessities of life like tasty, nourishing food. We may build and enjoy relationships of love and of business as well, and be grateful that we have them. Still, we must not overstretch our souls by too strongly desiring even good things outside our control. Epictetus says that when we can enjoy the

---

3  Diogenes the Cynic and Heraclitus the pre-Socratic philosopher, who along with Socrates and Zeno, were considered the closest thing to Stoic sages, godlike in their indifference to things outside their control.
4  Simplicius, v.I, 41.

banquet of life, giving thanks for the good things that come our way, we are fit to eat as guest of the gods. Still, if we can train ourselves to become unmoved by even the finest delicacies of things outside our control, then we will have become rulers of ourselves, and in that respect, like the gods who rule over the universe.

Indeed, a recurring theme for Epictetus in the *Handbook* and the *Discourses* is the goal of the Stoic to *follow the will of, share in fellowship with,* and *become like* "the gods," or "Zeus" as the supreme Father God. A touching anonymous epitaph found in the writings of St. John Chrysostom and Macrobius reads as follows: "Slave, poor as Irus, halting as I trod, I, Epictetus, was the friend of God."[5]

> (16) When you see someone wailing in grief because his child has gone away or he has lost his property, don't get carried away by the impression that the external situation is bad, but be ready to say to yourself that what saddens him is not merely the situation itself (since others would not be crushed in similar circumstances), but his judgment about it. By all means, show him sympathy, and groan along with him, if need be, but *do not moan on the inside.* Ω

REMEMBER THE OTHER SWIVEL CHAIR WITH THE *GRIEVING person mourning* loudly? Of course, you do! You even showed her sympathy by placing your hand on her shoulder. Still, memory images aside, does this lesson sound to you like another hard one? Should a good Stoic just *pretend* to care for a mourner, making an *outward display* of sympathy, while remaining *unmoved on the inside?* This calls from some nuanced and very important distinctions.

I recall as a student of Adler University in the 1990s an Adlerian *bon mot* we heard from our professors time and time again. The psychology school's namesake, psychiatrist Alfred Adler, had said that for therapists to be maximally effective with their clients, they must "see with their eyes, and hear with their ears." A healer must be empathetic, striving to grasp from the patient's perspective what he is going through. Now, Epictetus himself said "the lecture room of the philosopher is a hospital";[6] as a young man he was one of Musonius Rufus's "patients," so to speak, and he reported this cherished memory:

---

5  Oldfather, v.1, 7.
6  *Discourses* 3.23.30 in Oldfather v. 2, 181.

> Rufus used to say: "If you have time enough to praise me, then I know what I am saying is worthless." And after saying this, he went on to say things that caused each one of us who sat there to think that someone at some time had given him revealing information about us: he grasped our circumstances so well, and he placed our faults before our eyes so effectively. Students, the philosopher's school is a doctor's office.[7]

Apparently, Epictetus's revered teacher saw with his students' eyes and heard with their ears, and Epictetus fully agreed with his medical analogy for philosophy.

As for this chapter's most straightforward lesson, Epictetus reminds us once more that it is irrational and mistaken to become devastated by any external thing, even something as unwanted as the loss of a loved one or a large financial loss. He reinforces the point that it is our beliefs or judgments that determine our reactions and not just the events themselves by pointing out that different people will react very differently to similar losses. Clear enough.

He concludes, though, by asking us to show sympathy to a grieving person, and perhaps even moan along with him if the circumstances seem right for it, but not to weep or moan "inwardly" as well. Epictetus was certainly not the type to going around saying "I *feel* your pain!" and neither would he advise us to do so. He advises us to *acknowledge* their pain, to try to comfort them, but not to *feel* it too, thus needlessly disturbing ourselves.

Indeed, this very issue is a timely one within the modern medical and healing professions. In preparing to give a talk on burnout among physicians and other healthcare workers at the Catholic Medical Association's annual conference in 2019, I learned some studies suggested that excessive or inappropriate empathy with their patients' suffering helped produce physician burnout. Indeed, in recent years a lot of thought and research in medical practice has gone into making fine and important distinctions between concepts like "affective empathy," "cognitive empathy," "behavioral empathy," "moral empathy," "sympathy," and "compassion."[8] One

---

7  Epictetus *Discourses*, 3.23.29–32, as translated in Cynthia King, *Musonius Rufus: Lectures and Sayings* (North Charleston, SC: William B. Irvine, Pub./CreateSpace.com, 2011).

8  See, for example, David Jeffrey, "Empathy, sympathy and compassion in

bottom-line conclusion has been that true empathy that helps people in distress without distressing health-care providers themselves is a nuanced set of *skills* with key features as follows:

• Connection: involving emotional sharing with the patient in a two-way relationship.
• Clinical curiosity: to gain insight into the patient's concerns, feelings and distress, giving patients a sense that they matter.
• Another-orientated perspective: the doctor tries to imagine what it is like to be the patient and to see the world from the patient's perspective.
• Self–other differentiation: this respects the patient as an individual with dignity.
• Care: acting appropriately on the understanding gained to help the patient.[9]

Note the attention to genuine connection, concern, and caring, to seeing with the patient's eyes, but without losing sight of "self-other differentiation." I think old Epictetus would agree with the importance of such features of empathy not only for doctors healing patients' bodies or philosophers healing students' minds, but for any of us who would care to think and act like a Stoic to provide real care and comfort to any suffering person—without adding ourselves to the disabled list.

> **17** *Remember that you are an actor in a play that is determined by the Playwright. He determines if it's short or long. Whether he wants you to play a beggar, a lame man, a ruler or a private citizen, what is up to you is to play your assigned part well.* Ω

IN A SENSE, EPICTETUS ANTICIPATED SHAKESPEARE BY fifteen hundred years in declaring "All the world's a stage." Now, in addition to our banquet metaphor for life he gives us that of the stage. The Playwright, of course, refers to God. We didn't get to write the play, determine our part, or where it will end, but it is up to us to play our assigned role as well as we possibly can.

---

healthcare: Is there a problem? Is there a difference? Does it matter?," *Journal of the Royal Society of Medicine*, vol. 9, issue 21, 2016. https://journals.sagepub.com/doi/full/10.1177/0141076816680120.
9   Ibid.

This should not suggest a complete predetermination or predestination, however. While none of us chooses our parents (remember the lesson Mr. Universe taught me?), our race, our inherited traits, or the time, social class, or location into which we are born, the most important things still remain up to us.

To borrow from my doctoral school's namesake once more: "The important thing is not what one is born with, but what one makes of that equipment."[10] We can indeed "ad lib" to some extent, since the Playwright has given us the capacity to control our thoughts, tongues, and actions.

Modern *Handbook* commentator Keith Seddon makes an interesting point here about the parts of scripts of our lives that do remain outside of our control, perhaps one that we've all considered a time or two in our lives, about how chance events can have such profound consequences throughout the course of our lives.

Hmm, if I hadn't spent that quarter on a memory book in 1978 would I be writing this book right now? If my workout buddy and mentor or my future wife hadn't walked into the gym where I worked in the early 1980s, how different would my career and my family life have been? Indeed, it is the Playwright who provides us with all kinds of scenery, props, and co-stars, and yet the kind of life story we play out with them is largely up to us.

Ancient *Handbook* commentator Simplicius provides some beautiful insights of his own. The Playwright or Director will assign each actor his or her role, but it is the function of each actor to play that assigned role to the best of his or her ability. Indeed, "for this reason a slave or a madman in a play is often well-received, and a wealthy man or general or king poorly received, when the former act their given roles well, and the latter badly."[11] (I don't know about you, but for me, Levar Burton as the slave Kunta Kinte in *Roots*, and Jack Nicholson as madman Randle McMurphy in *One Flew Over the Cuckoo's Nest* are modern proofs in Simplicius's ancient pudding!)

Simplicius says it works just this way in real life too. Indeed, how many wealthy men, generals, or even kings of Epictetus's day are as known or as revered in our day as that self-same poor, lame, ex-slave who played so well the roles that the Playwright assigned him?

---

10   Heinz L. Ansbacher and Rowena R. Ansbacher, eds., *The Individual Psychology of Alfred Adler* (New York, NY: Harper & Row, 1956), 176.
11   Simplicius, v. 1, 105.

⑱    When a crow croaks in an ominous way, don't let the impression carry you away with fear, but tell yourself that ominous signs do not affect you, but only perhaps your paltry body or your petty possessions, reputation, or children, or wife. For *all signs are good signs if you wish, since it is up to you to find benefit from whatever life should bring.* Ω

NOW LET'S SEE WHY WE MEMORIZED THAT BLACK CROW *croaking* in our fireplace. The eminent 19th-century Epictetan scholar Adolf Friedrich Bonhöffer noted that the vast majority of ancient Stoics believed in the "mantic," that is, divination or prophecy, because of their "mystical-pantheistic doctrine of the universe . . . which promoted the supposition that every coming event has a sign."[12] Further, "herein Epictetus again shows himself a genuine and legitimate Stoic" for believing in it without doubt.[13] The cawing of a crow was seen as an ominous portent in Epictetus's time and culture, much like the black cat crossing one's path that most of us are probably familiar with.

Now, those of us who are not superstitious and see such things as chance, meaningless events can easily say to such impressions: "Ha, you are nothing to me!" Yet Epictetus's lesson is deeper still. He tells us that even those who *do believe* in ominous portents can look at them and say, "You are nothing to me!" This is because such portents can only predict or foretell events that are outside our control, pertaining to things like our bodies, reputations, families, fortunes, etc. Indeed, he tells us that we can transform any ostensibly ominous portent into something auspicious or positive, since it is within our power to fortify our *prohairesis* and build our characters by confronting and enduring or conquering all manners of external adversity. (Perhaps here Epictetus anticipates Nietzsche's "What does not kill me makes me stronger!")

⑲    *If you would be invincible, enter no contest that you cannot win.* Don't be carried away by appearances and think someone who has gained honor, power, or a good reputation is necessarily rendered happy. If what is truly of value is what is truly up to you, there is no

12  Adolf Friedrich Bonhöffer, *The Ethics of the Stoic Epictetus: An English Translation*, William O. Stephen, trans. (New York, NY: Peter Lang, 2000), 75.
13  Ibid.

room for envy or jealousy. You will not desire to become a general, a legislator, or a leader, but you'll desire to be free. *To become free you must not set your sights on things outside your control.* Ω

REMEMBER THAT ENORMOUS *1ST-PLACE TROPHY* IN THE living room doorway? In this passage Epictetus tells us how we can never suffer defeat: "You can't lose if you don't play," we might say! He advises us not to stretch out our desires and strive and compete for outward things that may falsely appear to be worthwhile, but which are outside our own control and are ultimately up to others. In modern vernacular, he advises us to get out of the "rat race" and strive for what truly befits a human being. In doing so we will not experience frustrated desires for trivial things and neither will we suffer envy or jealously when others acquire positions that garner honor from others.

Envy and jealousy are harmful emotions that arise when we believe others have good things that we lack. According to Simplicius, "jealousy is distress at another's good and envy is a seething wish to become equal to someone who is regarded as good."[14] Epictetus would certainly steer us far away from any emotional distress, not to mention any desire that "seethes"!

Finally, if we pursue only what is under our control, exercising our *prohairesis* about what really matters, we will become not only *free* from undesirable emotions, we will become *invincible* and win that 1st place trophy of a happy, virtuous life.

> ⑳ *Remember that insults don't harm you, only the judgment you make that they are insulting.* Note well that when someone bothers you, it is really your own belief that produces your discomfort. So then, don't get carried away by appearances and act too swiftly when insulted or annoyed. If you pause to cool down and reflect on the realities beneath the appearances, you will regain your self-control and composure. Ω

DO YOU RECALL HOW THAT *HECKLER HURLED* THAT *TOMATO* into the Exit sign over the door? This image should serve to remind us of Epictetus's first explicit lesson on how to bear up to insults

---

14 Simplicius, v. I, 107.

from others without becoming perturbed. And is this not a lesson so badly needed in our day when so many people "troll" internet sites, happily hurling scurrilous slurs seeking to rile people up, and when so many others appear to collect injustices and insults, searching for ways they may become aggrieved through direct slights or the most subtle of "micro-aggressions"?

I don't know about you, but I was old enough to grow up hearing the old saying, "Sticks and stones may break my bones, but words can never hurt me!" I think Epictetus would agree, though he would never advise a person to speak to others in language intended to upset or harm them (nor to hurl sticks or stones at them either). He seeks to buttress our characters so that insulting words from others will indeed not hurt us, and while sticks and stones may in fact break our bones, this self-described "lame old man," whose own leg was broken, can help us bear up with physical injury as well.

Now, as to the mechanics of how we can achieve invincibility not only from our own frustrated desires, but from abusive actions of others towards us, we must remember once more our fundamental lesson from *Handbook* chapter 5, that we are not disturbed by things or events, but by our beliefs or judgments, by what *we tell ourselves* about these events.

Further, the first step in the process is simply to slow down, to delay our emotional or behavioral response to give our rational minds a chance to come into play. Have you heard of the time-worn advice for the angry to count to ten before responding to the person who angers them, or to get a good night's sleep before you fire off an angry email? This kind of delay is very useful in controlling our responses to insults, especially if we take that time to look at the insult through Stoic lenses, lenses that see we cannot control another's behavior, we can control our own behavior, and indeed, in some misguided way, what the insulter said to us somehow made sense to him. (There is more to come on that idea when we get to Marcus Aurelius.)

And here's one last thing to consider for now. While we pause to reflect, we also ought to consider whether what we took as an insult to us happened to be *true,* providing us an opportunity for a lesson we need to learn about ourselves. (For an interesting twist on this idea, stay tuned for *Handbook* chapter 33.)

AND SO ENDS OUR MEMORY TOUR AND WHIRLWIND commentary on *Handbook* chapters 11–20. Can you remember the mnemonic images and the lessons they suggest for all the first twenty chapters now? If not, don't forget the handy-dandy master mnemonic table at the end of Part I.

## MORE WORDS FOR WOULD-BE MODERN MEMORY MASTERS

PLEASE ALLOW ME TO CLOSE WITH A FEW ADDITIONAL comments for any budding memory master who'd care to think like a Stoic.

First, please note that the *memory images* I've chosen are quite arbitrary. They are simply the first things that pop into my mind when I read the *Handbook* chapters and zoom in on key words and ideas. Hopefully they're working well for you too, but if you should come to craft memory images of your own, do know that they tend to be even more powerful, since they draw from the natural associations that spring from *your* own knowledge base.

Second, it is probably obvious by now that my suggested *images* (mnemonic table column two) and the suggested *lesson* for each *Handbook* chapter (column three) are certainly not complete. Many of the *Handbook* chapters have multiple lessons, which you could easily embellish with additional mnemonic images of your own, if you should so choose. Indeed, your imagery system could gradually grow throughout the years as you read and re-read the *Handbook*.

I'll end with one very simple example regarding that *1st-place trophy* in our 19th location. If you would care to remember that in chapter 19 Epictetus teaches us not only how to become *invincible* by never entering the wrong kinds of contests that we can never win, but also that in doing so we can overcome disturbing emotions like *envy* and *jealousy*, you could simply imagine that the plaque at the trophy's base shows the letters *NV* (for envy) within a red circle with a diagonal slash.

# CHAPTER 3

# FROM DEATH TO DUTIES

## (Handbook *Chapters 21-30*)

*"Our duties are generally measured by our social relationships."*

Handbook Ch. 30

## MEMORY TOUR:
### HANDBOOK CHAPTERS 21–30

A S YOU ENTER THE DINING-ROOM DOORWAY (location **㉑**), you are quite surprised to see *your own headstone* sitting there with a *calendar* on the floor right in front of it. Next, you spy standing on a chair at the head of the table **㉒** several *people laughing aloud at your beard.* (If you are like me, you didn't even realize you had one.) Balancing precariously atop a wall thermometer off to the left **㉓** are another group of *people,* some *smiling* and some *frowning* at you. Below, upon the seat at the left of the table **㉔** a most boisterous person mostly boisterously bellows *"What a splendid seat!"* Looking next to the seat at the foot of the table **㉕**, you realize it is actually a massive *gilded throne,* sitting upon a massive *bathroom scale.*

Upon the seat on the right **㉖** sits a *slave boy* deliberately *smashing two mugs.* As you peer into the image in the mirror upon the wall **㉗** you feel as if you're in the middle of a Robin Hood movie scene, as an *arrow* whizzes by your ear and *sticks inside a target's bull's eye.* Above a portrait on another wall is mounted a light **㉘** and it shines upon an odd little scene in which *you handcuff yourself and turn yourself over to a judge.* (Did you do something illegal we don't know about?) At this point, you decide you've had enough of this room, but blocking the doorway out **㉙** is the massive ancient Olympic wrestler *Milo, playing the trumpet* along with his pet *monkey.* Finally, who should be standing right in front of them on an "exit mat" **㉚** but *your own father and brother.*

57

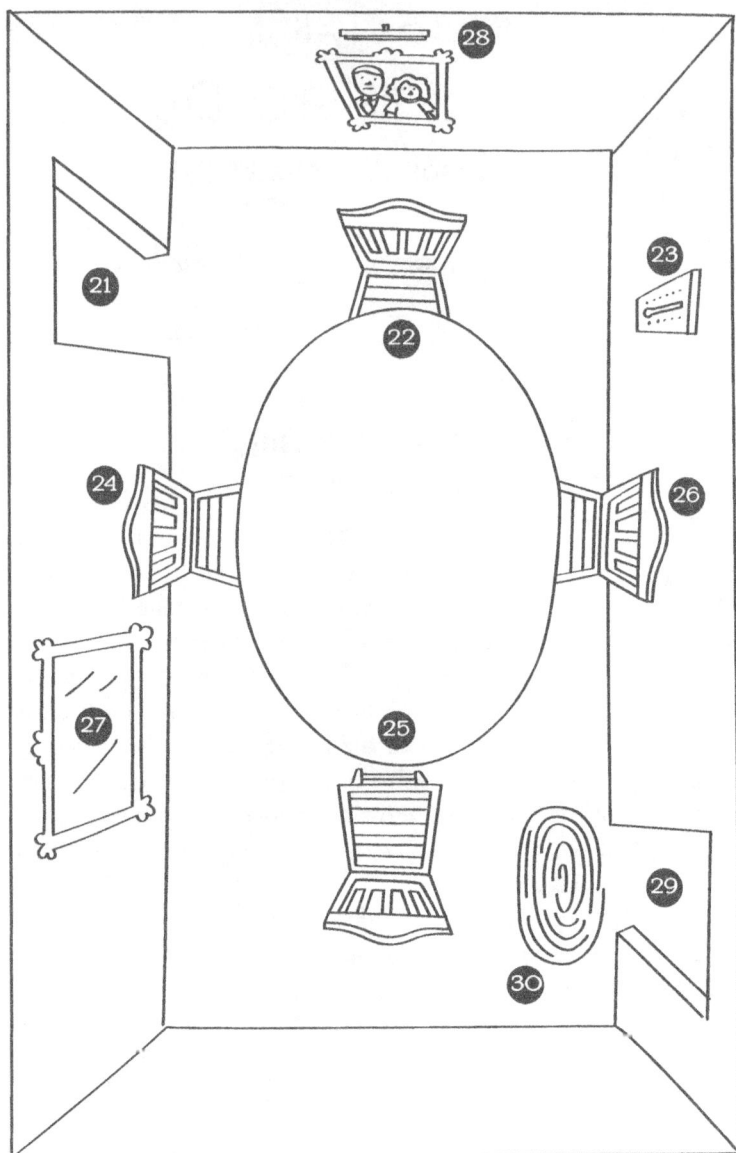

| LOCATION/<br>*HANDBOOK* CHAPTER | IMAGE | LESSON |
|---|---|---|
| ㉑ DINING-ROOM DOORWAY | *Calendar and your headstone* | Memento mori |
| ㉒ HEAD OF TABLE | *People laugh at your beard* | Philosophers expect ridicule |
| ㉓ THERMOMETER | *People smile or frown at you* | Please your higher self |
| ㉔ SEAT ON LEFT | *"What a splendid seat!"* | Love your rightful place |
| ㉕ FOOT OF TABLE | *Gilded throne sits in scales* | Weigh all honors good or bad |
| ㉖ SEAT ON RIGHT | *Slave boy breaks two mugs* | Break your double standards |
| ㉗ MIRROR ON WALL | *Arrow in target's bull's eye* | Nature does not miss |
| ㉘ LIGHT OVER PORTRAIT | *Your body handed to judge* | Hold your judgment dear |
| ㉙ DOOR OUT | *Milo and monkey play trumpet* | Stop monkeying around |
| ㉚ EXIT MAT | *Your own father and brother* | Honor your highest duties |

## THE LESSONS BEHIND THE IMAGES:
## *HANDBOOK* CHAPTERS 21–30

> ㉑  *Don't try to avoid thinking about things that appear terrible, like death or exile, but look at them squarely every day and you will not be carried away by contemptible thoughts or petty desires.* Ω

AS SOON AS WE ENTERED THE DINING ROOM, THERE WAS your own *headstone* with a *calendar* laid out in front of it. Is the thought of looking at your own headstone at all disconcerting? It certainly was to Dickens' Ebenezer Scrooge, but it also helped lead to his "Aha!" moment in recognizing the need to reform his life while he still had the chance.

Here, Epictetus explicitly advises us to think about our own inevitable death on every day of the calendar as a powerful spiritual exercise. It's referred to in Latin as *memento mori*, "remember you will die," words a slave would whisper into the ear of triumphant Roman generals in the midst of their grand victory parades.

Its purpose was to rein in the overweening pride of *arrogantia* or *hubris,* and Epictetus argues that it will rein in all manner of vice and inappropriate desires. There is a strong parallel in Scripture as well: "In all you do, remember the end of your life, and then you will never sin" (Sir. 7:36).

Epictetus advised the same for exile, hopefully an event few of us need face in our time, but a real possibility in Epictetus's day. Indeed, he set up his school in Nicopolis, Greece, after he was exiled from Rome, along with other philosophers. The Emperor Claudius exiled Seneca to the island of Corsica where he stayed for about eight years. Epictetus's own teacher, Musonius Rufus, was exiled three times by various Roman emperors, and of his twenty-one extant lecture fragments, the lengthiest one is lecture 9, "Is Exile an Evil?" Rufus answers "No!" and proceeds to quote Euripides: "As all the heavens are open to the eagle's flight, So all the earth is for a noble man his fatherland."[1]

So then, Epictetus advises us to remember and ponder every day whatever might seem most terrible to us. It will calm our fears to remember that nothing is truly terrible for us if it lies outside our control, and it may inspire us to noble actions if we remember that our opportunities to perform them will one day be over.

> **22** *If you love philosophy brace yourself for ridicule and abuse* from those who will call out, "Here comes the philosopher! Look at his nose in the air!" But don't reject philosophy and don't put on airs either. Stick to your worthy aspirations as if you were assigned to them by God. If you stick to your principles, those who laugh will later admire you, but if you cave in, then you'll be laughed at twice over. Ω

HOW STRANGE THAT AT THAT HEAD OF THE TABLE SAT *people laughing at your beard.* (Stranger still if you are a clean-shaven man—or a woman.) The beard is used here as the classic symbol of the ancient philosopher. Musonius's lecture 21 waxes eloquent about manly beards, comparing them to the crest of a rooster or the mane of a male lion. He also notes they serve the practical purposes of protecting the chin and making it easy to identify a person as a male. In the words of Epictetus in response to an

---

1  Cited in Lutz, 57.

interlocutor: "'Come then, Epictetus, shave off your beard.' If I am a philosopher, I answer: 'I will not shave it off.' 'But I will take off your neck.' 'If that will do you any good, take it off.'"[2]

Well, it appears that Seneca was clean-shaven, Epictetus makes it quite clear elsewhere that there is far more to a philosopher than a long beard, and this lesson is about far more than beards, but hopefully our little discussion of beards will at least help lock in this mnemonic image.

As for the lesson behind the image, note that now Epictetus addresses us not merely as any man or woman on the street, but as budding lovers of philosophy. If we have strived to apply his earlier lessons, people might notice a change in us, and some might find this threatening. Perhaps our drinking and carousing buddies will wonder why we're concerned with virtue and things of the mind now and not only pleasures and things of the body. They might even feel slighted, looked down upon, and decide to make fun of us. So, what are we to do?

Well, hopefully we will apply our previous lessons and not become disturbed by laughter or insults. Further, we will not pretend to be more advanced in philosophy than we truly are or try to convey a sense of our superiority over the unclean masses bereft of philosophy's graces. Indeed, we should remember that God has called us to nobler things. If we stay the course and endure their laughter with good grace, someday our hecklers may become our admirers (and perhaps be drawn toward philosophy too).

If we let their laughter get the best of us and abandon philosophy then they may laugh at us twice, first for thinking we could become philosophers, and second for abandoning ostensibly lofty goals due to something as trifling as ridicule (which as every Stoic knows, is something outside our control, and should be "as nothing" to us).

---

**23** In the same vein, if you abandon your principles in hopes of pleasing others, you have lowered your standards and lost your way. *Be content then to be a philosopher, whether you please others or not.* And if you would be a philosopher, appear one to yourself, and you will become capable of living a life in pursuit of wisdom. Ω

---

2   Oldfather, v. 1, 23, *Discourses* 1.2.

RECALL THAT SURROUNDING THE WALL THERMOMETER *people* were either *smiling* or *frowning* at you. Ideally, it did not bother you much. Lest he give us the impression in the last lesson that we should be overly concerned whether or not other people approve of us, he reminds us that our goal is to pursue and live a life of wisdom, regardless of whether it pleases others or not. A philosopher does not base her actions on whether or not they please the judgments of others. If others admire one's pursuit of virtue, that is certainly a nice side effect. If others do not, that should in no way deflect us from our path to what is true and good.

Ultimately, the opinions of true importance are our own true opinions of ourselves. To quote Shakespeare's Polonius: "To thine own self be true." Epictetus would have us be true to the noblest selves we can be. If we can honestly maintain we are doing our best to become philosophers, someday we'll wake up and find that we are (whether we're bearded or not).

24 Don't fear that you will receive no honors and be a nobody if you don't obtain some high public position or get invited to fancy parties. You think lack of honors a bad thing? How can *you* be in a bad or shameful state because of the actions of *others?* You worry that you won't be able to help your friend if you don't gain an office or accrue great wealth? Perhaps your friends even encourage you to do so that they might become a citizen or get some cash from you. If you can do it in an honorable way while maintaining self-respect, perhaps you will choose to do so, but such wishes of theirs are not up to you. Your friends will be better off with an honest, trustworthy friend than with a friend who has forsaken his dignity for wealth or for office. *Strive to be a good citizen in as humble a position as may befit you and you will serve yourself, your friends, and your city best.* Ω

AS YOU SAT DOWN UPON THE CHAIR AT THE RIGHT OF the dining room table, amazed at its beauty and comfort, you could not help but exclaim *"What a splendid seat!"* Well, our summary above is less than half the length of one of the longest *Handbook* chapters, so I direct you to the *Handbook* itself, when you have the chance. Still, even in our brief abridgement, many lessons are there to be found.

Now, the lesson encapsulated by our mnemonic image (and exclamation) is to come to love our own rightful place, rather than constantly striving for higher ones, higher ones at least in the eyes of the world, and perhaps in the eyes of one's friends. We don't *need* offices, power, or wealth to be the *somebody* God made us, a person with a spark of the divine in our *prohairesis.*

Epictetus recognizes that we might think of the good we could do for our friends if we made such worldly advances. He warns us too that some of our friends might well encourage us to obtain such positions—because of what could be in it for them! This is not to say that accepting certain promotions, striving for new positions or offices, or perhaps becoming an entrepreneur, may not land us in our rightful place, but we will know for sure such strivings are not right for us if we must engage in any vicious or undignified behaviors to obtain them. He advises us that we will truly be most useful to all as friends and as citizens if we do our honest best in whatever position best suits us.

In this chapter we clearly see that the Stoic does not think "It's all about me!" The Stoic does not selfishly pursue wealth or honor at the expense of honesty and dignity. Further, the Stoic does not embrace a naïve altruism either, "doing good" for others through disreputable actions, thinking that good ends justify evil means.[3] Indeed, if we do our honest best in whatever our fitting position might be, regardless of how lofty or humble, we will best serve ourselves, our friends, and our nation. So, whatever our place in life may be at this moment, Epictetus would have us do our best to make it a splendid one!

---

㉕ *If someone else has been given a greater honor than you, a higher place at the table, or perhaps he, and not you, has been sought out for advice, ask yourself if the honors are good or bad. If they are good, you should be glad that the other has received them. If they are bad, then you don't need them.* Remember too that you are in no position to

---

3  The great Socratic friend of the Stoics, Cicero, provides another insight worth pondering in his *De Amicitia* (On Friendship). Some friends might want us to assume some high position, thinking that we, in return, might raise them up as well. Cicero advises as follows: "Now, in the first place, you must render to each friend as much aid as you can, and, in the second place, as much as he whom you have to assist has the capacity to bear." Cicero, *On Friendship*, W. A. Falconer, trans. (Harvard University Press, Cambridge: MA, 2001), 181–83. Not only should we be careful to seek the right place for ourselves, we should exercise care that we do not elevate friends to a height holding burdens they cannot bear up to.

demand an equal share if you did not do the same things to acquire things outside of your control. After all, how can a person who does not hang around a powerful person's door all day have the same share as the person who does? You'll be unjust and greedy if you expect to get things you haven't paid for. If somebody pays an obol for a head of lettuce don't think you are worse off than him if you did not pay and were not given the lettuce. The other guy has his lettuce, and you still have the obol that you did not pay. It works the same way for banquets and grand parties. If you are not invited, it is because you did not pay the inviter's price in praise or attention. While the person who paid that price got the meal and drinks you got something too, the fact that you didn't flatter someone or have to spend the evening hanging around hangers on. 🜨

WE IMAGINED THE CHAIR AT THE FOOT OF THE TABLE AS a *golden throne* sitting upon massive *bathroom scales*. The golden throne represents high honors while the scales remind us of the price we must pay for such honors. Perhaps a ruler sits upon that throne. If that ruler be a wise philosopher-king, you should rejoice that such a good man has attained such a well-deserved honor. If the ruler sitting there fears for his own life due to would-be usurpers, as if the sword of Damocles dangles above his head, be glad that you were not so honored.

Those, of course, are extreme examples. We will never have the choice of whether to strive for the throne of a Roman Emperor like Marcus Aurelius or of a Sicilian King like Dionysius, but we all must choose what kinds of positions or honors we will strive for—or not. We build here on the theme of Epictetus's last chapter. We should not only avoid striving for externals like honors from others, we should recall that those who obtain them often pay a dear price, things like flattery and sycophancy which demean one's self. What price must one pay, for example, to run for a political office or to gain party invites from the in crowd?

In Epictetus's day, many people actually arrived at the doorsteps of powerful people early in the morning to accompany them and sing their praises all day, in hopes of some kind of personal gain. In our day, there are still so many ways we can obsequiously agree with and flatter people of power or influence for our own gain. (In fact, I bet you can think of several slang and vulgar terms commonly used to describe such behaviors and the people who perform them, from "boot licker" on up.) Epictetus would not have us be in their number, because such a price is too high for any external honor.

Further, he would not have us feel that we have lost out on anything because we will not pay such a price. It's up to us. Do you want a head of lettuce bad enough that you are willing to pay an obol for it, or not? (I just did an internet search, and as of today, the lettuce would cost about $1.99.) If you're hungry, hand over two bucks and enjoy. If you're not, hang on to them for something else, but don't envy the guy eating his!

So, to paraphrase O. Henry just a bit, Epictetus offers sage advice here for everything from cabbages to kings. For any tangible good or honor we seek, we should place it in our Stoic scales to determine whether it is good or bad and whether it's worth the price. In the words of the ancient Romans—*Caveat emptor!*[4]

> ㉖ It is possible to discern the will of nature by things in which we do not differ from one another. Your friend's slave boy breaks his mug and you tell him. "It's just one of those things, shrug it off!" How do you act when *your* mug is broken? Take this small lesson and apply it to big things. When a friend's wife or child dies, don't say, "Such is life," and when yours does you wail out "Woe is me!" *Remember then how you feel when you hear of such things that have happened to others.* ㉛

DO YOU RECALL THE CHAIR ON THE RIGHT ON WHICH A *slave boy broke two mugs?* When the little child broke one mug in our front yard back in *Handbook* chapter three, he served to remind us to always consider the nature of things, like the fact that mugs are breakable! Now our mnemonic slave boy is breaking *two mugs* to encourage us to smash our *double standards*, by feeling, acting, and speaking quite differently whether the mug is ours or somebody else's. Of course, the more important the thing that is broken or lost, the more important this lesson becomes. How easy to give advice after someone else's loss and how hard to put ourselves in other people's shoes.

In the 1940s, British philosopher Bertrand Russell made famous what is called "emotive [or emotional] conjugation," in which we can easily find ourselves setting up not only double but *triple-standards*

---

4 Let the buyer beware!

so to speak. Here were two of his examples: "*I* am firm, *you* are obstinate, *he* is a pig-headed fool." Another was "*I* have reconsidered the matter, *you* have changed your mind, *he* has gone back on his word."

Note well how the language is altered in such meaningful ways as we move from the 1st to the 3rd person. I can't help but think that we see such conjugations in action almost every time we hear a prominent politician (as I'm sure was the case back in Epictetus's day too). We must be careful we do not make such mistakes in our own thoughts and words. We can exercise such care precisely by heeding Epictetus's advice to remember the things in which we do not differ from one another, that is, the things that are common to us all in our human nature, including this erroneous tendency to shift our evaluations, statements, and advice to make ourselves sound better or to treat our own losses as if they were greater than similar losses experienced by others.

> **27** *Just as a target is not set up in order to be missed, neither are things that exist in nature bad or evil in themselves.*[5] Ω

REMEMBER THAT *ARROW* WHIZZING BY YOUR EAR AND lodging into the *bull's eye* in the center of the mirror? Well, Epictetus is always advising us to follow nature because nature does not miss! Indeed, he would seem to agree with the oft-repeated lesson of Genesis 1 that all that God has made is good. Every single thing that exists or occurs has its place in the overall order of the universe and is not bad or evil in itself. What matters to us is what we make of the things that exist and the events that occur.

It was decades ago now when what looked to me like two innocent little sweat bees buzzed nearby as I removed a lawn mower from a hatchback, intending to mow my aging parents' lawn. "I won't bother them, and they won't bother me," I thought to myself. Lo, the little darlings were no sweat bees but yellow jacket hornets and their arrows did not miss their mark on my thigh, as I explained to an urgent care physician a few hours later.

As we'll see when we get to the "exit mat" in this room, Epictetus himself tells us we must honor and care for our parents, yet nature itself had gotten in my way. What horrid little flying things!

---

5  This translates the entire one-sentence chapter.

Of course, despite the swollen, painful leg, that event was not truly evil, or even bad, and I'm thankful for yellow jackets. My mother, you see, owned farm land, and one of the yellow jacket hornet's roles is to feed their children with insects that love munching on crops. They also eat houseflies that can spread disease.[6] Further, the two that double-teamed me taught me about my own allergic reaction to such stings, so I'll know what to do in the future.

We should remember that nature does not miss the target, and even if we *are* the target, nature may be teaching us painful but valuable lessons. It's up to us to learn from them.

> **28** Think how angry you would be if someone turned over your *body* to any person who happened to cross your path. Well then, why are you not ashamed to your turn over your *mind* to any person who happens along, so that when he insults or slights you, you allow your thoughts to become disturbed and upset? Ω

IT WAS AN ODD AND A PERSONAL MEMORY IMAGE, WHEN the light above the mirror shined upon the scene of *you handcuffing yourself and turning your body over to some judge.* Now you see why we imagined it, and doesn't Epictetus make a really good point? Could he see the future, or perhaps human nature has simply not changed too much in the last 2,000 years? Here is another, and not the last, chapter that addresses insulting behaviors from others, and that does so with a most striking image.

Surely, we would not hand over our *hand* or an *eye* to any Tom, Dick, or Harry, Sue, Tish, or Sherry passing by, and yet how often do we hand over our *minds* to some irate disgruntled customer, or perhaps some internet troll? When we come to *Handbook* chapter 33 we'll encounter a wonderful little Epictetian rejoinder to insults, but here is a rejoinder that first comes to my mind as a fitting example of this chapter's lesson.

To paraphrase to my best recollection a scene from Ayn Rand's novel, *The Fountainhead,* architectural critic Ellsworth Toohey has spent years writing negative columns attempting to crush the career of the maverick architect, Howard Roark. Toohey eventually

---

6 Of course, even the lowly housefly has its role to play in the broader ecosystem, by eating things like waste and rot, and feeding perhaps more lovable creatures like frogs.

meets Roark face-to-face and asks Roark what he thinks of him. Roark calmly responds, "But I don't think of you." Roark was not one to hand over his mind to another.

> **㉙** *If you set your sights on some goal, think out in advance the long sequence of behaviors that must lead up to it and follow it.* You would wear the glorious laurel wreath of the Olympic athlete? It's a fine thing indeed, but are you willing to eat a strict diet, train relentlessly, forgo wine, turn yourself over to the orders of a trainer, and be willing to dislocate your shoulder, sprain your ankle, wrench your spine, eat a mouthful of dirt, and after all that suffer defeat? Do you want to compete in the pentathlon or to wrestle? Well then, inspect your own nature. Look at your arms and your thighs and your back. Are they suited to such pursuits? Think about such things, and then go for it if you still want it. Otherwise, you'll become like the child who will be a gladiator one day, a trumpeter the next, and an actor the day after that, or indeed like a monkey who does what he sees. Find the pursuits that are truly fitting for you and then pursue them if you are willing to pay the price. *Ultimately, your heart must be set either on externals or on your ruling principle. It's up to you whether you choose the role of a philosopher, or that of a non-philosopher.* **Ω**

SO HERE IS WHY *MILO,* THE GREATEST OLYMPIC WRES- tler, and a *trumpet-playing monkey* were there at the site of the doorway. Now, philosophy is the love of wisdom and one of the four cardinal virtues is *phronesis* (prudence or practical wisdom). Though Epictetus does not explicitly name it, he enumerates several of what philosophers like Aristotle, Macrobius, and St. Thomas Aquinas described as parts of prudence, or additional virtues necessary to exercise it fully. Among these that Epictetus addresses are *circumspection*, looking around to consider all that the task entails, *understanding* the nature of the course of action one is considering to pursue and the nature of oneself as the would-be pursuer, exercising *foresight* regarding possible outcomes, and *caution*, taking the time to think and *reason* all these things through before leaping into action.

Epictetus advises us to employ prudent thinking to determine just which kinds of pursuits will lead us toward a fulfilling life. He also further develops the theme of remembering to weigh and consider the price we must pay for preferred external things. Epictetus cherished things of the mind, but, though they are externals, he did not disparage the things of the body. And as a man immersed in Greek thought and culture, he thought an Olympic victory a very fine thing. He knew well though that not everyone has what it takes to make it to the top in such an arduous endeavor. A person must be willing to do whatever *is within his control* to achieve athletic excellence, be it suffering deprivations, pain, injuries, eating dirt, and perhaps still encountering defeat. Yet, even that is not enough. The things of one's own body *outside of one's control,* like the skeletal structure and natural muscle lengths of relevant body parts, must be suited to the task at hand. (Epictetus anticipates the advice I would receive from a Mr. Universe in 1978!) The body naturally suited for distance running will not fare well in Olympic wrestling (not to mention Sumo wrestling on the other side of the world), and vice-versa.

Epictetus advises us to look at our true levels of desire and our own natural suitability for whatever activity we decide to pursue, lest we become like a child who plays soldier one day, trumpeter the next, like a monkey who imitates whatever catches his attention. Of course, Epictetus speaks of more than merely sports or hobbies. He would have us become not dilettantes in fickle pursuit of sundry externals, but philosophers in constant pursuit of the things that matter the most, the rational, *prohairetic* things of our *hêgemonikon* or "ruling principle."

As intelligent beings blessed with the divine spark of reason, we all possess the natural capacity to pursue philosophy. It is up to us to determine if we are willing to pay the price, and if we do, we will find it far more valuable than any Olympic crown of olive leaves (or even a modern gold medal).

**30** *We find our true duties by examining our social relationships. You have a father? Then take care of him. "But he is not a good father." Did nature determine you would have a good father? No, only that you would have a father. "My brother has harmed me." Well then, maintain your brotherly relation with him. Focus not on what he has done, but on how you can keep the responses you choose in harmony with nature. Another person can't truly harm you unless you allow it. You are harmed when you choose to think you* *have been harmed.* So then, keep this in mind, indeed, make it a habit, as you consider what duties to expect from your neighbor, your fellow citizen, or your commanding officer. Ω

HERE'S WHY *YOUR FATHER AND BROTHER* WERE WAITING for you at the "exit mat." Epictetus has taught us so many valuable lessons on how we should *think* (with a view to the true nature of things) and what we should *desire* (virtue and things that are up to us), and now he gives us the golden key to determining what we should *do. Appropriate actions or duties are determined by the nature of our human relationships and roles.*

Do you remember our favorite actor at the *piano* illustrating the lesson of *Handbook* chapter 17 to play well the *role* the Playwright has assigned us? Here he zooms in on the most intimate and enduring roles we play throughout our lives, our roles within our own families. He reminds us that the family we are born into is outside of our control. Nature says we must all have fathers (and mothers, of course), but not necessarily that they will be good ones. Good or not, it is still up to us how we act toward them. Many of us have brothers or sisters as well, and again, we do not get to choose them! Even if they should act maliciously toward us, we should remember they cannot truly harm us and we should not try to harm them, but to act as good persons ourselves, helping them where we can, and deflecting their slings and arrows if need be.

Perhaps they will learn lessons from our good actions and be inspired to shape up their acts. All the better if that should happen, but whether it does or not, we have our own role to play as best we can.

If I might digress just a bit, consider how modern Stoicism-inspired cognitive therapies first developed through the work of formerly psychoanalytic practitioners like Albert Ellis and Aaron Beck.[7] While psychoanalytic therapies tend to place great weight on the psychological influences of our early family environments, Epictetus and his modern cognitive offspring would remind us that even if we did have far less than desirable fathers or mothers who raised us up, it is up to us as adults to determine how we will treat them, and to what extent we choose to allow their past behaviors to

---

7 As we will flesh out in more detail when we get to chapter 15.

influence our current thoughts, emotions, and behaviors. Valuable lessons can be learned from less-than-ideal experiences. It also calls to my mind the old story of two brothers, one an alcoholic, and one a teetotaler. When the first was asked why he was an alcoholic, he responded that his father was an alcoholic. When the second was asked why he did not drink at all, he responded that his father was an alcoholic. Their father did not cause their behavior, but the *judgments* they made about his behavior did.

Epictetus would have us remember our extra-familial roles and relationships too, as neighbors, citizens, or perhaps even soldiers, as the case may be. Whether or not they act appropriately toward us, it is our duty to act toward them as befits a lover of wisdom and of his fellow man.

SO ENDS OUR CHAPTER 3. DO YOU RECALL ALL THE *locations* and *images* in our dining room? Do those images call to your mind at least one sound Stoic lesson? And while you are at it, are the first 20 *Handbook* lessons still locked in too? If not, I direct you to the table at the start of this chapter or the master table at the end of Part I. When you've finished, please join me again as we strive to keep building our moral character by bolstering virtues from piety to modesty.

# CHAPTER 4

# ON BUILDING
# ONE'S CHARACTER—
# FROM PIETY TO MODESTY
### (Handbook *Chapters 31-40*)

*"Decide right now what kind of a character you will build and maintain whether you are alone or with other people."*

Handbook Ch. 33

## MEMORY TOUR:
### HANDBOOK CHAPTERS 31–40

N EXT, WE MOVE INTO OUR MNEMONIC STUDY where we will study the *Handbook's* 31st to 40th lessons. Let's pick up a piece of pie, a cup of tea, and head on in.

Upon a massive L-shaped writing desk **31** sits Olympian *Zeus* himself (you can tell by the thunderbolt in his right hand). You find yourself offering him your *pie* and *tea*. Upon the leather chair **32** sits a replica of the ancient *Temple* of Apollo at Delphi, and atop the steps *Apollo* himself *throwing somebody out!* The computer monitor **33** is turned on to some kind of raucous chat room where *Socrates* and *Zeno* stare back at you *in silence.* On the wall on the left sits a copy of Raphael's famous painting **34** "The School of Athens." Plato's right hand points up to the heavens, and Aristotle's points out to the earth, as they usually do. You notice too, however, that in their left hands, each man is holding a *water clock.* Next you spy a beautiful Greek urn **35**, and the scene painted on it depicts a dramatic *unveiling* of a *bust of Zeno.*

Sitting on a shelf is a stack of Stoic books **36**, which should come as no surprise in this study. Oddly enough though, the book spines are decorated to depict the image of an *Epicurean philosopher*

*chewing on a huge leg of lamb* (which was apparently finger-licking good!). Now, who should be squeezing into the chair of the left ③⑦ but *Peter Pan* himself, and your high school *principal*. Next to the chair is a floor lamp ③⑧, and a military *commander* is hopping around it on one foot, since he just *stepped on a nail*. Strangely enough, the right arm of the right chair ③⑨ is transformed into a mountain *cliff*, and some poor *guy* steps right off it. Last, but not least, sitting upon a pedestal, mighty Atlas himself kneels as he holds a world globe on his back ④⓪. As you peer into the globe, however, you are surprised to see not oceans and continents, but a stage with a *young girls' beauty contest* in progress.

| LOCATION/ HANDBOOK CHAPTER | IMAGE | LESSON |
|---|---|---|
| ③① DESKTOP | *Giving Zeus pie and tea* | Don't blame the gods or fate |
| ③② LEATHER CHAIR | *Apollo as temple bouncer* | Create your own fortune |
| ③③ COMPUTER MONITOR | *Zeno and Socrates silent* | Imitate Socrates or Zeno |
| ③④ PICTURE OF PHILOSOPHERS | *Two water clocks* | Think twice, then act or not |
| ③⑤ GREEK URN | *Bust dramatically unveiled* | Never hide what's right |
| ③⑥ STOIC BOOKS | *Climber chewing lamb leg* | Etiquette over selfishness |
| ③⑦ LEFT CHAIR | *Peter Pan and your principal* | Fill your true role |
| ③⑧ FLOOR LAMP | *Commander steps on nail* | Protect your Prohairesis |
| ③⑨ RIGHT CHAIR | *Man walks off cliff* | Attend to your true needs |
| ④⓪ ATLAS HOLDS GLOBE | *Young girls' beauty pageant* | Honor women's virtues |

## THE LESSONS BEHIND THE IMAGES: HANDBOOK CHAPTERS 31–40

③①     We best show piety to the gods when we hold true *beliefs* about them—that they exist and administer the universe justly, and when we submit our *wills* to their judgment, accepting that the universe is as it is for a purpose and whatever happens does so for a purpose. In this way, you will not blame the gods or accuse them of neglect. *To achieve such piety, we must detach our ideas of what is good and what is bad from what is not up to us, and focus our thoughts every day on the things that are up to us.* Otherwise, we will seek out the gods to blame, when we focus only on externals that seem evil and purposeless at the surface level, and when not seen in the light of the grander scheme. We cannot have pious feelings toward the gods if we erroneously believe they are causing us harm. When we properly tend to our desires and aversions in accordance with reason and nature, we show piety to the gods. Further, it is always appropriate to make libations[1] and sacrifices and to give

---

1   A portion of a drink, most often wine, that pious Greeks would pour out in offering to the gods before they drank the rest. (Some ancient sources tell of some stingy, rather less than pious people had who mastered the art of a quick flick of the wrist that would spill merely a drop.)

the gods first-fruits according to the traditions of our fathers, and to do so with pure hearts and with liberal generosity. Ω

OUR MNEMONIC IMAGE OF OFFERING *PIE* AND *TEA* TO *ZEUS* himself sitting on the desk should call to mind Epictetus's call to *piety* to the gods. Now, while our focus is clearly on Epictetus's ethics, rather than his natural theology, I should briefly note once more that different Stoics had different conceptions of the divine. The Stoics did not deny the gods, and some saw the reality of a single God. Aided by reason but lacking in divine revelation, they had varied conceptions of God that captured pieces and parts of the truths of His nature. Epictetus's natural reason did lead him to God, whom he sometimes calls God and sometimes Zeus, the chief of the Greek gods whose name essentially means God—*Theos,* or, in Latin, *Deus,* as in deity.[2] In *Discourse* II.14.11, Epictetus provides some of the reasoning that led him to a Divine Being who governs the universe. He also stressed God's ultimate importance there:

> Now the philosophers say that the first thing we must
> learn is this: That there is a God, and that He provides
> for the universe, and that it is impossible for a man to
> conceal from Him, not merely his actions, but even his
> purposes and his thoughts.[3]

Epictetus stresses the importance of a proper understanding of the existence and justice of God, coupled with a desire to follow his will in all that we do. He reiterates previous lessons that if we trust in God's Providence, we will not blame him for anything that happens. He has given us dominion over our own *prohairesis,* and for that greatest of all goods we should show our gratitude through participating in traditional acts of religion that honor him.

If you will recall *Handbook* chapter 30's emphasis on what we owe our parents, we see in this chapter a further development of the classical virtue of *piety.* A primary object of piety is the

---

2  In commenting on this *Handbook* chapter, philosopher Keith Seddon notes that the terms "gods," "God," and Zeus are virtually interchangeable for the Stoics, and "the Stoics also identify God with providence, fate, reason, nature, and the world itself." Keith Seddon, *Epictetus' Handbook and the Tablet of Cebes: Guides to Stoic Living* (New York, NY: Routledge, 2005), 120.
3  Oldfather, v.l, 301.

honor we owe our parents for giving us life and nurturing us. In Virgil's *Aeneid*, the hero Aeneas was often called "the pious." Early in the narrative we see him carrying his aged father Anchises upon his shoulders, guiding him to safety through the burning streets of Troy (as Aeneas holds the hand of his own young son). Another object of piety is our nation or country, often referred to as a "fatherland" or "motherland." Indeed, in chapter 30, Epictetus speaks of our roles as citizens too. Piety's highest object of all is God, the Father of us all, he to whom we all owe our being.

In a very real sense, key themes of *Handbook* chapters 30 and 31 are summed up in this brief line from St. Thomas Aquinas in his treatment of the virtue of piety: "Man is debtor chiefly to his parents and his country, after God."[4] Hopefully, handing Zeus some pie and tea will help us remember the kind of debts we should gladly strive to repay God, within the limits of what's up to us.

> **32**    Would you go to a fortune-teller? Bear in mind that even if their predictions are right, they have nothing of value to tell you. *You have no need of a fortune-teller to tell you to always do what is right and just, regardless of what the outcome might be.* Remember how that great diviner, Pythian Apollo, threw out of his temple a man who did not help his friend when he was being murdered.[5]

SO, THIS WAS WHY WE SAW THE GREEK GOD *APOLLO THROW a man out of his temple* that sat in the leather chair. The idea should not be completely unfamiliar. All four gospels tell us Jesus Christ expelled money-changers from his Father's temple, because they turned a house of prayer into a den of thieves. According to a Greek myth, two friends were beset by robbers on the road. One man, rather than risking his own life in helping defend his friend who was being attacked, continued to the temple of Apollo, god of reason, to ask for his advice. Why was he thrown out? We have already been given the divine spark of reason and should all know that we must do what is right, whether or not it could prove harmful to us, and whether or not we will ultimately succeed. (This is

---

4   Thomas Aquinas, *Summa Theologica*, IIa-IIae, Q. 101, a. 1.
5   The story refers to the god Apollo at the Oracle of Delphi and the idea that one should not need a fortune-teller to know that one should defend one's country or one's friend despite possible harm to oneself.

also referred to as "natural law.") Acting according to right reason is always up to us, and this is what God expects of us.

Now, I've just summarized a portion of *Handbook* 32, and Epictetus also cites Socrates' advice never to consult an oracle about the *outcome* of an action we know we should perform because it is morally right. Simplicius sums it up like this: "At any rate, both Epictetus and Socrates seem to have forbidden us to ask about things that the soul can know about in itself."[6]

Some well-meaning teachers tell students there are no stupid questions. Epictetus and Socrates might disagree!

> **㉝** *Decide right now what kind of a character you will build and maintain whether you are alone or with others.* Be silent when you can. Listen more than you speak. Stick to your bare needs for bodily things like clothing, food, drink, housing and possessions. Get rid of anything you hold just for the sake of reputation or luxury. As for sex, stay pure before marriage, but don't be angry with those who do not abstain, and don't boast about your abstinence. If someone tells you that somebody else is saying bad things about you, don't defend yourself, but merely say, *"That person obviously did not know about all of my other faults, or he would have brought those up too."* When you have to go to public events don't get carried away by the mob, but maintain your honor and dignity. *When you are about to meet someone of prominence, ask yourself, "What would Socrates or Zeno have done in this situation?"* Expect to be shunned or ignored if you desire or need to call on a person of importance, and do not be distressed if you are told he isn't home or if he pays you no attention. In conversation, don't carry on about your own deeds and accomplishments. It is not as pleasant for others to hear what has happened to you as it is for you to talk about it. Avoid too becoming a buffoon or slipping into vulgarity. When another person uses foul language in your presence, tell him you do not appreciate that if the opportunity arises, and if not, you can get your message across by your silence or your frown at his words. **Ω**

WHEN WE LOOKED UPON THE COMPUTER MONITOR ON THE desk, we beheld some kind of raucous chat room in which *Zeno and Socrates* looked out at us in *silence.* Even our condensed summary of

---

6 Simplicius, v. 2, 86.

*Handbook* chapter 33 is so chock full of lessons, we might imagine that Zeno and Socrates are remaining silent so they don't miss a single point. Epictetus has given us a fairly extensive primer on some fundamental do's and don'ts of proper Stoic behavior.

Starting with the "don'ts," Epictetus warns us of the faults of inconsistency in our behaviors, of excessive chattiness, of buffoonery, of sexual incontinence, of boasting about sexual continence, of becoming upset by insults, of seeking idle entertainments, of flattery, of disdain, of talking too much about oneself, and of vulgar language.

As for some of the "do's," Epictetus exhorts us to develop a consistent character of integrity, so we act the same way whether we are alone or with others, to cultivate the habit of silence so we can learn from others and maintain our dignity, to respond to insults with calm good humor, to think about how Socrates or Zeno might behave when we are about to meet a distinguished person, to discourage foul language in our presence, by open correction if circumstances warrant, or at least by silence or frowning in response to its use.[7]

For the sake of brevity, I'll zoom in on Epictetus's advice regarding insults. He said that if we are told someone has spoken poorly of us, we should respond as follows: *"That person obviously did not know about all of my other faults, or he would have brought those up too."*

I can't help but love that response. First of all, it is very likely absolutely true! It also bespeaks humility, self-awareness, and humor. Such a total lack of defensiveness shows that one has received no injury at all, that one, like Zeno and Socrates before him, has successfully donned the armor of philosophy and become invincible (at least in regard to petty insults).

---

7   Here's a hopefully fun, little coincidence. When I spoke at the Stoicon X Milwaukee in 2019 one of the brief "lightning round" speakers spoke of the benefit we can obtain from reading good biographies, and he mentioned Ron Chernow's *Grant*. I happened to have recently finished the book myself, and being of a similar mind with Epictetus and Ulysses S. Grant on the subject of cussing and swearing, this quote from Grant comes to mind whenever I read *Handbook* 33: "I never learned to swear. When a boy I seemed to have an aversion to it, and when I became a man I saw the folly of it. I have always noticed, too, that swearing helps to rouse a man's anger; and when a man flies into a passion his adversary who keeps cool always gets the better of him. In fact, I could never see the use of swearing. I think it is the case with many people who swear excessively that they do not mean to be profane; but, to say the least, it is a great waste of time."

> **㉞**   *Be on your guard when faced with apparent pleasures. Don't be carried away by first appearances, but wait for a while and give yourself time to think. Then call to mind two times, not only the time in which you'll enjoy that pleasure, but the time afterwards when you'll berate yourself for your action. Then imagine instead how you will be truly pleased and worthy of self-praise if you refrain from it. If there are times when it is reasonable to indulge in a particular pleasant action, even then, don't get carried away by its charm, pleasure, and attractiveness, but also keep in mind how much better it is to win victory over your desires for pleasure.* Ω

REMEMBER RAPHAEL'S *SCHOOL OF ATHENS* UP ON THE WALL, and how Aristotle and Plato were holding *water clocks*? In the actual painting, they are surrounded by a large group of philosophers including Socrates, Diogenes, and possibly our own Stoic Zeno. Plato (patterned after the face and body of Leonardo Da Vinci), points toward the heavenly realm of the forms or ideas, while Aristotle points out toward the earth, since he believed our knowledge is built from the evidence that comes in from our senses.

Now, the primary reason I used this painting is because it really does sit in this spot in my actual study. The reason Plato and Aristotle are holding water clocks is to remind us of Epictetus's fundamental piece of advice for controlling our desires for pleasures, which is to keep *two times* in mind, the time spent enjoying the pleasure, and the time afterward when we will face the consequences. Indeed, he has given us a powerful tool to rein in vices like gluttony and lust, if we train ourselves in its use.

How tasty that jelly-filled donut looks, and we've only had a couple of glazed ones so far. Imagine its exquisite flavors washed down by cold milk or hot coffee. And yet, a few minutes later, how much will we enjoy that temporary abdominal bloat, sure to be followed by more permanent abdominal fat? How beautiful that man or woman appears, but how would it impact our spouse if he or she were to find out that we had engaged in improprieties? How would it impact our relationship with our spouse even if he or she did not know? How would this look in the eyes of God?

Recall that in *Handbook* chapter 10, Epictetus told us we have the power to deal with the appearance of an attractive person. We must remember we have *self-control*. Here he gives us a technique to help develop it by using our powers or reason and imagination to bring the powerful negative consequences of illicit pleasures to the forefront of our minds.

Further, he cautions us not to be overcome and carried away even by appropriate pleasures, like perhaps just that first donut. Those who think like a Stoic will be too busy pursuing virtue to spend too much time seeking pleasures, and we will often be much more pleased with ourselves when we flee from fleeting pleasures.

> **㉟** *If you determine that it is right to do some action, then never try to hide it, even if others might misinterpret it and think you are up to no good. If it is not the right thing to do, then don't do it. But if it is, why should you be afraid of those who criticize you wrongly?* Ω

WHY WAS OUR GREEK URN ON THE SHELF NOT DECORATED with armored warriors (as is the real one on my shelf), but with a *bust of Zeno* being *dramatically unveiled*? Well, Zeno was so right in starting Stoic philosophy and we should never hide what is right! To adapt a modern commercial phrase, Epictetus proclaims: "Just do it!—if it is right; Just don't do it!—if it is wrong." It appears that St. Thomas Aquinas would agree, for he later summarizes the fundamental precepts of the virtue of justice as "Do good and do not do evil."

Notice how Epictetus exhorts us in yet another way not to be carried away by first impressions or appearances, but to stand fast and drill deep down to the level of underlying truths. If you have determined what is right and morally just for you to do, then do it, even if others may not understand and may criticize you. Hopefully we are all learning how to bear criticisms and insults by now. Further, if it's wrong, do not do it, even though it might win you praise.

> **㊱** *Think of your actions in their complete context and moderate them accordingly.* When you have a meal with others, remember not only the pleasure and nourishment that would come from grabbing an overly large portion, but also the respectful behavior you owe to your host. Ω

NEXT, WE CAME TO THE STACK OF BOOKS WITH THAT strange picture on the side binding of an *Epicurean* chewing on a *massive leg of lamb*. Well, the Epicureans placed *pleasure* as the highest value, as opposed to the Stoics who prized *virtue.* I chose this image partly because there is a popular misconception that the Epicureans encouraged over-indulgence in simple bodily pleasures, encouraging things like gluttony, but as we'll see when we come to Seneca, who frequently cites Epicurus, even they prized most highly the nobler pleasures of the mind.

Even more should those who would think like a Stoic moderate desires for bodily pleasure by considering them in their overall context, remembering that it is more important to properly exercise one's *prohairesis* by respecting one's host (and other guests) by not reaching out for an undue portion. We exercise our power of prudence when we consider events in their complete context and we exercise our power of continence when we rein in our desires for huge, tasty portions. And of course, this applies to far more than legs of lamb. As Epictetus has told us before, we should not stretch out our desires for things outside our control, but should accept with grace and gratitude whatever allotment comes our way.

㊲ *If you take on some position or project beyond your true capacity, you will bring disgrace on yourself,* and by taking on an inappropriate role, you will be neglecting to take on a role that truly is fitting for you. Ω

AH! YOU HAVE DEDUCED WHY WE PICTURED YOUR HIGH school principal sitting with Peter Pan on the study's left chair? Then you have heard of Laurence Peter's modern management concept called the "Peter Principle" (as explained in his partially tongue-in-cheek book of the same name). Namely, people within an organizational hierarchy tend to get promoted due to successes in previous positions until they attain a level *beyond* their true capacities, to their "level of incompetence"—and that is where they tend to stay!

How intriguing that 1900 years before Peter, Epictetus warned us not to promote *ourselves* to the level of our incompetence! We should not desire roles we do not have the capacities to perform. Rather, we must know ourselves and assess our true capacities. Perhaps we can become more capable over time for some desired position with proper training and experience and render ourselves fit for some higher role. Until that time should come, if we occupy a role that we can perform well, we should do our very best at it. In that way we will serve ourselves and others best.

**38** *Just as when walking you are careful not to step on a nail or twist your ankle, pay as much attention not to bring harm to your ruling principle.*[8] *If we exercise such care with every action, we will act more securely.* Ω

REMEMBER THAT *MILITARY COMMANDER* HOPPING AROUND the floor lamp because he'd just *stepped on a nail?* Thankfully, people don't step on nails very often, because we tend to be reasonably careful of our *bodily integrity* and we "watch our step" while we walk. We should be just as careful before performing any action that could puncture or twist our *moral character.* It's like the lesson he taught us about insults back at the light over the portrait in the dining room. We wouldn't willingly hand our bodies over to a judge, and neither should we hand over our *prohairesis* to anyone who judges us. So, too when we commence to judge whether or not we will perform a particular action, we take care to keep our souls safe from harm at least as much as we would our bodies.

**39** *Regarding your possessions, the body provides the true measure of your needs, as the nature of the foot calls for the need for shoes. To get carried away beyond true need is to walk over a cliff.* Even with shoes, if you go beyond the measure of the needs of the foot, you will think you need gilded shoes and then shoes with purple embroidery. The sky is the limit once a thing moves beyond its true measure. Ω

OUR NEXT IMAGE WAS NO CLIFF-HANGER, BECAUSE WE know the little *man walked right off that cliff* that grew from the right chair's arm. Epictetus tells us again and again not to get carried away by our first impressions or by our desires, for to do so could lead to moral suicide. Remember to ask yourself the true nature of things. What is the nature of shoes? They serve to protect the feet, not to broadcast their owner's lofty opinion of himself to the world. If we are too focused on acquiring and displaying externals, our desires will become further and further removed from nature and will lead us to a fall. Attend to your true needs as a person of character.

---

8   In Stoic psychology, the *hegemonikon* is the essential part of the soul that can discern the good and choose to act upon it. Various translations use "ruling principle," "governing principle," "ruling faculty," or simply "mind."

**40** Females are called "ladies" or "mistresses" right after they turn fourteen. If they see they are valued as nothing but bedmates for men, they place all their focus on their appearance and place all their hopes on luring a man. *We should rather take care to make clear to young women that they are valued not only for their attractiveness, but for appearing modest and showing self-respect in their dress and manner.* Ω

THIS IS WHY WE PICTURED NOT CONTINENTS, BUT A *TEEN-age beauty contest* depicted on the globe Atlas held on his back. Two millennia before the "Me Too" movement Epictetus made clear that any person of moral character should value women for far more than their bodies. Further, young girls should be encouraged to focus not only on displaying their physical attractiveness to men, but on displaying virtues like modesty, which bespeaks their self-respect. We could expect as much from Epictetus, whose mentor, Musonius Rufus, declared:

> Rather than educating men and women differently concerning the most important things in life, we should teach them the same. If anyone asks me what knowledge guides this education, I will say to him that just as no man would be properly educated without philosophy, so no woman would be either.[9]

OKAY, SO THAT'S A WRAP FOR *HANDBOOK* CHAPTERS 31–40 on virtues from piety to modesty and many in between. Can you recall the study's locations, images, and central lessons? If not, as you know so well by now, *repetitio mater memoriae.* In our next chapter, we'll move outside for a breath of fresh air to our memory house's most memorable porch.

---

9 Cynthia King, *Musonius Rufus: Lectures and Sayings* (North Charleston, SC: William B. Irvine, Pub./CreateSpace.com, 2011), 33.

# CHAPTER 5
# TENDING THE TEMPLE OF THE BODY AND MIND
## (Handbook *Chapters 41–50*)

*"It is the mark of a small mind to be excessively focused on the concerns of the body, with excessive exercising, eating, drinking, and sexual activity."*

*Handbook* Ch. 41

## MEMORY TOUR:
### *HANDBOOK* CHAPTERS 41–50

I INVITE YOU NOW TO WALK WITH ME OUT TO the porch. Your very first glance reveals that this is no ordinary porch attached to my house, but the famous *Stoa Poikile*, the "Painted Porch" in Athens, Greece upon which Zeno taught, and from which the Stoics took their name!

You first notice an odd sight upon the front steps (location **41**) where an enormous *bodybuilder* with a very *tiny head* stands there flexing and staring at his muscles. Upon the porch and off to the left, sitting atop a short pedestal, is a bust of Zeno himself **42**. You spy *yourself* right behind it, smiling and gently *patting the back* of a person who just *insulted* your honor! How odd that a pillar just to the left **43** depicts your own *brother*, but instead of arms he has *handles* protruding from his side. Leaning against the left wall **44** a *sneering miser looks down*. What an odd thing, you think next, for the beauty-loving ancient Greeks to adorn the frieze above the left wall **45** with a *smelly wino lying in a gutter*.

Above the apex of the porch, you see a starry night **46** and two people crouched on the peak. The *person on the left is looking right over Socrates' head*, paying him no attention. At the right frieze **47** you see another friend and hero of the Stoics, *Diogenes the Cynic, hugging one of the statues* depicted in bas-relief. Can't

imagine what Diogenes looked like? Well, the word Cynic came from the Greek "cyon," meaning dog (similar to the Latin *"canis"* from which we derive "canine"). Just picture a *man* with the *head of a dog* hugging the statue. Right underneath, standing in front of the right wall base ㊽, you find *three people* standing there, one *short*, one of *medium* height, and one *tall*. In front of the right pillar ㊾ is yet another great Stoic, and one of Epictetus's favorites, *Chrysippus.* He's *writing* something down on a tablet, unfortunately quite *illegibly.* (If you're having trouble forming a mental image of Chrysippus, feel free to simply substitute a person you know named Chris.) Finally, to our great surprise, who should stand teaching in the center of the Stoa ㊿, but, straight from Nicopolis—*Epictetus* himself! He calls *you* up to stand by him and *hold* for him some *stone tablets.*

| LOCATION/ HANDBOOK CHAPTER | IMAGE | LESSON |
|---|---|---|
| ④① STOA STEPS | *Microcephalic bodybuilder* | Mind your mind |
| ④② BUST OF ZENO | *You pat insulter's back* | "It seemed that way to him" |
| ④③ LEFT PILLAR | *Your brother with two handles* | You can choose which handle |
| ④④ LEFT WALL | *Sneering miser looks down* | You aren't what you own |
| ④⑤ LEFT FRIEZE | *Smelly wino in gutter* | Give benefit of doubt |
| ④⑥ STARS ABOVE APEX | *Person peers over Socrates* | Don't claim to love wisdom |
| ④⑦ RIGHT FRIEZE | *Diogenes hugging it* | Don't put on a show |
| ④⑧ RIGHT WALL BASE | *Three persons of rising height* | Signs to gauge progress |
| ④⑨ RIGHT PILLAR | *Chrysippus writing illegibly* | Don't parse or parrot, but live |
| ⑤⓪ EPICTETUS'S BODY | *You stand by stone tablets* | Hold these principles sacred |

## THE LESSONS BEHIND THE IMAGES: *HANDBOOK* CHAPTERS 41–50

④① *It is the mark of a small mind to be excessively focused on the concerns of the body, with excessive exercising, eating, drinking, and sexual activity. You must keep these things in their proper place, doing them in passing, but focus your attention fully on the ruling part of your soul.* Ω

AS WE STEPPED OUTSIDE OF OUR MEMORY HOUSE FOR A breath of fresh air, we found that our porch is indeed the great "Painted Porch" in Athens from which the Stoics took their name.[1] As a former contestant in and current practitioner of bodybuilding myself, I suggested with a hint of hesitation our man of all brawn and no brains (the massive *bodybuilder* with a *tiny head*) on its ancient steps. This, of course, is an exaggerated reminder of Epictetus's solid

---

I   Our version is greatly simplified and modified for our mnemonic needs, but if you'd care to see what remains of this porch in our day, I highly recommend this video tour courtesy of "Stoic Dan." https://www.youtube.com/watch?v=4iCMKsrm2bc.

advice that if we place too much focus on things of the body, we will remain underdeveloped in the things that matter the most, the things of the mind, and chiefly our moral purpose.

We see a similar theme in the writings of Seneca, who counseled in his 15th letter to Lucilius that a man should not devote too much time to caring for his body, because regardless of how powerful and muscular a man may become, he'll never be a match for a first-class bull!

No, humans are meant for higher things. St. Paul joins in as follows: "Train yourself in godliness; for while bodily training is of some value, godliness is of value in every way, as it holds promise for the present life and also for the life to come" (1 Timothy 4:7–8).

So, does Epictetus tell us to disregard our bodies altogether? Of course not, since we recall that he himself told us that just because he cannot become a Milo does not mean he will not take proper care of his body. Seneca goes on to prescribe simple, time-efficient exercises that will train the body without robbing time from training the mind. St. Paul goes on to write: "I pommel my body and subdue it, lest after preaching to others I myself should be disqualified" (1 Cor. 9:27).

So then, Epictetus is *not* telling us we cannot exercise proper care and concern for our bodies. Indeed, what is or is not excessive will depend upon the roles we have been assigned or chosen. An Olympic or professional athlete can certainly devote significant amounts of time and effort to making the body swift, skilled, enduring, and strong. A professional chef or perhaps a crafter of fine whiskeys (sadly, this "water of life" was apparently unknown to the ancient Greeks and Romans) can appropriately devote considerable time and effort to perfecting his or her skills. Still, whatever our roles in life may be, we must all give more care to the development of our minds and moral character than to any bodily concerns. Training our *prohairesis* will bring us and our neighbors the greatest rewards.

42 *If someone insults you or treats you badly, remember that he believes it is right for him to do so.* He acts according to *his* perspective and not according to *yours*. If he interprets your words or actions wrongly, it is he who is harmed and deceived. *If you keep this principle in mind, you will be gentle with those who abuse you, saying to yourself every time, "It seemed that way to him."*

DO YOU RECALL THAT, BEHIND THE BUST OF ZENO TO THE left, you *patted* (not smacked) *the back* of a *person who insulted you?* How interesting that the Stoics are often mischaracterized as people focused solely on their own concerns while so many of Epictetus's *Handbook* lessons teach us that in keeping ourselves undisturbed, we always give others the benefit of the doubt and do our best to maintain amiable social relations. Here again, as we saw in *Handbook* chapters 20, 22, 28, 33, and 38, Epictetus counsels us on how to behave when injured, insulted, criticized, mocked, slighted, or otherwise abused by others. I find his advice so wise and powerful as I ponder them in my recliner, but what a bear to put into practice when actually faced with such behavior from others!

It is not easy to overcome our own defensiveness, our tendency to feel moral indignation and to desire revenge, but it is well worth the effort to remember once more the lesson of *Handbook* chapter 5 that we are disturbed not by things (including insults), but by our judgments about them. When insulted, we should also recall the lesson of *Handbook* chapter 3, to consider the nature of things. Any person who insults us is a rational being who has his own reasons for acting as he does. Perhaps he (or she, of course) has made erroneous judgments about us, is carried away by first impressions, and has little knowledge of how to control his emotions and how to play well with others. This does not mean *we* should become disturbed because of that person's disturbance. Neither does it mean we should hold that person in disdain. Indeed, according to Simplicius, Epictetus equips us with the capacity to treat those who insult us "gently and magnanimously."[2]

What a lofty thing it would be to train oneself to calmly respond when abused by others "It seemed that way to him." It calls to my mind these words in response to the most heinous of all abuses: "Father, forgive them; for they know not what they do" (Luke 23:34).

> **43** *Everything has two handles, and only one of them is suitable for carrying. If your brother harms you, don't grab hold of the handle that he treated you unjustly, but instead grab the handle that he is the brother who was raised with you. In this way you will grasp the handle that is suitable to carry this situation.* ♑

---

2 Simplicius, v. 2, 111.

SO THIS IS WHY YOUR POOR *BROTHER* STOOD THERE AT the left pillar not with two arms but with *two handles* protruding from his side! Epictetus's lesson reminds me of the famous slogan of Father Flanagan's Boys Town (and the beautiful song from the 1960s): "He ain't heavy, he's my brother!" We will best be able to play our roles as brothers, to care for and carry our brothers, if we choose not carry around the baggage of any harm or injustice he may have done us.

The lesson, of course, is just as applicable to sisters, and I imagine that this lesson will hit home (so to speak) with any readers who have any siblings. As natural as brotherly and sisterly affection may be, and as blood is thicker than water, it is certainly possible that due to our lifelong familiarity with them (and the relative unlikelihood of severing our bonds forever), we may be more likely to lash out at our siblings than at others.

Further, the lesson applies to all other people and situations as well.[3] Before we act in response to any other person or situation, we need to find the *correct handle* to, well—handle it correctly! Why just two handles? Modern *Handbook* commentator Keith Seddon makes the point that that while there may be *many* ways to understand any situation (as there are many sides to any story), there is only one *correct* one, the one befitting a Stoic! Many ways to interpret behaviors or situations will lead to anger, sorrow, anxiety, or other sorts of disturbance. The Stoic way is to grab the handle that reflects the true nature of the other person or situation, along with one's own true roles and duties, foremost of which is to maintain one's *prohairesis,* unperturbed, while enjoying a good flow of life. (So, the next time your sibling and anyone else begins to get on your nerves, just imagine two handles protruding from their sides and *gently* grasp the one Epictetus would!)

**44** These are invalid statements: "I'm richer than you; therefore I am better than you," or "I'm more eloquent than you; therefore I'm better than you." Here are their valid forms: "I'm richer than

---

3 Building on the base of this *Handbook* lesson, psychiatrist Ronald Pies has crafted a wonderful practical guide to key Stoic lessons, rich in the wisdom of Marcus Aurelius and peppered with Judaic and Christian insights. I direct readers to his *Everything Has Two Handles: The Stoic's Guide to the Art of Living* (Lanham, MD: Hamilton Books, 2008).

you; therefore my property is greater than yours," or "I'm more eloquent than you; therefore my manner of speaking is superior to yours." *You are neither your possessions nor your speech.* Ω

AT THE LEFT WALL A *SNEERING MISER* LOOKS DOWN UPON you. Obviously, he thinks he is better than you, but in reality, he is only richer. Riches are external things that are not up to us, and are therefore indifferent. We could also imagine a great orator by the miser's side, looking down at us too because his voice is more powerful and melodious, but again, good for him perhaps, but there's far more to a person than eloquent speech.

I first encountered the Stoics in the early 1980s through the writings of psychologist Albert Ellis. As I prepared a research paper for a clinical psychology course on his Rational-Emotive Behavior therapy, I scoured the library for virtually anything written about it, in the days of yore before the Internet. I've not been able to track it down again, but I recall an article by Ellis or another REBT practitioner on the then hot topic of "self-esteem." The gist of the article was that we should all give ourselves the unconditional self-esteem that is due to every person and not go around berating ourselves or comparing ourselves to others. The key recommendation was not to rate oneself as a global, capital "I" at all, but to think of oneself as a series of many lower case "i's" in one's many roles.

So, in Epictetian terms, if one failed at becoming rich or a renowned public speaker, one would not think "I" am a failure, but perhaps "i" as a businessman or "i" as an orator are not so hot, but come to think of it "i" as a friend, or "i" as a parent, or "i" as a Parcheesi player am really not so bad. We all have many "small i" roles to play, but the only utterly essential "capital I" role regards our "capital P," not Parcheesi, but *Prohairesis*. What we really are down deepest is our moral character. We need not berate ourselves if others with more worldly success look down upon us. Neither should we look down upon others if we should prove successful in indifferent things. One form of vanity, you will recall from *Handbook* chapter 6, is to boast about trivial things.

**45** Does a man bathe too quickly? Don't say he bathes badly, but that he bathes quickly. Does someone drink a great deal of wine? Don't say he is a wino, but that he drinks a great deal of wine. *You do not know the other person's reasons for his actions, so how can you know from outward appearances whether his actions were done badly?* Ω

SO, THIS IS WHY WE IMAGINED THAT THE GREAT SCULP-tors and painters of the *Stoa Poikile* (Micon of Athens and Polygnotos of Thasos, to be exact) choose to depict a *wino in the gutter* upon the left frieze! Epictetus, like Jesus Christ, warns us to be very careful when we judge. And do you remember Bertrand Russell's "emotional conjugation"? We must train ourselves to give others the benefit of the doubt, since we do not know the reasons for their behaviors as well as we know our own. There may be a good reason for a person to drink a lot of wine, and even if not, as we learned with the insulter behind Zeno's bust, whatever the reason a person does something that looks bad to us, that person does so because in some way, correct or not, it makes sense to him.

St. Thomas Aquinas chimed in on this topic 1200 years later when examining the virtue of justice:

> He who interprets doubtful behaviors for the best, may happen to be deceived more often than not; yet it is better to err frequently through thinking well of the wicked man, than to err less frequently through having an evil opinion of a good man, because in the latter an injury is inflicted, but not in the former.[4]

Now, as for the bather, I recall years ago reading one of Mark Twain's books wherein Huck Finn, I believe, made loud splashing sounds with his hands in a bathtub, pretending, for his guardian's sake, to be taking a bath. At that same time, I heard splashing in our own bathtub and found one of our young sons pulling the same prank! Now that he's an adult I'm not sure of his bathing habits, but he does appear clean, and his wife (our illustrator) has not complained, so I give him the benefit of the doubt. Of course, such benefits should be given for all kinds of behaviors besides ostensibly drinking too much or bathing too little.

---

4 *Summa Theologica*, IIa-IIae, Q. 60, a. 4.

**46** *Would you be a philosopher? Then never call yourself one, and don't talk a great deal about it among non-philosophers, but rather show your philosophy through your actions.* Don't give a discourse on proper eating at a banquet, eat properly at a banquet. Remember how Socrates was so free of ostentation and self-importance that when people came to him asking him to introduce them to philosophers, he took them. Socrates did not mind being overlooked, so why should we? Also, if philosophical talk crops up in the conversations of non-philosophers, be hesitant to put your two cents worth in, spewing out what you have not yet fully digested. When someone says you don't know anything and it doesn't bother you, then you will know you are making a good start in philosophy. Sheep don't show how well they have eaten by vomiting up their grass before their shepherd, but by digesting their food and producing wool and milk. So too for you, *don't regurgitate philosophical propositions to non-philosophers, but show them the actions such propositions produce in one's life, once they are digested.* Ω

WHY DID WE IMAGINE SOMEONE *LOOKING OVER SOCRATES* at the stars in the sky above the porch's apex? Because Socrates did not mind being overlooked! This calls to mind a similar event in the life of St. Thomas Aquinas. A religious brother visiting the Dominican convent at Paris chanced upon Thomas upon arriving and ordered Thomas to guide him around the city, chiding him at times for walking too slowly. The brother was later aghast when he learned that the man who so humbly submitted to his commands and withstood his rebukes was the world's most renowned philosopher and theologian!

So, Epictetus makes clear that for those who would live like a Stoic, actions speak much louder than words. He would also have us practice humility, especially in regard to our mastery of philosophy. Moreover, to add icing to the cake, he gives us the wonderful image of the absurdity of a sheep vomiting up grass in front of its shepherd. (In fact, I think I'll add this one to the mnemonic, by having Socrates pet one!)

This last lesson from this chapter has special relevance to our very endeavor of committing the gist of the *Handbook* to memory. Our goal should be not only to *regurgitate* its lessons backward and forward, but to *chew* on them, *digest* them, and *live* them.

**㊼** *When you have trained yourself to live simply according to bodily needs, don't boast and show off about it.* If you drink only water, then drink it, but don't look for every opportunity to tell people you drink only water. Discipline yourself for yourself and not for outward show. *Don't go around hugging statues! Instead, if you are very thirsty, take some cold water into your mouth and spit it out when no one is looking.* **Ω**

OUR IMAGE OF THE *DOG-HEADED MAN HUGGING THE STATUE* is an allusion to the Cynic Diogenes, who reportedly would train himself in toughness and make a show of it by hugging cold statues displayed outdoors in public places. And this in the midst of winter! While Diogenes had his point to make, Epictetus writes elsewhere that few are called by God to the extreme asceticism of the Cynic, but, echoing his teacher Musonius Rufus, he notes that Stoics would do well to train themselves privately in physical discipline and self-denial, in acts as small as denying oneself a drink of water when thirsty.[5] Quite interestingly, fifteen centuries later, across the Atlantic in Peru, friends of St. Rose of Lima reported that denying herself water when thirsty was among her ascetical practices.

So, how might we apply this in our own lives today? We can certainly deny ourselves water sometimes if we'd like, though hopefully not to the point that we dehydrate and damage our bodies. Other simple practices in self-discipline might include taking cold showers now and again or, to start simply, perhaps refusing to turn on your car's heater or seat-warmers on a cold day. My own favorite form of physical self-discipline is the occasional performance of "super slow" strength training movements, taking a full 10 seconds to raise the weight on each repetition and a full 10 seconds to lower them, feeling them all the way over the course of at least a full minute or two. Of course, this might smack of showing off, since I'm not very good at hiding the pain! What ascetical practice might you try to practice *when nobody's watching* to gain more control over yourself?

---

5  In an interesting aside, Keith Seddon points out that in *Discourse* 3.12.10 Epictetus actually recommends that one *imagine* oneself hugging such a statue when insulted or abused to cool and curb anger. Again, *imagination* can play a vital role not only in the art of memory, but in the art of living!

**48**    *The condition and character of those uneducated in philosophy:*

* Never to look for good or harm to come from themselves, but to expect them to come from others.

*The condition and character of those educated in philosophy:*

* Always to look for good or bad to come from within oneself.

*Signs of progress in philosophy:*

* To blame or praise no one.
* Never to talk about oneself as accomplished or learned.
* When faced with failure, to look to oneself for the reasons.
* When praised by another, to smile to oneself and take it lightly.
* To move through life carefully like an invalid whose limbs are healing and are not yet strong.
* To eliminate selfish desires and to seek to avoid only things contrary to nature.
* To diminish impulsive behavior.
* To care not if others consider you foolish or ignorant.

*In a word, the person progressing in philosophy watches himself as if he were an enemy lying in wait.* Ω

THE *THREE PERSONS* AT THE RIGHT PILLAR OF *PROGRES-sively greater size* are there to remind us of our goal to grow our *prohairesis* through philosophy, as we progress from the uneducated *beginner* to the *prokopton* (one making progress) with an eye toward the towering and elusive goal of the *Stoic sage*. As for the seriousness of our endeavor, Epictetus compares it to a war in which our greatest enemy lies within. He has laid out the signs so clearly that I'll provide little comment but to suggest that we all look over his list to carefully assess where we are now and what we must master to progress.

**49**    Don't put on airs that you can explain the great works of a philosopher like Chrysippus,[6] but say to yourself that if Chrysippus had written more clearly himself, you would have nothing to boast about. What should we want? To understand nature and to live our lives in harmony with it. If we hear that Chrysippus knows and we can't understand him, then we seek out someone who

---

6   Chrysippus of Soli (279–206 BC), third head of the Stoic school, one of the most influential and the most prolific of the Greek Stoics.

can explain his writings to us. Now, when we do find someone who can explain him, we must live according to the things he has explained. If we are moved only by the excellence of the explanation, then we have become grammarians, not philosophers. *No, our task is not to read or explain Chrysippus, but to live our lives in harmony with the wisdom in his lessons.* Ω

AT THE SIGHT OF THE RIGHT PILLAR WE IMAGINED *CHRY-sippus* (or our friend *Chris*) *writing something illegibly* to help us lock in this important lesson. Here, Epictetus provides yet another variation on the theme that the Stoic seeks wisdom not merely to be knowledgeable or to be thought learned by others, but to *live out that wisdom* in his or her daily life.

I imagine that when Epictetus returns again and again to some central themes to examine them from different angles, certain of those angles might really hit home with different readers. This one has a special significance to me, since, as an author, I'm probably best known as someone who tries to explain the philosophical and psychological lessons of others—particularly the Stoics and St. Thomas Aquinas. Lo, if I should think this some grand thing, does Epictetus burst my bubble! No, my writing is worthwhile only if it should serve to help others live by the wisdom those teachers expound (and help me live by it too).

Epictetus holds a warning for philosophical writers and for modern professional philosophers. When academic philosophers gain the reputation of helping students come to doubt their very existence, rather than giving them guides toward flourishing, virtuous living, they have abandoned true love of wisdom and become mere players of word- and mind-games.

Indeed, he also holds up a warning for every person who would think like a Stoic—and live like one. Though I hope our memory practices are indeed fun and game-like in some ways, we must remember that they are but means to a far higher end. We should strive not merely to become memory masters, but masters of the Stoic art of living.

50 *When presented with valid principles, treat them as if they were the law and it would be sacrilegious to go against them. Pay no*

> *attention if others speak poorly about you, since their words are not within your control.* Ω

HERE'S WHY YOU IMAGINED STANDING NEXT TO *EPICTETUS*, *holding stone tablets* for him. We pictured him much like Moses holding the Ten Commandments etched in stone. Valid ethical principles, like those of this *Handbook*, should be treated as inviolable moral laws from God Himself. Such is the nature of natural law. We must hold fast, stand by, and live by Stoic truths, regardless of what others might think. The Stoic, of course, focuses on what is up to us, and the opinions of others are not up to us. Living according to such truths is indeed a sacred thing, since it aligns our wills with the will of God.

## SECOND REHEARSE, REVERSE OF THE FIRST

OUR MNEMONIC TOUR OF THE *HANDBOOK* IS VERY NEAR its end—only three images and lessons to go! But before we conclude, let's assess how our memories are holding out. As for this chapter's lessons, can you work back from the *stone tablets* by Epictetus ⑤⓪, to the *illegibly writing Chrysippus* at the right pillar ④⑨, to the *progressively taller threesome* at the right wall ④⑧, to *Diogenes hugging the stature* on the right frieze ④⑦, to the *person looking over Socrates* at the apex ④⑥, to the *wino in the gutter on the left frieze* ④⑤, to the *sneering miser at the left wall* ④④, to your brother with two handles at the left pillar ④③, to you patting an insulter's back at the bust of Zeno ④②, all the way back to the microcephalic bodybuilder on the steps ④①? If so, *kudos!* If not, take another peek or two at the master chart to master this chapter's contents.

We've done so much memorizing that it's just about time to start living, "*by Zeus,*" as Epictetus would say, so let's get down to the business of living in our next chapter as we conclude the *Handbook.*

# CHAPTER 6

# THE TIME TO BEGIN LIVING WELL IS NOW, BY ZEUS!

## (Handbook *Chapters 51-53*)

*"You have learned the right philosophic principles and agreed with them, so when are you going to put them into action?"*

*Handbook Ch. 51*

## MEMORY TOUR:
### *HANDBOOK CHAPTERS 51–53*

**W**E HAVE BUT THREE CHAPTERS OF EPICTETUS'S *Handbook* left. Let's see, just where shall we put them? Remembering that these memory methods are as flexible as one's imagination, we could put them virtually anywhere we wanted! We could add three more locations within the porch or start to form a new memory room. In my own previous memory books, I included a room with 20 locations since the subject matter at hand included 20 items. With but three items to go, I suggest we make this as simple as possible. Further, it seems fitting to me to conclude with our full focus on Epictetus himself. Let's see how simple this can be.

We simply move up a foot or so from the center of Epictetus's body to his partially beard-covered lips (location **51**). You see those lips blow a *whistle* and you look around to find our porch encircled by an athletic *stadium*. We move next to Epictetus's left hand **52** where we see him holding and *admiring* a sizeable *wisdom tooth*. Finally, we move to Epictetus's right hand **53** and who should sit at his right hand but his great hero Socrates who in turn reaches out with his hand almost touching the hand of Zeus! (It can't help but call to mind Michelangelo's famous *Creation of Adam* fresco adorning the ceiling of the Sistine Chapel.)

| LOCATION/<br>HANDBOOK CHAPTER | IMAGE | LESSON |
|---|---|---|
| 51 EPICTETUS'S LIPS | Whistle blows in stadium | Your life contest has started |
| 52 EPICTETUS'S LEFT HAND | Sage admires wisdom tooth | Seek truth before all else |
| 53 EPICTETUS'S RIGHT HAND | Socrates touches Zeus's hand | Follow God's good flow |

51 How long are you going to consider yourself unworthy of pursuing the best things and never going against the conclusions of reason? You have learned the right philosophic principles and agreed with them, so when are you going to put them into action? You are not a child anymore, but a full grown adult. If you procrastinate and make excuses for focusing day after day on non-essential things, you will live on in ignorance until the day you die. So, be a man! (or a woman!) *Declare to yourself today that you will always act according to what is right and best. If you find it hard, buck up! The contest is now, you are in the Olympic games of life today, and you cannot put things off anymore, delaying your progress for even one more day.* Socrates became perfect by paying attention to nothing but his reason in every life situation. *Even if you are not yet another Socrates, get out there and live like you want to become one.* Ω

AS WE ZOOMED IN ON EPICTETUS'S LIPS HE BLEW UPON A *whistle* and we found ourselves within an *Olympic stadium*. A few hundred years before Epictetus, Aristotle wrote of the Olympics in a somewhat similar way:

> As in the Olympic Games, it is not the most beautiful and strongest that are crowned, but those who compete (for it is some of these that are victorious), so those who act rightly win the noble and good things in life.[1]

Epictetus, like Aristotle, tells us we must take action and put our philosophy into practice, if we hope to achieve what is most worthwhile in life. We cannot win if we do not compete and the

---

I Aristotle, *Nicomachean Ethics*, 1.8 in *The Complete Works of Aristotle: The Revised Oxford Translation*, vol. 2, Jonathan Barnes, ed. (Princeton, NJ: Princeton University Press, 1984), 1736.

time to enter the lists is *now*. We have studied and memorized so many important Stoic lessons by now, and the worst time to begin to put them into practice is *tomorrow*, which, for all we know, may never come for us. But who are we to try? We are no Socrates after all—or Aristotle or Epictetus for that matter. Yet how will we progress and grow unless we strive to grow more like them? Some modern psychologists speak of "stretch goals," lofty goals that exceed our current grasp, but inspire us to surpass our current state as we build and stretch our capacities to attain them.

As we near the end of the *Handbook,* let's leave procrastination to the spectators on the sidelines, and make sure that *today is the day* we begin to strive to live like the Stoics, the unconquerable Milos of Olympian *prohairesis!*

> 52   In terms of the discipline of philosophy itself, the first important aspect is *applying fundamental principles,* such as "We should not lie." The second aspect is that of *logical demonstrations,* for example, about why one should not adhere to what is false. The third aspect is the *confirmation and explanation of the second,* for example, analyzing why some proof is a proof, or even what is a proof, and what are truth and falsity. Therefore, the first aspect gives rise to the need for the second and the second to the third. They follow logically. The most important, however, is the *first* aspect, and too often we focus merely on the third, neglecting the first altogether. Therefore, *we believe false things and act upon false beliefs, yet we stand quite ready to prove to someone that he should not believe what is false.* Ω

IN OUR PENULTIMATE *HANDBOOK* IMAGE, WE PICTURED Epictetus admiring a *wisdom tooth* held in his left hand. True wisdom is based on living the truth (tooth being our easily pictured sound-alike word). As I hinted at last chapter, perhaps many modern university students exposed to philosophy courses would conclude that Epictetus was quite prescient in describing the course of much of modern academic philosophy, with such a focus on words about words, arguments about arguments, and so little emphasis on what particular things are truly true or false, right or wrong, for those who would live good and thoughtful lives, informed by their pursuit of wisdom.

Now, Epictetus did indeed know and teach his students logical reasoning skills (the second aspect), as well as metaphysical, meta-ethical, and epistemological principles examining even the nature of truth itself (the third aspect), but such thinking serves primarily as a *means* to the *end* of *living* according to truth and nature, following the will of God. Thankfully, what remains for us of Epictetus's teaching is primarily about that first and foremost role and goal of philosophy, to guide us to practice the truths of wisdom in our daily lives.

As we imagine Epictetus admiring that wisdom tooth, we might note how St. Thomas Aquinas summarized a fundamental insight of Aristotle's contrasting true wisdom with lesser forms of knowledge: "The slenderest knowledge that may be attained of the highest things is more desirable than the most certain knowledge obtained of lesser things."[2] We might imagine Epictetus also chiming in: "To live a life guided by wisdom is more desirable than to be able to explain why one should do so, while one does not."

> **53** On a parting note, always keep these great thoughts *ready at hand to use them every day of your life:*
>
> (a) *Lead me thou on, O Zeus, and Destiny,*
> *To whatever goal you assign me.*
> *I will follow and not falter,*
> *But even if my will proves weak and craven,*
> *I'll follow anyway.*
>
> (b) *Whoever has rightly complied with necessity*
> *Is counted wise and skilled in things divine.*
>
> (c) *Well, O Crito, if it is pleasing to the gods, then let it be so.*
>
> (d) *Anytus and Meletus can kill me, but they cannot harm me.* Ω

LAST, BUT FAR FROM LEAST, WE SAW *SOCRATES* SITTING at Epictetus's right hand *raising his own hand* upward *toward the outstretched hand of Zeus,* much in the way Adam reaches out toward the outstretched hand of God on the vault of the Sistine Chapel. In this final chapter, we are reminded of the nature of the *Handbook* itself, that we are to have these Stoic principles always ready at

---

2  *Summa Theologica,* Ia, Q. I, a. 5, citing Aristotle's *On the Parts of Animals.*

hand, and of *this* book as well, that they will be readiest at hand to use in our lives when we have taken the time and effort to inscribe them in our long-term memories. (Indeed, in chapter 13 we'll make the effort to memorize these four quotations verbatim.)

The first of these lines (a) is a brief excerpt from Cleanthes' (331–232 BC) *Hymn to Zeus*.[3] Cleanthes followed Zeno and preceded Chrysippus as head of the Stoic school at Athens and clearly shared with Epictetus a personal sense of God as well as our call to follow His will in the actions of our daily lives.

The second lines (b) are from a fragment 965 of the Greek tragedian Euripides (480–406 BC). It reiterates Cleanthes' sentiments and emphasizes our need to go with the flow of "necessity" or God's Providence. As Epictetus taught us in *Handbook* chapter 8, our wishes will always be granted when we wish events to happen as they really do happen.

The third line (c) is based upon Plato's *Crito*, 43d, and the last (d) upon Plato's *Apology*, 30c-d, both of which are presented as quotations from Socrates. (These are my translations after consulting several modern English translations and the original Greek in Oldfather.) Socrates, like Epictetus, strives to please the gods and follow their will since they are good and we share a spark of the divine.

And finally, we circle back to the lesson of *Handbook* chapter five, the foundation of modern cognitive psychotherapy: "People are disturbed not by things, but by their judgments about things." Epictetus's first example of this principle was that Socrates did not fear death, and the parting lesson of the *Handbook* harks back to Socrates' lesson in his own words. Anytus and Meletus were his primary accusers in the trial that lead to his death sentence. Socrates knew they could kill his body, but could not touch his inviolable *prohairesis*. Would that we learn to think the same!

Simplicius, a non-Christian neo-Platonist, ended his own massive commentary on the *Handbook* with a prayer of his own to the "Lord, father and guide of reason in us," as well as to "the Savior" that we might apply these lessons and live lives guided by truth and reason. Remembering Epictetus's ultimate goal to follow God, we might conclude by recalling one simple petition

---

3  Seneca also cites it in *Letter 107*.

from the Savior Himself: "Thy will be done, on earth, as it is in heaven" (Matt. 6:10).

AND SO ENDS OUR MEMORY TOUR OF EPICTETUS'S *Handbook.* Do you know all 53 images and key lessons now? Will you work to keep them ready at hand and ever in mind to pursue a life of virtue and joy? The answers are up to you, but for now, before we delve into the silver-tongued wisdom of the Stoic Seneca, let's review the entire *Handbook* memory tour at one glance.

And here's one last thought before we review. If you find you can recall our images within their locations, but some do not readily trigger the *Handbook* lesson for that chapter, be sure to put *your own imagination and memory* to work by adapting or expanding on the images in ways that will best call to *your mind* the lesson *at hand.*

# EPICTETUS'S HANDBOOK
## MNEMONIC MASTER CHART

| CHAPTER/LOCATION | MNEMONIC IMAGE | HANDBOOK LESSON |
|---|---|---|
| ❶ FRONT DOOR | *Jet fighter control panel* | Dichotomy of control |
| ❷ DOOR MAT | *"Dee Sire!"* | Discipline of desire |
| ❸ GLASS PANEL | *Child with broken pot* | Knowing the nature of things |
| ❹ PORTRAIT ON BACK WALL | *Bubble bath* | *Premeditatio malorum* |
| ❺ GUN RACK | *Socrates with "B" leaves* | Beliefs mediate emotions |
| ❻ CENTER OF FOYER | *Horse* | Horse sense over vanity |
| ❼ CHANDELIER | *Sea captain* | The shortness of life |
| ❽ MIRROR ON WALL | *Birthday cake candles* | How to fulfill your wishes |
| ❾ CUSHIONED BENCH | *Yoda: "Pro hairy, he is!"* | *Prohairesis* rules! |
| ❿ DRAWER IN BENCH | *He-Man: "I have the power!"* | We have many powers |
| ⓫ CENTER OF LIVING ROOM | *Store "Returns" counter* | How to handle loss |
| ⓬ PICTURE WINDOW | *Slave with wine bottle* | Freedom is not free |
| ⓭ SOFA | *Socrates in a dunce cap* | Focus on what really matters |
| ⓮ COFFEE TABLE | *You sit on it in shackles* | How not to enslave yourself |
| ⓯ RIGHT SWIVEL CHAIR | *Banquet feast on cushion* | Etiquette for dinner & life |
| ⓰ LEFT SWIVEL CHAIR | *Bereaved person moaning* | Don't moan on the inside |
| ⓱ PIANO | *Your favorite actor* | Play your role well |
| ⓲ FIREPLACE | *Croaking crow* | It's all good |
| ⓳ LIVING-ROOM DOORWAY | *Giant 1st place trophy* | How to be invincible |

| | | |
|---|---|---|
| ㉑ **EXIT SIGN DOORWAY OUT** | *Heckler throws tomato* | How to deflect all insults |
| ㉑ **DINING-ROOM DOORWAY** | *Calendar and your headstone* | Memento mori |
| ㉒ **HEAD OF TABLE** | *People laugh at your beard* | Philosophers expect ridicule |
| ㉓ **THERMOMETER** | *People smile or frown at you* | Please your higher self |
| ㉔ **SEAT ON LEFT** | *"What a splendid seat!"* | Love your rightful place |
| ㉕ **FOOT OF TABLE** | *Gilded throne sits in scales* | Weigh all honors good or bad |
| ㉖ **SEAT ON RIGHT** | *Slave boy breaks two mugs* | Break your double standards |
| ㉗ **MIRROR ON WALL** | *Arrow in target's bull's eye* | Nature does not miss |
| ㉘ **LIGHT OVER PORTRAIT** | *Your body handed to judge* | Hold your judgment dear |
| ㉙ **DOOR OUT** | *Milo and monkey play trumpet* | Stop monkeying around |
| ㉚ **EXIT MAT** | *Your own father and brother* | Honor your highest duties |
| ㉛ **DESKTOP** | *Giving Zeus pie and tea* | Don't blame the gods or fate |
| ㉜ **LEATHER CHAIR** | *Apollo as temple bouncer* | Create your own fortune |
| ㉝ **COMPUTER MONITOR** | *Zeno and Socrates silent* | Imitate Socrates or Zeno |
| ㉞ **PICTURE OF PHILOSOPHERS** | *Two water clocks* | Think twice, then act or not |
| ㉟ **GREEK URN** | *Bust dramatically unveiled* | Never hide what's right |
| ㊱ **STOIC BOOKS** | *Climber chewing lamb leg* | Etiquette over selfishness |
| ㊲ **LEFT CHAIR** | *Peter Pan and your principal* | Fill your true role |
| ㊳ **FLOOR LAMP** | *Commander steps on nail* | Protect your *Prohairesis* |
| ㊴ **RIGHT CHAIR** | *Man walks off cliff* | Attend to your true needs |

| | | |
|---|---|---|
| **40 ATLAS HOLDS GLOBE** | *Young girls' beauty pageant* | Honor women's virtues |
| **41 STOA STEPS** | *Microcephalic bodybuilder* | Mind your mind |
| **42 BUST OF ZENO** | *You pat insulter's back* | "It seemed that way to him" |
| **43 LEFT PILLAR** | *Your brother with two handles* | You can choose which handle |
| **44 LEFT WALL** | *Sneering miser looks down* | You aren't what you own |
| **45 LEFT FRIEZE** | *Smelly wino in gutter* | Give benefit of doubt |
| **46 STARS ABOVE APEX** | *Person peers over Socrates* | Don't claim to love wisdom |
| **47 RIGHT FRIEZE** | *Diogenes hugging it* | Don't put on a show |
| **48 RIGHT WALL BASE** | *Three persons of rising height* | Signs to gauge progress |
| **49 RIGHT PILLAR** | *Chrysippus writing illegibly* | Don't parse or parrot, but live |
| **50 EPICTETUS'S BODY** | *You stand by stone tablets* | Hold these principles sacred |
| **51 EPICTETUS'S LIPS** | *Whistle blows in stadium* | Your life contest has started |
| **52 EPICTETUS'S LEFT HAND** | *Sage admires wisdom tooth* | Seek truth before all else |
| **53 EPICTETUS'S RIGHT HAND** | *Socrates touches Zeus's hand* | Follow God's good flow |

# PART II

# MEMORIZE SENECA'S LETTERS!

*"The Moral Letters, or Letters to Lucilius, are Seneca's best-known writings today. The letters include some of Seneca's most memorable sayings, and remain one of our best sources for understanding Stoic philosophy."*
Donald Robertson[1]

*"Considered en masse, the letters form a fruitful and helpful handbook, of the very widest scope and interest."*
Richard M. Gummere[2]

---

1   Seneca, *Letters from a Stoic: The Ancient Classic*, with introduction by Donald Robertson (West Sussex, UK: Capstone, 2021), xxix.
2   In Loeb, *Epistles*, xiii.

# CHAPTER 7

# GAIUS LUCILIUS JUNIOR, "YOU'VE GOT MAIL!"

## ON LEARNING, LIVING, AND GIVING PHILOSOPHY

### (Letters 1–10)

*"The very first thing philosophy promises to give us is fellow-feeling, a sense of sociability and sympathy with all other human beings."*

*Letter 5*

## WELCOME BACK TO THE HOUSE OF MEMORY!

B Y NOW, YOU'RE PROBABLY BEGINNING TO FEEL at home in our house of memory, but feel free to refer back to the pictures as necessary. It takes some time and practice to learn the mnemonic rooms "by heart," but once you do, you'll be better able to appreciate their full power. And in the chapters that lie ahead, we'll have plenty of practice!

Now that we've used the method of loci to build our house of Epictetian wisdom, we'll see how those same rooms can be remodeled from a Grecian to a Roman decor, so to speak, allowing us to house a virtually limitless amount of new information. Are you familiar with the child's toy for drawing or writing with a plastic stylus and thin plastic sheet covering a wax tablet? Just lift the sheet and the lines disappear, allowing for a brand-new message or picture. The method of loci works something like that toy. In fact, ancient Romans called it "mental writing." We can "lift the sheet" and write all kinds of new information on our memories. With the child's toy, the older impressions, though no longer visible on the sheet, do remain embedded in the wax. So too when we use our mental locations for new information: the older information is still embedded in the wax of our memory and can be recalled when we want if we rehearse it now and again.

So, our next step is to "lift the sheet" on the five rooms (okay, four rooms and one porch) we used to house the lessons of Epictetus's *Handbook* to inscribe new images and new lessons from a new Stoic—Lucius Annaeus Seneca (c. 4 BC–AD 65). But first we'll address this perhaps surprising question: Was our Seneca the Stoic *also* a memory master?

## SENECA: STOIC *AND* MEMORY MASTER?

OPEN UP ONE OF THE MODERN CLASSICS ON THE ANCIENT art of memory, flip back to the index, and you will find our Stoic Seneca referenced several times. Did Seneca *practice* the classical art of memory? Did he *write* about it? It appears we cannot be sure, but there are several tantalizing leads suggesting that perhaps he did both.

• The 12th-century scholar, John of Salisbury, wrote as follows: "Seneca most readily promised to teach the art for furnishing memories, of which I certainly wish I were a master; but as far as I know, he did not actually teach it."[1]

• In the 16th century, one Johannes Spangerbergius wrote in his "little book" on "artificial memory" that Seneca was among the foremost ancient exponents of the art of memory.[2]

• The 18th-century scholar, Ottaviano Diodati, in his article on the art of memory for Dennis Diderot's *Encyclopédie,* listed Seneca as one of the ancients who possessed a prodigious memory.[3]

• The 20th-century historian, Paolo Rossi, noted that Seneca, "in his discussion of the memory of kindnesses received in *De beneficiis* III, 2–5 touches on the themes of 'frequency' and 'order' of memory acts."[4]

• The 21st-century *Letters* translators Margaret Graver and A. A. Long note that in his letters, Seneca "is constantly quoting poetry," especially Virgil, Ovid, Horace, and Lucretius. Further: "The comparison with surviving texts of those authors suggests that he quotes from

1 Cited in Mary Carruthers, *The Book of Memory: A Study of Memory in Medieval Culture* (New York, NY: Cambridge University Press, 1990), 146.
2 Cited in Paolo Rossi, *Logic and the Art of Memory: The Quest for a Universal Language,* Stephen Clucas, trans. (Chicago, IL: University of Chicago Press, 2000), 69.
3 Ibid., 233.
4 Ibid., 11.

memory, for there are several instances in which he substitutes a word or splices together two similar passages."[5]

Has a complete Senecan memory treatise perhaps been lost to history, as 3rd-century historian of philosophy, Diogenes Laertius, suggests may be the case for Aristotle? Who knows?

To make one last intriguing point, 20th-century memory historian Frances A. Yates notes that Seneca the Elder, our Seneca's *father,* "a teacher of rhetoric, could reportedly repeat two thousand names in the order in which they had been given; and when a class of two hundred or more students or more spoke each in turn a line of poetry, he could recite all the lines in reverse order, beginning with the last one said and going back right to the first."[6]

Well, we know that the elder Seneca was not the fan of Greek philosophy his second son would become, but he appears to have been a man of prodigious natural memory, honed and perfected by the memory arts. Perhaps he passed his knowledge of mnemonic aids to our Stoic Seneca, but whether he did or not, it's time for *us* to grow in our mastery of memory methods and in our mastery of Stoic principles by applying our locations to brand new nuggets of solid, Stoic wisdom. We now commence our memory tour of the first 50 of Seneca's remarkable letters to his friend Lucilius.

## MEMORY TOUR FOR SENECA'S LETTERS 1–10

AS YOU RING THE DOORBELL AND THE FRONT DOOR ❶ opens, you are shocked to see a *flying clock* zip right past you! You hesitate to step on the doormat ❷ inside because it is covered by a magnificent multi-colored *illuminated book.*[7] When you look out into the front yard through the glass panel ❸ next to the door, who should you see but *your own best friend.* Though the image

---

5  Lucius Annaeus Seneca, *Letters on Ethics,* Margaret Graver & A. A. Long, trans. (Chicago, IL: University of Chicago Press, 2015), 8–9. (They mention as well a caution Seneca provides when discussing memorization. We will address it when we get to letter 33.)

6  Frances A. Yates, *The Art of Memory* (Chicago, IL: University of Chicago Press, 1966), 16. (Citing from Marcus Annaeus Seneca, *Controversiarum Libri,* Lib. I, Praef. 2.)

7  Have you ever seen one of these gorgeous multi-colored medieval books? If not, sometime check out online the Book of Kells, perhaps the most famous of all. This gorgeous 8th-century illustrated book of the gospels is housed inside the magnificent Trinity College Library in Dublin, Ireland.

may be a bit disturbing for those who have not yet achieved the equanimity of a Socrates, the portrait on the wall ❹ depicts *your own tombstone*. On a less somber note, right under the gun rack ❺ you spy *Seneca* himself *embracing several strangers*.

Next, you see perhaps the strangest sight of all. Are you familiar with the Transformers of cartoon and big screen movie fame? They are giant alien robots that can transform and disguise themselves as things like cars and planes. Well, anyway, for a reason I will reveal later, in the center of the foyer ❻, a massive, smiling Transformer robot opens up his metal skull and *hands you his metal brain!* As you look overhead you realize that the round chandelier ❼ is actually a mini-replica of the Roman *Coliseum* and from the tumult you hear and the dust you see rising, you surmise that a *riot* has broken loose inside. Next you peer into the mirror ❽ and see not yourself, but a most *beautiful woman* holding a *golden chain*. Upon the cushioned bench ❾ you spy an ancient sculptor chiseling out the form of a magnificent human being with a big smile on its face. Finally, when you open the drawer ❿ of the cushioned bench, who should you see but *you, talking to yourself.* (Perhaps you've been practicing too many mnemonics.)

| LETTER/LOCATION | IMAGE | LETTERS LESSON |
|---|---|---|
| ❶ FRONT DOOR | *Clock flies out at you* | *Tempus fugit!* |
| ❷ DOOR MAT | *Illuminated book* | Reading the wisest authors |
| ❸ GLASS PANEL | *Your best friend* | Fostering true friendships |
| ❹ PORTRAIT ON BACK WALL | *Your own headstone* | Overcoming fear of death |
| ❺ GUN RACK | *Seneca embraces strangers* | *Gemeinschaftsgefühl!?* |
| ❻ CENTER OF FOYER | *Transformer gives you brain* | Joys of sharing wisdom |
| ❼ CHANDELIER | *Riot inside the Coliseum* | The dangers of crowds |
| ❽ MIRROR ON WALL | *Woman with golden chain* | Philosophy makes us free |
| ❾ CUSHIONED BENCH | *Sculptor sculpts a human* | Making new friends |
| ❿ DRAWER IN BENCH | *You, talking to yourself* | Trust your true self |

Before we proceed to the lessons behind the images, let me note once more that we have 124 letters from Seneca to Lucilius. Modern translators Margaret Graver and A. A. Long note Seneca may have written even more letters since the Roman author Aulius Gellius quoted a line from the *22nd* book of letters while extant editions end with book *20*. Nonetheless, Graver and Long's English translation is about 500 pages long and the Loeb Classics edition in three volumes, with both the Latin and an English translation, weighs in at nearly 1,400 pages.

So, to keep *this* book briefer than the *Letters* themselves (not to mention Diderot's *Encyclopédie*), I will present a complete memory tour for only the first 50 letters, though at the chapter's end I will provide suggestions for readers who would care to test their memory powers on all 124. Note well too that the majority of Seneca's letters are considerably longer than Epictetus's *Handbook* chapters, and I will zoom in on only *one* key lesson from each of them. So, keep in mind that I will be "cherry-picking," so to speak, but only because Seneca's orchards of sweet *bon mots* and sage lessons rival the extent of his own extensive orchards of real trees he mentions now and then. My intent is both to provide readers a sample of memorable lessons and to whet readers' appetites to feast on the *Letters* themselves.

Finally, again in the spirit of brevity, and to enhance the efficacy of our mnemonic efforts, my commentaries will tend to be briefer than those for Epictetus. (At least that is the plan!) As was the case with the *Handbook* chapters, you will know you have reached the end of my brief quotations from Seneca (cobbled together after perusing the original Latin, the Richard M. Gummere translation in the Loeb edition, and the translation of Graver and Long) when you reach the omega sign (Ω). So now let's get down to business. As Seneca soon will tell us, times a' wastin'.

## THE LESSONS BEHIND THE IMAGES:
## (ON LEARNING, LIVING, AND GIVING PHILOSOPHY)
## LETTERS 1–10

**1** My dear Lucilius, do what you write about doing: seize every hour. Lay hold of today and you will not depend so much on tomorrow. While you procrastinate, life speeds by. Ω

WE IMAGINED A CLOCK FLYING BY US OUT THE FRONT door because *"tempus fugit!"* (time flies!), or as Seneca put it *"vita transcurrit"* ("life speeds by"). The phrase *tempus fugit* gained fame through Virgil's poems the *Georgics,* where it appears as *"fugit inreparabile tempus"* ("it escapes, irretrievable time"). Clearly, Seneca agreed.

The Roman poet Horace, Virgil's contemporary, died when Seneca was but a child. Perhaps his most enduring saying, still visible today on coffee mugs and tee shirts, was *"Carpe diem!"* (Seize the day!). He ended the phrase with words meaning "to the least extent possible trusting in the next one." So, I think it is safe to say Horace also inspired Seneca in this letter. Of course, he indicates that his friend Lucilius had written first to him on the theme and Seneca writes not *carpe diem* but *"omnes horas complectere,"* "lay hold of or grab every hour."

If you'll pardon the personal note, this idea has impacted me personally two times as a writer. My first published work was an essay written in a class in my freshman year of college entitled "A Minute Saved is a Minute Earned." It was a meditation on Benjamin Franklin's famous saying "A penny saved is a penny earned," and with a temporal twist *à la* Horace and Seneca it focused on not wasting precious time.

Twenty-five years later I read these words from Seneca himself: *"Nihil minus est hominis occupati quam vivere"* ("There is nothing the busy man is less busied with than living").[8] By this he refers to the person who is *too* busy, who has scheduled life in such a way that there is too little time for leisure, reflection, and seizing the hour. Like Socrates said: "The unexamined life is not worth living." Having gone through a doctoral program while working full-time, doing college teaching on the side, and raising young boys with my wife, I decided to take Seneca's advice, stopped teaching, and reduced as many unnecessary commitments as possible.

With a new abundance of free hours to seize, within six months my readings and reflections on the Stoics, Aristotle, and St. Thomas Aquinas had restored my belief in the reasonableness of God after twenty-five years of atheism. Just a few months later I would write my first of twenty-three books over the next sixteen years (with four more in the works after this one).

So, my story aside, I wonder if you've considered how many hours *you* let fly by without grasping hold of them before they flee? What would happen if you seized them? Would you contribute more accomplishments in your field of interest? Would you grow ever more toward thinking and living like a Stoic? Would you more fully relish your key roles and relationships during your limited time on earth to become a better spouse, parent, friend, or citizen? The time is now to ask such questions and think about them. *"Tempus fugit!"*

8 Seneca, *Moral Essays*, vol. 2, *On the Shortness of Life* vii, 3 (Cambridge, MA: Harvard University Press, 1935), 305.

**2** Always read authors of established worth; and if ever you desire a change of pace, always come back later to the proven masters. Ω

THAT *ILLUMINATED BOOK* ON THE DOORMAT SERVES AS A reminder of the beauty and the value of masterful classic books. As a modern writer who mostly just passes on the wisdom of the giants who came before him, I might worry that Seneca's statement could lead readers to cast *this* book aside (but as one who tries to think like a Stoic, I will not worry about things outside of my control, like your reading choices). Still, if you should decide to keep reading this book for a while, I cannot encourage you highly enough to soon return to the works of the great masters themselves, like Seneca and the other Stoics. And seriously, in my own study of the Stoics, I find my interest is most piqued and my knowledge grows best when I do just as Seneca advised, always returning to the Stoic masterworks themselves after reading modern works about them. That way I get the best of both worlds (though to me the oldest of those worlds is also the "best-est").

**3** Take time to ponder whether or not to admit a person into your friendship; but when you've decided to make him your friend, welcome him with all your heart and your soul and speak freely with him as you would with yourself. Ω

THIS IS WHY WE SAW *YOUR BEST FRIEND* THROUGH THE glass panel out in the front yard. Don't have a best friend at the moment? Seneca suggests that if you would think and act like a Stoic consider seeking one out (with care). Much in keeping with Aristotle's description of true *virtuous* friendships, based not only on pleasure or usefulness, but the mutual admiration and cultivation of each friend's moral character, and in line with Cicero's emphasis on the true *harmony* and *intimacy* that should exist between close friends, Seneca recommends that when a person has been *judged* of worthy character to enter our circle of friends we should speak to that friend as we speak to ourselves, in keeping with the ancient description of a friend as a "second self," of two friends as "one soul in two breasts." (Stay tuned for more insights on friendship when we get back to that sculptor on the cushioned bench!)

> ❹  One cannot live a life free of worry if one thinks too much about prolonging it, believing that living through a great number of consulships is some kind of great blessing. Rehearse this thought to yourself every day and you will face your last day with serenity. Ω

YOUR TOMBSTONE WAS DEPICTED ON THE PICTURE ON THE wall in keeping with Seneca's advice to remember always that your days in life will end. Worrying about it will not prolong it, and even if it did, a long life is not necessarily a great blessing, but a life of virtue *is*, regardless of its length or brevity. When it comes to living the good life, Seneca certainly favors quality over quantity.

> ❺  The very first thing philosophy promises to give us is fellow-feeling, a sense of sociability and sympathy with all other human beings. Ω

NEXT, AT THE GUN RACK, WE SAW *SENECA* HIMSELF *embracing a group of strangers.* The fifth letter is full of important lessons and I have zoomed in on what I consider the most essential one. Consider again that sometimes the Stoics are caricatured as rather self-absorbed individuals, concerned with what is under *their* control, with the welfare of others little more than an afterthought. Here though, Seneca says the *"primum"* (primary or very first) thing philosophy should give us is a sense of community and concern with our fellow human beings. Anyone who would think like a Stoic should think about that for a while!

Ah, but where does that ridiculously long German tongue-twister, *Gemeinschaftsgefühl* (ge-mine-shafts-ge-full) come in as our suggested take-home message for this chapter? As a graduate of Adler University in Chicago I cannot read this line of Seneca's without thinking about Austrian psychiatrist Alfred Adler's fundamental criterion of mental health. It is usually translated as "social interest," meaning a community feeling and sense of connectedness with and concern for others.

Adler is often connected with his concept of innate human "striving for superiority," whereby we constantly seek to grow in our powers, as even in infancy we strive to control our own bodily movements. We happen to find this very idea in the first sentence of this letter from Seneca: "You are hard at work, forgetting about

119

everything else and sticking to the single task of making yourself a better person every day. This I approve, and rejoice in it too."[9]

Still, "social interest," was, in fact, Adler's *primary criterion* for mental health (as it is for philosophy for Seneca). How do we determine if a person strives for superiority in a healthy way or becomes a better person every day? By seeing if their actions serve to benefit others. According to Seneca (whom Adler had credited in his writings), the same criterion could be applied in determining whether or not a person is thinking and acting like a Stoic.

Seneca also gives some specific advice on how one can live as a philosopher when most of one's fellows do not. The lives of philosophers should not be *opposed* to the lives of the masses, but marked by the pursuit of *higher* goods. The student of philosophy should be in outward appearance like his fellow man, but different inwardly because of the true goods he seeks. We should dress neither ostentatiously nor shabbily. We should not try to dress and behave in ways diametrically opposed to the masses, lest we repulse or scare away the very people whose lives we seek to improve.

**6**  I enjoy learning so I can teach.

SO, WE FINALLY FIND OUT WHY THE *TRANSFORMER* IN the middle of the foyer gladly *handed his brain to you.* Here we have one particular example of social interest in practice. Seneca loves to learn because he enjoys sharing with others the wisdom that has so benefited him. Twelve centuries later, St. Thomas Aquinas would craft an eloquent phrase that would become one of the mottos of his own Dominican order (an order with special devotion to study, teaching, preaching, and community life): "For even as it is better to enlighten than merely to shine, so it is better to give to others the fruits of contemplation than merely to contemplate."[10] (Perhaps we could also picture a brilliant. warming light coming from the Transformer's brain!) The better we become able to think like Stoics the more we'll enjoy sharing benefits with others, perhaps not often through overt teaching or preaching, but through the calm way we live our lives and the warmth that we radiate toward others.

---

9  Graver and Long, 31.
10  *Summa Theologica*, IIa-IIae, Q. 188, a. 6.

⑦   Do you ask what you should avoid above all else? Crowds. ☜

LET'S SEE WHY WE HEARD A RIOTOUS TUMULT WITHIN
the chandelier that became the Colosseum. We are easily influenced
by others, and massive crowds encourage vices either obviously
or subtly without our conscious awareness.[11] The worst kind of
crowd in the first century of the Roman Empire was the crowd at
the gladiatorial games. One would come home from such spectacles
more selfish, cruel, and inhuman. Seneca talks about stopping in
during the lunch hour, hoping to find some relaxing, light-hearted
entertainment to provide relief from the morning's bloodshed and
gore, but finds it is even more cruel and sadistic.

Here he sees, not trained and armored gladiators, but criminals
pitted against one another without a bit of armor to protect them
from excruciating blows and stabs. In the morning men are thrown
to lions and bears, but at noon they are thrown to the spectators,
many of whom prefer such butchery. Spectators expect every last
criminal to die at each other's hands, save for the lone survivor who
will still face some other form of savage execution. "Kill him! Beat
him! Burn him!" they cheer, as they ask among themselves why some
man seems so cowardly or unwilling to murder his foe. Some will
defend their actions, saying these men have been murders. Seneca
retorts rhetorically to a spectator: "Granted that, as a murderer, he
deserved this punishment, what crime have you committed, poor
fellow, that you should deserve to sit and see this show?"[12]

We are influenced by the company we keep. Even men like Socrates or Cato might have been shaken had they spent their time
among the unthinking multitude. A single example of vice can
harm us. One friend with luxurious habits can help us to grow soft
and flabby. Never underestimate, then, the powerful influence of a
mob. The student of philosophy should learn to be content retiring
within himself and seeking out the company both of those who
can lift him up and improve him and of those whom he might be
capable of improving. After all, people learn as they teach.

---

11   Though Seneca wrote these words in the 1st century, they seem more
timely than ever within the last few years of the 21st century as so many
massive gatherings of protest have erupted into riotous violence.
12   Seneca, *Epistles 1–65*, volume 1 of 3, trans. R. Gummere (Cambridge, MA:
Harvard University Press, 2006), 33.

**8** If you wish to be truly free, you must become the slave of Philosophy. Ω

REMEMBER THAT *BEAUTIFUL WOMAN* WITH A *GOLDEN CHAIN* in the mirror? Well, her name is *Sophia*, short for *Philosophia*.[13] So, once we have withdrawn from the crowd, how should we spend our time? Our personification of philosophy reminds us of her unique beauty and promise for any who seriously pursue her. Seneca's statement is one of many quotations he borrows from Epicurus. Though Seneca disagrees with the Epicureans, who placed pleasures higher than virtues, he is always quite ready to endorse them on particular issues where they've hit the nail of truth on the head. The only way we will attain true liberty, true freedom from anxiety, anger, sadness, greed, and all manner of ill-feeling and ignoble behavior is by becoming the "slave" of the truth of philosophy, pursuing her every day while willingly donning her chains of gold.

**9** The sage does not make friends so they can sit beside him in his illness or to attend to his needs, but to have someone he may sit beside and care for. Ω

WE IMAGINED A *SCULPTOR SCULPTING A PERSON* ON THAT cushioned bench to remind us of our task to make friends. In letter 9, Seneca considers how a person who is self-sufficient would still desire to have friendships by summarizing three key points:

1. Seneca posits, like a good Stoic, that a self-sufficient person does not *need* friendships, but still *desires* them. Indeed, he supplies the very graphic example of the loss of a limb or even of one's eyes through war or some accident. Surely a wise man would prefer to have all his parts, but will still seek maximum happiness with the parts of him that remain. When such a man loses a friend, he bears it with composure.
2. He agrees with the positions put forward by Aristotle and Cicero, and contrary to Socrates suggestion in Plato's

---

13 Wisdom has also been famously personified as a beautiful woman in the Old Testament book of Wisdom and in the 6th-century philosopher Boethius's powerful book *The Consolation of Philosophy*.

*Lysis,* that *friendships are not born of need, but rather, of a superabundance of virtue.* Here, he explicitly contradicts a saying of Epicurus to the effect that we seek friends to stay by us when we are ill and to help us when we are in need. Seneca proclaims, rather, that *we seek friends in order to have someone to sit by when sick and to help when in need.* (This point is so noble I suggest we embellish our memory image by having the sculptor sit down by the statue and tenderly place a thermometer in its mouth!)

3. Virtue concerns only that which is within our control, and not the happenstance of fortune. Therefore, the man who builds friendships based on *virtue,* rather than the *desire for gain,* is immune to the changes and chance happenstance of fortune, and in that sense he remains self-sufficient.

Seneca has been referred to as a "silver-tongued" orator and he is known for the *bon mots* that enrich his writings. One such phrase appears in this letter when Seneca advises Lucilius to replace lost friends with new ones. He offers a phrase that the Stoic philosopher Hecato of Rhodes (ca. 100 BC) declared to be as potent as any witch's love potion: *"If you would be loved, love."*

---

**⑩**  I dare to entrust you to your own self. 🄌

---

LET'S SEE WHY YOU WERE *TALKING TO YOURSELF* WITHIN that drawer in the bench. Seneca tells Lucilius a story that comes from the great Cynic, Crates of Thebes, our Stoic founder Zeno's first mentor in philosophy. Crates once saw a young man out walking by himself and asked him what he was doing all alone. The man replied, "I'm talking to myself," to which Crates replied, "Pray be very careful then. You are talking to a bad man!"

Though I can't recall exactly who it was, perhaps Jack Benny or Rodney Dangerfield, a variation of this story made its way to American comedy routines in the 20th century. The comedian said something along these lines: "I like talking to myself because I enjoy conversing with a higher class of people!"

Seneca starts this letter by commending Lucilius for avoiding crowds, and jests that he would rather have him speak to nobody else but him, so he wouldn't have to share him. The serious message is that he detects Lucilius's progress in philosophy and trusts him to profit from periods of solitude and self-reflection. Hopefully, we are beginning to think like Stoics too, and perhaps one day, Seneca would entrust us to ourselves as well.

## YOU KNOW THE DRILL

ALL RIGHT THEN, YOU KNOW THE DRILL. DO YOU HAVE the key images and lessons from *Letters* 1–10 locked tightly within the recesses of your mind? If so, let's move on. If not, rehearse them again a time or two and we'll meet you in the next chapter.

# CHAPTER 8

# FROM ROSY CHEEKS TO CONSISTENT HOBGOBLINS

## MINDING NATURE WHILE NURTURING YOUR MIND

### (Letters 11–20)

*"No boxer can step into battle with high spirits who has never been beaten black and blue."*

*Letter 13*

## MEMORY TOUR
### FOR SENECA'S LETTERS 11–20

IN THE CENTER OF THE LIVING ROOM ⓫ YOU spy a *statue of yourself.* You must have found it embarrassing, because your *cheeks are red.* As you look out the picture window ⓬, a smiling *old man cavorting in a tree house* waves at you. Meanwhile back on the living room sofa ⓭ sits a *black and blue boxer* (though his bruising does not seem to bother him). Right in the center of the coffee table ⓮ a little *woman* walks into a little *cave.* And who should be sitting in the right swivel chair ⓯, but a large *muscle man* intently *reading a book.*

Moving along to the left swivel chair ⓰ you see he's been joined by a *cobbler* busily *cobbling a sole.* How strange to see at the piano ⓱ a well-dressed *rich man grabbing at pennies* within its change slot. (It must be a player piano this time.) You notice the Christmas *stockings* hung from the fire place ⓲ have just started to *smoke.* Then you decide you've had enough of the room, but notice the living room doorway ⓳ is completely blocked by a giant *spider's web.* When you look up at the exit sign over the exit door ⓴, you spy a *hobgoblin scurrying away,* not at all daunted by the spider's web!

125

| LETTER/LOCATION | IMAGE | LETTERS LESSON |
|---|---|---|
| ⑪ CENTER OF LIVING ROOM | *Your statue with red cheeks* | The limits of human nature |
| ⑫ PICTURE WINDOW | *Old man in tree house* | How to enjoy aging |
| ⑬ SOFA | *Black and blue boxer* | Challenges build strength |
| ⑭ COFFEE TABLE | *Woman walks into cave* | The solace of philosophy |
| ⑮ RIGHT SWIVEL CHAIR | *Muscleman reading book* | Good care of body and mind |
| ⑯ LEFT SWIVEL CHAIR | *Cobbler cobbles a sole* | Philosophy builds the soul |
| ⑰ PIANO | *Rich man grab at pennies* | How to laugh greed away |
| ⑱ FIREPLACE | *Stockings begin to smoke* | Prepare for feast or famine |
| ⑲ LIVING-ROOM DOORWAY | *Spider web* | The webs of our desires |
| ⑳ EXIT SIGN DOORWAY OUT | *Hobgoblin scurries away* | Consistency for big minds |

## THE LESSONS BEHIND THE IMAGES:
## MINDING NATURE WHILE NURTURING YOUR MIND
### LETTERS 11–20

⑪ For no amount of wisdom can remove the natural weaknesses of the body. Our inborn tendencies can be diminished to some extent, but not completely overcome. ☒

THE *STATUE OF YOURSELF* IN THE LIVING ROOM'S CENTER had *rosy cheeks* to remind us of Seneca's lesson that many of our natural body functions, like blushing, act reflexively and may never be completely under our control. (Of course, we will all recall that in the very first *Handbook* chapter, Epictetus listed the body as something outside our control.)

Now, this lesson really hits home for me because of my ruddy complexion and lifelong capacity to blush on a dime, so to speak, especially in social situations. I mentioned before that I was able to *diminish* the extent of my blushing, but more importantly to keep it from hindering me in public speaking, by changing my judgment about it. "So I'm turning red—so what!" My cheeks might

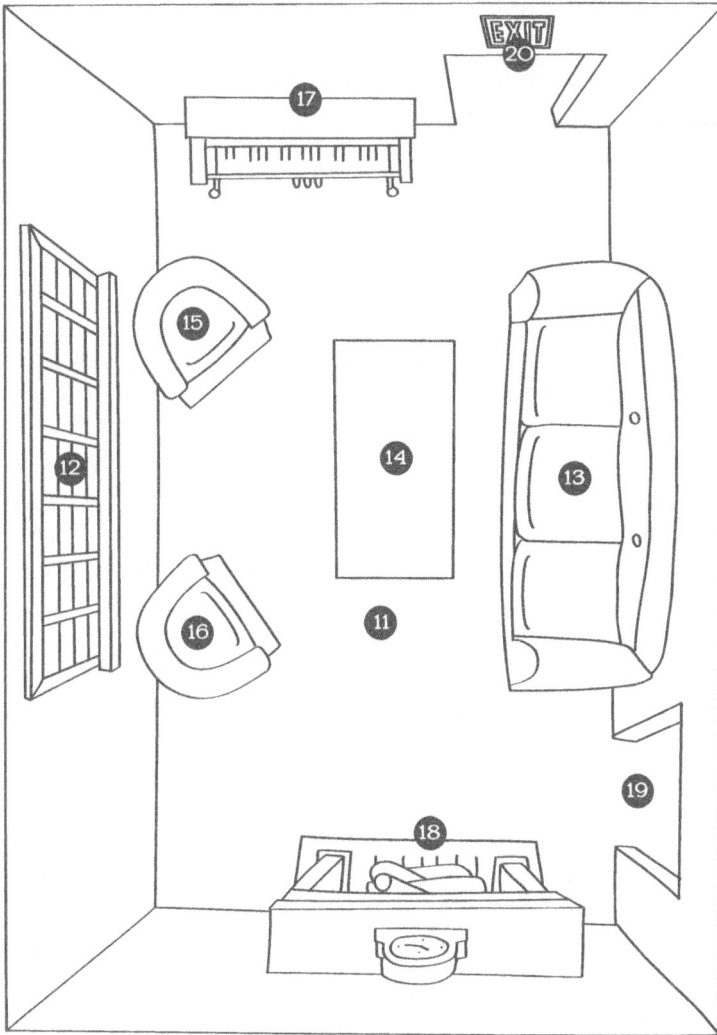

still turn a little rosy when I give a talk, but I always still get the job done now.

Seneca's advice should warn us against unrealistic, perfectionistic expectations of what thinking like a Stoic can do for us. We will still have some instant bodily and emotional reactions, be it blushing for some, to a rapidly climbing heart rate and breathing when suddenly faced with a dangerous situation for virtually everyone. Further, through individual genetics, some people will be far more sensitive and reactive in some reflexive behaviors than others.

Modern neuropsychologists distinguish between lower, sub-cortical brain circuits that respond without conscious awareness to outside stimuli and higher cortical brain circuits where conscious awareness and judgment come into play. The lower brain circuits will go their own merry way and operate as they do in those who think like a Stoic, but the *judgments* we make, *even about our own physiological reactions*, are what make all the difference.

---

**12** How sweet it is to have tired out one's appetites and left them behind! Ω

---

SO WHY WAS THAT *OLD MAN HAPPILY CAVORTING IN THAT tree house* we saw through the picture window? Because he has discovered how to enjoy aging by living like a Stoic! Having hit 60 myself, I find this one of Seneca's most engaging letters. Writing in his 60s, Seneca considered himself to have attained old age (and he would never live to see 70). In *Letter 12* he tells Lucilius the signs he sees of his own advancing age. He visits his old country estate and finds the old house in a state of dilapidation. This is the house that grew under his own hands, and yet stones of his age are crumbling to pieces. He scolds the caretaker for the state of a row of trees that are gnarled and shriveled and bear no leaves. He tells them they need to have the ground under them loosened and they need to be watered. The caretaker tells him he has done all that, but to not avail, because the trees are simply old. (Seneca lets us in on his secret that he himself had planted those trees.) He then asks the caretaker about the identity of a rickety old slave who comes into view, a man who looks like he's knocking at death's door. The old man himself replies to Seneca: "Don't you know me, sir? I am Felicio; you used to bring me little images. My father was Philositus the steward, and I am your pet slave."[1] Seneca says the man is crazy, or has become a boy again, since his teeth are falling out (but he knows that the slave tells the truth).

Seneca muses that the old country homestead of his youth revealed to him his age wherever he turned, but he is not despondent. Rather, he urges us to love and to cherish our old age.

---

1  Gummere, *Epistles*, vol. I, 67.

6666666

Fruits are most welcome when almost over; youth is most charming at its close; the last drink delights the toper,—the glass which souses him and puts the finishing touch on his drunkenness. Each pleasure reserves to the end the greatest delights which it contains. Life is most delightful when it is on the downward slope, but has not yet reached the decline ... How comforting it is to have tired out one's appetites, and to have done with them![2]

Those who would live like a Stoic will have plenty to remain happy about, even as we grow as old as dirt.

> ⑬  No boxer can step into battle with high spirits who has never been beaten black and blue. ♊

IT'S PRETTY STRAIGHTFORWARD NOW WHY WE SAW THE *black and blue boxer* sitting on the sofa *unfazed by his bruises.* To some philosophically-minded readers, perhaps Nietzsche's famous phrase will again come to mind: "That which does not kill me makes me stronger." Seneca said in this letter that our fortitude increases through facing challenges. This letter is actually a quite lengthy one. Its heading in Gummere's Loeb edition is "On Groundless Fears," and in Graver and Long's translation "Anxieties about the Future." Seneca warns how, for example:

> the mind at times fashions for itself false shapes of evil when there are no signs that point to any evil; it twists into the worst construction some word of doubtful meaning; or it fancies some person's grudge to be more serious than it really is, considering not how angry the enemy is, but to what lengths he may go if he is angry. But life is not worth living, and there is no limit to our sorrows, if we indulge our fears to the greatest possible extent.[3]

He also expounds on a remedy, explaining how to "let prudence help you, and contemn fear with a resolute spirit even when it is in plain sight."[4] Any reader who suffers from anxiety would do well to ponder the Senecan insights in this letter in full.

---

2  Ibid., 69.
3  Gummere, vol. I, 80–81.
4  Ibid., 81.

**⑭** Let us take refuge in philosophy... for philosophy is peaceful and minds her own business. Ω

HERE, ON THE COFFEE TABLE, WE SAW THAT *LITTLE woman* enter that *little cave.* Upon closer inspection, we recognize her as the beautiful *Philosophia* we first met in the mirror of letter 8. In letter 14 Seneca reflects on how philosophy provides us safety and refuge in the midst of our tumultuous world. Though he would have us engage benevolently with our fellow man and cultivate intimate friendships, he warns against the perils of too much social engagement, and he names three perils as foremost: *"odium, invidia, contemptus"* (hatred, envy, contempt). It is the study and practice of philosophy that will spare us from these grave threats to human fellowship, for as he states so eloquently, "philosophy is peaceful and minds her own business."

**⑮** There are brief and simple ways to train the body, so as to save time, which we should keep in strict account. But whatever you do, come back quickly from body to mind, for the mind must be exercised day and night and will flourish through regular training. Ω

THIS IS WHY A *BODYBUILDER* SAT *READING* IN THE RIGHT swivel chair.[5] You may recall the microcephalic bodybuilder we encountered in 41st chapter of the *Handbook*, which also addressed the theme of training both mind and body, keeping in mind that the mind is of primary importance. Why, I even told you then that the topic would come up again in Seneca's letter 15. So, I won't reiterate the points we considered before, but I will highlight something new.

Note that Seneca, in the first century, wrote about time-efficient exercises that can train the body swiftly, leaving plenty of time for proper care of the mind. Well, in the twentieth century,

---

5  I can't help but reveal why this image popped into my head. Upon the right corner of my writing desk sits a free-standing frame with a photo of my wife holding our American Eskimo dog Mindy. Sitting on top of the frame is a small replica of Rodin's Thinker, joined by a small green Incredible Hulk sitting down reading a book! They are my simple daily reminders to love, think, read, lift—and take care of the dog.

strength-building methods known as High Intensity Training (HIT) and endurance-building methods known as High Intensity Interval Training (HIIT) were independently developed and found very effective. (Indeed, as an inveterate weight lifter, I've applied HIT methods for over 40 years now.) They are effective methods of very brief, intense, and infrequent training that leave plenty of time and energy for other pursuits. (I now train seven days a week, and if my workouts were not so brief, I would not be writing my 23rd book!) Here's where to go if you'd like to learn more about HIT and HIIT—from a Stoic perspective.[6]

> **⑯** Philosophy molds and develops the soul. It orders our life, guides our actions, and tells us what we must and must not do. It sits at the helm and guides our course among the waves of uncertainty. Ω

IT SEEMS OUR *COBBLER* IN THE LEFT SWIVEL CHAIR WAS cobbling not a *sole,* but a *soul.* I love this beautiful little paean to philosophy in its roles as the builder of noble souls and as a trustworthy guide through the uncertainties of life. A letter with many life lessons, it contains one of my favorite ostensibly humble Senecan self-disclosures. He tells Lucilius not to marvel at any genius of his own, "for as yet I am lavish only with other men's property."[7] Further, "whatever is said well by anyone belongs to me."[8] He had been quoting Epicurus again and essentially points out to Lucilius that to think like a Stoic is to seek out, recognize, and broadcast *truth,* regardless of whether its source is inside or outside of one's own school.

In one of the most profound sections of this letter, Seneca addresses the possible roles of God and fate or chance in the choices and actions of our lives. He concludes as follows: "She (Philosophy) will encourage us to obey God cheerfully, but Fortune defiantly; she will teach us to follow God and endure chance."[9]

---

6   See Kevin Vost, *"Show Me Your Shoulders! The Stoic Workout"* online at https://modernstoicism.com/show-me-your-shoulders-the-stoic-workout/, or in print as a chapter in *Stoicism Today: Selected Writings,* Vol. 3, edited by Leah Goldrick and Gregory B. Sadler (Modern Stoicism, 2021), 82–91.

7   Gummere, 107.

8   Graver and Long, 63.

9   Gummere, 107.

⑰  The Stoic, with a free and happy spirit, will laugh at the rustlings and gropings of those who are greedy for wealth, saying "Why do you postpone living? Are you waiting for some interest to come due? Wisdom's rewards are immediate." Ω

REMEMBER THE PLAYER PIANO AND THE *RICH MAN GROPING for pennies* in its coin slot? Though Seneca himself did indeed acquire great wealth earlier in his life, a key theme in this letter is to train oneself to be satisfied with just the few material goods nature truly requires. In this excerpt he also ties this lesson of the folly of pursuing inessential externals to the first letter's prescription to always make good use of our time. Time will fly past us with little reward unless we spend it seeking wisdom. So, get thinking like a Stoic and stop postponing living!

⑱  Even in the midst of the holiday season, as people revel with their party hats, we might do best at this time to train ourselves to reign in our desires for simple pleasures, precisely when others are indulging them. ▣

THE SATURNALIA WAS THE ANCIENT ROMAN FESTIVAL OF the god Saturn, marking the month of December as a time for reveling and making merry, much like our modern-day Christmas season. Epictetus mentions it in his *Discourses* I.29 in a most humane little bit of advice: "When children come up to us and clap their hands and say, 'This is the good Saturnalia,' do we say to them, 'The Saturnalia are not good'? By no means, we clap our hands also."[10]

Seneca jests that December, the month of the merry-making Saturnalia, used to be a month but had become the whole year! He points out to the mature adult Lucilius that festival seasons can provide great times to train oneself in becoming indifferent to simple, frivolous pleasures. In recommending wearing coarse clothing or eating cheap simple foods for some period of days, Seneca's advice may well call to mind Christian practices of self-denial in the season of Lent before Easter. And indeed, in the early history of the Church, Advent too, the season in November and December that precedes Christmas, was, like Lent, widely recognized as a time of fasting, prayer, and self-denial.

---

10  Oldfather, v.1, 191.

Seneca's reason for recommending such self-denial was to allevi-ate anxieties about poverty. When the person of means who worries about losing his fortune purposely gives himself a taste of living with little, he may ask himself "Is *this* what I was so worried about?"

> **⑲** Just as there is a web of the sequence of causes from which fate is spun, so too, there is a sequence of our desires, for one begins where the previous one ends. **Ω**

SURELY YOU DIDN'T FORGET THAT HUGE *SPIDER'S WEB* blocking the living room doorway to the dining room. As for the lesson captured in our arachnoid image, perhaps we have all pon-dered at one time or another the vast web of causes and effects that stretch throughout time. A standard theme in any science fiction story involving travel backward in time is that the slightest alteration of any seemingly trivial event could trigger a cascade of subsequent effects that could drastically alter the future. How often, though, do we consider *not external events,* but *our own role as causal agents* in setting up far-reaching webs of cause and effects?

Seneca warns Lucilius not to strive too hard for worldly success and prosperity, citing a line from perhaps a lost tragedy called *Prometheus:* "Lightning strikes the loftiest peaks." Those who seek the highest place may, through their own desires, make themselves the targets of destruction.

Indeed, in the years before he wrote these letters, Seneca had climbed to the heights of worldly power in the court of the Emperor Nero, and although Seneca would later leave Rome and seek a retirement of solitude and study, Nero's bolt did eventually seek him out with an order to commit suicide, which he did on April 12, AD 65. The lesson here for all of us is to consider what kinds of webs our desires may be spinning for us.

> **⑳** This is the chief task and proof of wisdom, that words and deeds should be in accord, that a person should be the same in all places, and always the same. What is wisdom? Always wanting the same things, and always rejecting the same things. **Ω**

ANY CLUE YET WHY WE IMAGINED A *HOBGOBLIN SCURRYING away* at the exit sign? Well, among the most famous sayings of

American poet-philosopher (and admirer of the Stoics[11]) Ralph Waldo Emerson is this one: "A foolish consistency is the hobgoblin of little minds, admired by little statesmen, philosophers, and divines." Emerson's graphic image warns of a *foolish consistency* of the kind that refuses to remain open to the facts of reality, making one unwilling to change one's prior beliefs, even when they are proven wrong. I simply could not resist the image of a hobgoblin for this letter, but we must remember that Seneca endorses a *wise consistency*, which we might call *integrity*. The person with this kind of consistency is the person whose words and actions are aligned, the person who "walks his talk."

One who would think like a Stoic is not fickle, focusing on virtue part of the time and on frivolous externals the rest of the time. While we don't have the space to deal with it extensively here, I'll note that I addressed this issue in more detail in *The Porch and the Cross*. Stoics like Musonius Rufus, Epictetus, and Marcus Aurelius did indeed exhibit the kind of integrity and consistency Seneca praises, but there are mixed opinions on whether Seneca himself was the opposite, a hypocrite, the prime example of a man who did *not* practice what he preached to others, the rich man who praised poverty, the lustful man who counseled self-control, the proud man who feigned humility. For some, it is almost as if there were two Senecas, the rich, powerful, and conniving politician, and the humble, noble man of letters and of high-minded moral philosophy. Indeed, various contemporaries, historians, and centuries of later thinkers have argued on both sides that the one or the other represents the real Seneca.

It makes most sense to me to think of Seneca as a predominantly honest and genuine man who, at least in his later years, truly sought to practice what he preached about a life devoted to philosophy and virtue, but who was hemmed in, overwhelmed, and, as we noted above, eventually extinguished by the noxious, notorious, and nearly inescapable environment in which he placed himself, the web he weaved from his desires through his youthful passion for worldly success. Whatever your opinion may be, we might all heed the advice of St. Thomas Aquinas (who himself quoted from Seneca himself quite profusely): "Do not place value

11   See, for example, Donald J. Robertson, *Emerson on Stoicism*, https://medium.com/stoicism-philosophy-as-a-way-of-life/emerson-on-stoicism-c7f77d8141fd.

on who says what, but rather, commit to your memory what true things are said."[12] Seneca's lessons are always worth remembering.

SO ENDS OUR DISCUSSION OF LETTERS 11–20. HAVE you inscribed them in your memory banks? Have you written them on the tablets of your heart?

12   From *A Letter from St. Thomas's to Brother John on How to Study*, as translated in Kevin Vost, *How to Think Like Aquinas* (Manchester, NH: Sophia Institute Press, 2018), 17.

# CHAPTER 9

# FROM SELENE TO SOCRATES

## LET YOUR LIGHT SHINE UNTO DEATH

### (Letters 21–30)

*"Above all else, dear Lucilius, learn how to experience joy."*
Letter 23

## MEMORY TOUR
### FOR SENECA'S LETTERS 21–30

A S YOU STEP INTO THE DINING-ROOM DOORWAY ㉑ you are soothed by *moonlight,* then suddenly invigo-rated by dazzling *sunlight.* Oddly enough on the chair at the head of the table ㉒ sits a *donkey,* but only its left *half.* You notice that the thermometer on the wall ㉓ has transformed into a bottle of *Joy dishwashing liquid.* You begin to sit down on the seat on the left ㉔ but notice that sitting upon it are a metal *can* and a document containing *your Will.* Glancing down at the foot of the table ㉕ you think you've seen a *winged angel,* but he tells you he's your *"Guardian Stoic."*

Good thing your Guardian Stoic is near, for upon the seat on the right ㉖ sits the *Grim Reaper* with his sickle. What do you see in this mirror on the wall ㉗? A *key with a capital "V"* written on it, a *peace symbol* ㉘, and another bottle of *Joy.* When you look at the light above the portrait ㉘ it shines on the *floor* which *splits open wide* and *you begin to run.* As you reach the door out ㉙ you are blocked by an *artist* painting a *wisdom tooth.* (To make sure we don't forget this, the artist is not painting to scale. That wisdom tooth takes up the whole canvas!) Finally, as you glance down at the exit mat ㉚ you see that it is decorated with a work of art far more impressive than any wisdom tooth. It's the famous 18th-century *painting of Socrates' death scene.*[1]

---

1  Not familiar or you'd like a refresher for forming your image? A simple internet

137

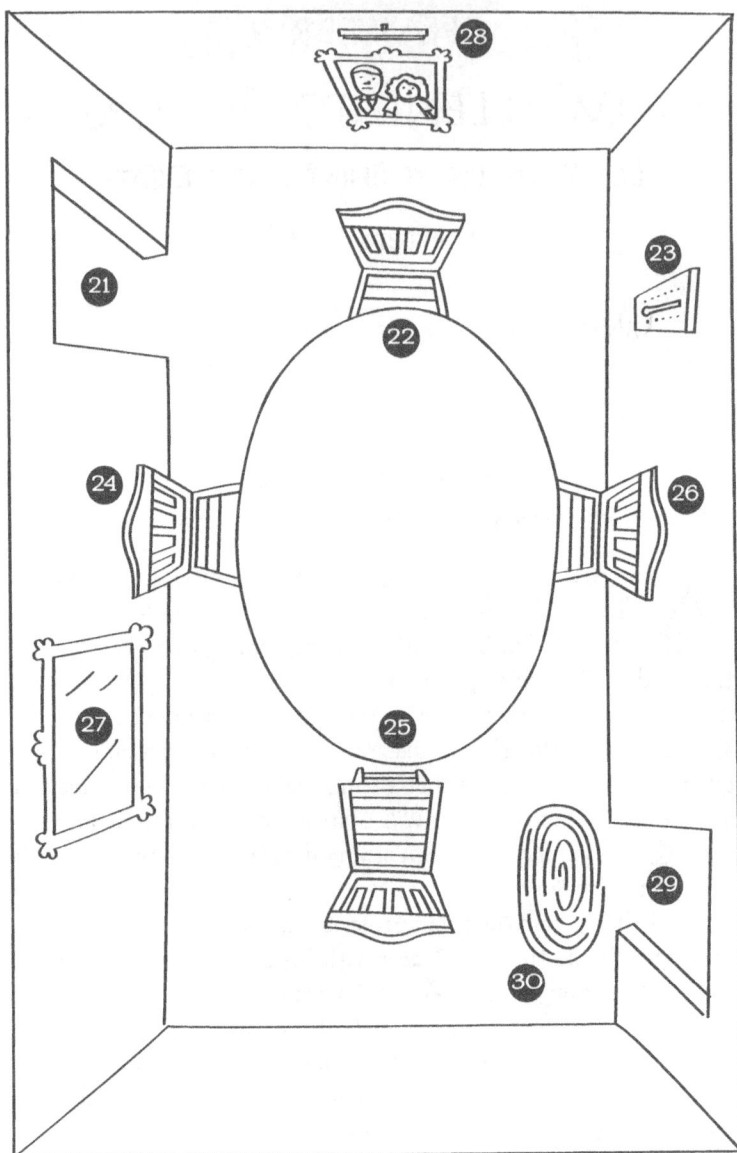

It's time now for the chart that summarizes our tour. Once you've got them all down pat, let's dig into the sublime lessons behind the bizarre images.

search for Jacques Louis David "Death of Socrates" will take you right to it.

| LETTER/LOCATION | IMAGE | LETTERS LESSON |
|---|---|---|
| ㉑ DINING-ROOM DOORWAY | Moonlight then blinding sun | Study will makes you shine |
| ㉒ HEAD OF TABLE | Left half of a donkey | Give your all to what matters |
| ㉓ THERMOMETER | Bottle of Joy cleaner | Learn to feel joy |
| ㉔ SEAT ON LEFT | A can and a will | The present conquers fears |
| ㉕ FOOT OF TABLE | "Guardian Stoic" with wings | Choose a noble guardian |
| ㉖ SEAT ON RIGHT | Grim Reaper with sickle | Treat each day as your last |
| ㉗ MIRROR ON WALL | V key, peace symbol, Joy | Virtue as key to peace and joy |
| ㉘ LIGHT OVER PORTRAIT | Ground opens. You run! | Our faults travel with us |
| ㉙ DOOR OUT | Artist paints wisdom tooth | How wisdom is an art |
| ㉚ EXIT MAT | Socrates' death scene | Live by welcoming death |

## THE LESSONS BEHIND THE IMAGES:
## LET YOUR LIGHT SHINE UNTO DEATH
## LETTERS 21–30

㉑    Our studies then can make us shine. ♎

AS WE ENTERED THE DINING ROOM DOORWAY WE WERE bathed in *moonlight*,[2] then suddenly showered with *sunlight*. Do you remember St. Thomas Aquinas's saying that it is better to shine forth your own light than merely to reflect the light from another source? Seneca makes the same contrast between reflected and self-generated radiance in this letter. As he advises Lucilius, if we seek to achieve truly honorable, noteworthy, memorable things, we will not achieve them by cozying up with and basking in the limelight of the rich, famous, and powerful. Indeed, they may well cast their shadow over us.

---

2 The "Selene" in our chapter title refers to the Greek Titan goddess of the moon. The Roman version of this moon goddess has a much more recognizable name, i.e.—"Luna."

Seneca proclaims, echoing lines from Epicurus and Cicero, that any fame based on *fortune* is destined to be very fleeting. On the contrary, for the person who builds upon his own *innate ability,* the respect he is granted will grow over time, and indeed, not only will honor accrue to the man himself, but to anything or anyone attached to his memory.

Later, we will contrast this passage with Aurelius's meditations on the fleeting nature of fame, but for now, I should note as well that Seneca tells Lucilius that due to these letters Lucilius's own name will be remembered as long as Seneca's is. (Nearly 2,000 years later, Seneca's words still prove true!)

㉒ A good person will not wear himself out with petty and contemptible labor or be busy merely for the sake of being busy. ♎

SO NOW LET'S FIND OUT WHY *HALF A DONKEY* WAS SIT-ting at the head of the table. In keeping with good decorum whilst sidestepping overt vulgarity, I will simply provide the title for this letter in the Gummere translation: "On the Futility of Half-Way Measures," and allow you to deduce the rest. Seneca advises Lucilius (and us, of course) not to do things half-way. To play on a less coarse common aphorism, "Anything worth doing is worth doing right." Seneca advises us not to waste time on dishonorable or frivolous pursuits, but to give our all to tasks that truly matter, like the pursuit of philosophy rather than mere prosperity.

㉓ Above all else, dear Lucilius, learn how to experience joy. ♎

NOW ON TO THAT BOTTLE OF *JOY* AT THE SITE OF THE wall thermometer. How contrary to the stereotype of the unfeeling (i.e., "stoic") Stoic to celebrate *gaudium* (joy) above all else! Indeed, Seneca exhorts his dear friend to set as his goal to learn how to experience the true joy that comes when one frees one's self from both the *hope* of external goods and from the *fear* of things like poverty or death. "The very soul must be happy and confident, lifted above every circumstance."[3] This is the promise of philosophy and it is fulfilled when one rejoices only in what comes from the best within oneself.

3 Gummere, 161.

And what is truly best? Real good "comes from a good conscience, from honorable purposes, from right actions, from contempt of the gifts of chance, from an even and calm way of living which treads but one path."[4] It is only a few who control themselves and their actions by a guiding purpose[5] while the rest are swept along aimlessly by the river of life, some through sluggish waters, and others in violent currents. (If you like Seneca's imagery here, feel free to imagine some non-Stoics immersed in water, grasping onto logs that flow past that bottle of *Joy*.)

**㉔** Let's think to ourselves that everything that *can* happen, *will* happen. Ω

OKAY, SO WHY ARE THE *CAN* AND THE *WILL* SITTING ON the left seat? Well, I will give psychoanalytic theorists credit for the idea that some of the lessons we learn in childhood can stay with us for the rest of our lives. I probably hadn't seen the program since the 1960s (until I tracked it down just now to double-check), but I recall an episode of the television comedy *Bewitched* in which Benjamin Franklin was transported to the 20th century. In one of his many quips, he says that he is not an optimist because optimists always expect the best and are often disappointed, while pessimists always expect the worst and are often pleasantly surprised!

I see some resonance here with this Senecan lesson on allaying anxieties about possible future perils. Instead of hoping that fortune does not bring us hardships, we should realize in advance that they may well come our way, and prepare ourselves to face them with dignity. I also see this lesson as a twist on the *Handbook's* eighth lesson that if we always wish to happen what actually does happen, we will never be disappointed and will always get our wish!

**㉕** Set as a guard over yourself the authority of some person of such character that in their presence even the basest scoundrel would not dare to do wrong. Then work to make *yourself* your own guardian. Ω

---

4 Ibid., 163.
5 Sounds a bit like Epictetus, no?

SO, THERE AT THE CHAIR AT THE FOOT OF THE TABLE was your winged "guardian Stoic"? Well, Christians believe God is omnipresent, and in the words of St. Thomas Aquinas, "He is by his presence in all things, as all things are bare and open to his eyes."[6] In addition, per Thomas, "each man has a guardian angel assigned to him. This rests on the fact that the guardianship of angels belongs to the execution of Divine providence concerning men."[7]

Well, though Seneca believed in divinity, he was not a Christian and did not believe in guardian angels. Still, he advised that we imagine we are watched by a person of impeccable character we would not want to let down. He provided noble Roman examples of Cato, Scipio, and Laelius. The lesson also has parallels with the modern Christian acronym WWJD?—"What would Jesus do?" Christians are called to imitate Christ and act as we believe he would. Seneca advises the same to those who would think like Stoics.

Which great philosopher might *you* choose to imagine is watching you and guarding you as you live your daily life and make important decisions—Socrates, Zeno, Rufus, Epictetus, Aurelius, or even Seneca himself? Can you imagine yourself becoming more and more like that great person—until you are fit to guard yourself?

> **26** You are younger; but so what? We don't know the number of years allotted to us. Who knows where death lies in wait for you; so be ready for it every day. **Ω**

WELL, ONE MINUTE WE ARE COMFORTED BY OUR GUARD-ian Stoic and the next minute, sitting in the next chair is the *Grim Reaper* himself reminding us that he awaits us all. *Memento mori* greets us again. We need to remember again and again that one day unbeknownst to us we must die.

St. Thomas More (1478–1535) had some interesting thoughts on the idea while he awaited his own death in the Tower of London, having placed his moral principles and duty to God above the will and commands of his erstwhile friend, King Henry VIII. He stated that the most profound of the ancient pagan philosophers considered philosophy, the love *(philia)* of wisdom *(sophia),* as a proper preparation or practice for the inevitability of death. As

---

6   *Summa Theologica,* Ia, Q. 8, a. 3.
7   *Summa Theologica,* Ia, Q. 133, a. 2.

death separates the soul from the body, the study of philosophy, by bringing the passions under reason's control, frees the soul from the dictates of the body's loves and affections while the two are still united. According to More, nothing more effectively severs our souls from the passions of our bodies than the thought of death, particularly our own death. Indeed, he said we should not casually contemplate the reality of our death, but should allow it to penetrate deep into our hearts through intense exercise of the imagination. (We might even include an image of the Grim Reaper.)

㉗ Virtue alone provides everlasting peace and joy. Ω

WHY DID THE LITTLE *KEY WITH THE "V,"* THE *PEACE SIGN* ☮, and the *Joy* appear in the mirror? Because Seneca says virtue (V for short) is the key to everlasting peace and joy. Early in the letter he builds on our last lesson about remembering our death by advising Lucilius to strive to let his faults die before he does. Faults are *vices*, dissipations or misdirections of our powers, while *virtues* perfect our innate powers as rational beings. The extent to which we can turn our vices into virtues is the extent to which we will experience tranquility and happiness during our brief stay on earth.

㉘ Though you may cross the sea and lands and cities fade away, your faults will follow you wherever you go. Ω

WHEN THAT LIGHT SHONE ON THE GROUND, A FAULT opened up and you ran. Seneca's lesson here is that we cannot run from our faults. It's much like the saying, "Wherever you go, there you are!" Indeed, a version is found in Thomas à Kempis's (c. 1380–1471) spiritual classic *The Imitation of Christ*, book 2, ch. 12: "Wherever you go, you take yourself with you" and this idea has also been attributed to Confucius (551–479 BC). Is this perhaps a case of great minds thinking alike? In any event, Seneca counsels that philosophy, not travel, will cure a disturbed mind. To quote yet another well-known aphorism: "You can't run away from your troubles."

Seneca does not brush aside travel though. He recommends that if we turn toward ourselves, the person we are matters more than any place we go, and we will find peace wherever we are. Indeed, perhaps echoing the advice of Rufus and Epictetus regarding exile, he advises: "Live in this belief: I am not bound to any one corner of the universe: this whole world is my country."[8]

> ㉙ Anything that comes about by chance is not an art. Now wisdom is an art and it should have a definite aim. Ω

SO, AT THE DOORWAY OUT OF THE DINING ROOM WE found our artist painting a giant wisdom tooth to remind us that *wisdom* is an *art*. And indeed, while Seneca did use the word *ars*, Graver and Long, unlike Gummere, chose to translate it as "skill." Now, *ars* is the Latin equivalent of the Greek *techne* for technique or craft, from which we get the English word "technology." So, while our image included a painter, a fine *artist*, we should still recall the broader meaning. Indeed, let's recall that through this book we are applying the *ars memoriae*, the "art of memory," which is indeed an "artificial," special technique or skill. If you'd like to embellish your memory image, please feel free to throw in an *archer* shooting an apple atop our artist's head, for an archer is the precise example Seneca actually used.

If we are to embrace philosophy and strive to think like a Stoic we should do so with a clear aim in mind, and if we hope to share our lessons with others, we must carefully select our targets. Seneca advises Lucilius not to waste his words on people who show no interest in moral progress. It parallels Jesus's words: "Do not cast your pearls before swine, lest they trample them under feet and attack you" (Matt. 7:6). Indeed, Seneca describes in detail attacks on the Stoics: "He'll scrutinize our school and find objections to throw at our philosophers—payoffs, girlfriends, gluttony. He'll show me one of them caught in adultery, another in a cook-shop, another in the palace."[9]

Rather than wasting arrows on inappropriate targets (let alone wasting pearls on swine), Seneca says a skilled archer should not *hit* the target only sometimes, but should *miss* it only once in a while. We might want to keep this lesson in mind should we so enjoying thinking like a Stoic we can't help but share our lessons with everyone we meet!

---

8  Gummere, 201.
9  Graver and Long, 99.

> **30** Death follows old age just as old age follows youth. The person who does not wish to die cannot have wished to live. Ω

FINALLY FOR THIS CHAPTER, UPON THE EXIT MAT, WE found a real work of art—David's *"Death of Socrates."* I encourage you to do a search and examine this beautiful painting sometime. Among the group of men in Socrates' prison cell at the time of Socrates' death, many cannot bear to look at him, including the jailer who hands Socrates the chalice of hemlock. Several look away. One man buries his face in his hands. A man at his side who looks to Socrates has a hand on Socrates' knee, as if to hold him there in their presence. Socrates himself, befitting his role as a hero to the Stoics, sits bolt upright in perfect posture, looking at his friends. While his right hand reaches for the chalice, his left points upward as he awaits his soul's release.

Epictetus had told us plainly that Socrates did not fear death. Here Seneca reminds us once more that we should not either. Indeed, he tells us that a deep immersion in philosophy can make us cheerful, even when death is in sight. We tend to fear things that are uncertain, but death is a certainty for us all. If death should come in old age, Seneca counsels that any pain it may bring will not last long; it may well bring a sense of relief to know that bodily pain will soon be no more. He opines that a very old person's soul is virtually "on his lips" and ready to leave the body with the slightest of force. He reminds us all as well that no season of life, from infancy to senescence, is exempt from death, so we should indeed meditate on it always, so we'll welcome it, and not fear it.

AND THERE WE HAVE IT FOR THIS CHAPTER, FROM Selene to Socrates, from Beethoven's "Moonlight Sonata" to Mozart's "Requiem Mass," so to speak, from the study of philosophy that will make our lights shine, to meditation upon death, which will make us fearless of the inevitable. Do you remember the locations, the images, and the lessons?

When you have them, let's move on to our next chapter where Odysseus awaits us, willingly tied fast to his ship's mast, so that he might think like a Stoic.

# CHAPTER 10
# FROM SIRENS TO CICERO
## (Letters 31–40)

*"Here is my wish: that you may gain such mastery over yourself that your mind, which is now pulled this way and that way by wandering thoughts, may come to a steadfast course, content in itself."*

*Letter 32*

## MEMORY TOUR
### FOR SENECA'S LETTERS 31–40

H OW ODD THAT THE MINUTE YOU ENTER OUR study, you get a taste of salty sea air and hear an indescribably haunting song. It makes sense the second you spy the scene on the desk top **31**, for there on a wine-dark sea is *Odysseus* himself, *lashed to his ship's main mast* so that he might hear the fabled *sirens' song* without coming under their power. Yet another boat sails down the seat of the leather chair **32**, as if it were part of the mighty Mississippi. But this time it's a *paddleboat*, piloted by none other than *Mark Twain* himself. Perhaps a strange screen saver, but on the computer's monitor **33** is the image of *a beautiful woman's ankle*. Right in the middle of the portrait of the philosophers **34**, blocking your view of Plato and Aristotle, stands *your favorite grade school teacher*, patting your friend *Will* on the back. (If you don't have a friend named Will, then imagine any Will you know or have heard of, like Will Rogers or William Shakespeare.) Who should appear on the Greek urn **35** but *Seneca himself, embracing his friend, Lucilius.*

Depicted on the cover of the stack of Stoic books **36** is an *old man* holding *a little baby.* You glance next at the left chair **37** and spy a gleaming 12-inch *ruler of solid gold* sitting on its seat. (Maybe King Midas touched it?) Up on top of the floor lamp **38**

sit *two female philosophers,* enrapt in deep *conversation.* Upon the right chair sits **39** a *Lives of the Eminent Philosophers* book. (Perhaps it is Diogenes Laertius's famous tome, and maybe the ladies are talking about that.) Finally, we spy Atlas holding up that globe **40** whilst the greatest Roman orator, *Cicero himself, slowly delivers a speech* right in front of him (never once offering to lend a hand).

So, let's see how we've done in navigating the study, before we dive into the lessons behind the images.

| LETTER/LOCATION | IMAGE | LETTERS LESSON |
|---|---|---|
| **31** DESKTOP | *Sirens sing to Odysseus* | Be deaf to evil influences |
| **32** LEATHER CHAIR | *Mark Twain guides riverboat* | Stay steady in your course |
| **33** COMPUTER MONITOR | *Beautiful woman's ankle* | Wisdom in breadth and depth |
| **34** PICTURE OF PHILOSOPHERS | *Teacher pats Will on back* | Will to be good |
| **35** GREEK URN | *Seneca and Lucilius armored* | *Gemeinschaftsgefühl* 2.0! |
| **36** STOIC BOOKS | *Old man holding baby* | Neither folly nor wisdom fears death |
| **37** LEFT CHAIR | *Glowing ruler stands out* | Make reason your ruler |
| **38** FLOOR LAMP | *Two women face to face* | Cherish wise conversation |
| **39** RIGHT CHAIR | *Lives of Philosophers book* | Great souls seek excellence |
| **40** ATLAS HOLDS GLOBE | *Cicero declaims to Atlas* | Speak slowly and clearly |

## THE LESSONS BEHIND THE IMAGES: FROM SIRENS TO CICERO LETTERS 31–40

**31** You will be wise if you stop up your ears, and don't merely stuff them with wax. You'll need a stronger sealant than that which Ulysses used for his comrades. Ω

HOW COULD WE FORGET THE IMAGE OF *ODYSSEUS* (ULYSSES in the Latin) *lashed to the mast* of his ship on the top of the desk? In the Greek mythology of Homer's *Odyssey*, the sirens were hideous creatures with the head of a woman and the body of a bird. Any sailors who heard their enchanting song would go mad, jump ship, and serve as a feast for the sirens. The ever-curious Odysseus had his sailors tie him to the mast so he could hear the song without endangering his life. As for his sailors, he had them stop their ears with wax.

Seneca refers to the story here as he further probes the theme of our seventh lesson on the danger of crowds. He praises Lucilius

149

for seeking out what is truly noble and best while trampling under his feet the petty, vulgar things that popular crowds deem good, and warns him of the need to ignore the enchanting voices of the crowd. He tells him he now recognizes him for who he truly is. Further, he warns that while the song Odysseus heard was alluring, it did not come at him from every side.

This rings even truer for us in the 21st century as we are constantly bombarded by popular culture from ever newer and more pervasive forms of media. If we are to become what we truly are at our best, we'll need to carefully monitor which voices from the crowd we allow into ears and our souls every day.

> **32** Here is my wish: that you may gain such mastery over yourself that your mind, which is now pulled this way and that way by wandering thoughts, may come to a steadfast course, content in itself. May you understand that truly good things belong to you as soon as you understand them. Ω

SO, WE COME TO OUR SECOND SHIP, THE *PADDLEBOAT* sailing along the leather chair. Now, Mark Twain was steering it for good reason. To give the gist of one of his stories, a boat's pilot has to leave the helm for a while and the man who is chosen to take his place has this habit of falling asleep. Right after the boat flawlessly passes the most treacherous bend on the river, the crew comes back and finds him fast asleep at the wheel. One man remarks something along these lines: "If he can pilot a boat that well while *asleep*, imagine what he could do if he was *dead!*"

Of course, Seneca's lesson has nothing to do with sleeping, but it is about steering a steady course in life. Still, thinking for a moment like another Stoic, Epictetus did say that the person rendered invincible by philosophy is the person "whom nothing outside his moral purpose can dismay," even if this person be "drunk," "melancholy mad," or "asleep"![1]

So, we might ask ourselves how far we progressed in guiding our life's ship by our moral purpose, steering clear from unnecessary externals to such an extent that we think and live like a Stoic even in our dreams.

---

1   *Discourses*, II, 17, Loeb edition.

㉝ A beautiful woman is not one whose ankle or arm is praised, but one whose overall appearance makes us forget to take note of her individual body parts. ♎

NEXT, WE CAME TO THE COMPUTER MONITOR WITH THAT odd screensaver of a *beautiful woman's ankle*. Seneca uses a simple physical metaphor here for a much more profound philosophical lesson, indeed, one that would-be memory masters should learn well. Seneca starts this letter by addressing and denying Lucilius's request that he continue to close each of his letters with a quote from a philosopher (as he did in *Letters* 1–29, though we rarely addressed them here, choosing to focus on other lessons of Seneca himself). Seneca warns here of relying too much on learning brief philosophical maxims or relying solely on summaries, rather than digging deep into the whole bodies of wisdom of wise philosophers. Pithy sayings are like beautiful ankles or arms, but what truly matters is how the parts fit together as a whole. He likens a philosophical masterpiece to a master plan carefully woven together, from which nothing can be removed without injury to the whole.

My suggestion then, building on Seneca, is to remember that the lessons we memorize in this book may be like free-floating ankles and limbs unless we use them to help walk us or pull us in to the original writings of the Stoics themselves. Remember well, that for every lesson we pull from each of Seneca's *Letters* many more have remained untouched (and we've hardly even mentioned his multiple *Moral Essays*). For every pithy paragraph of Epictetus's *Handbook* there are many wonderful pages in the *Discourses*. So, if we are to think like Stoics, we can still put our memories to the grindstones and lock in key lessons, just so we never forget to unlock and immerse ourselves in the beautifully rich writings that remain of the best of those men on the porch.

㉞ A proverb states "A job begun is a job half-done." Well, the job is more than half done for tasks involving the soul. The larger part of goodness is the will to be good. ♎

SO WHY WAS YOUR *FAVORITE TEACHER PATTING WILL ON the back* right in the center of the School of Athens portrait? As for the teacher, in this letter Seneca tells Lucilius he jumps for joy at the progress Lucilius is making in philosophy. While he pats Lucilius on the back, so to speak, he also pats his own back, claiming his student Lucilius as his own handiwork!

As for *Will,* we've highlighted Seneca's key lesson in this brief lesson summary, and perhaps it is summarized further by this popular modern catchphrase: "You gotta want it!" The key to becoming a good person is to want it dearly. If we will ourselves to be good above all else, and to refuse to do wrong, we will keep our words and actions in line and aimed straight at our noble goal, for "if a man's acts are not in harmony, his soul is crooked."

> **35** Make progress in philosophy, if for no other reason than that you will learn how to love. Ω

SENECA EMBRACED *LUCILIUS* IN THE ARTWORK ON THE urn to remind us of the simple lesson of the supremacy of neighborly love. I've summarized the lesson as *Gemeinschaftsgefühl* 2.0 to highlight the fact that Seneca once again places the knowledge of how to love as the highest aim of philosophy. The love of wisdom spawns the love of neighbor. He speaks of their friendship, of how they are growing to become "of one mind," as they share each other's strengths. When friends grow in philosophy each friend's growth brings joy and growth to the other. Indeed, Seneca exhorts Lucilius to make progress for Seneca's sake!

> **36** Infants, children, and those who've gone mad don't fear death. How shameful if we cannot use reason to achieve the peace of mind that ignorance or folly brings to them. Ω

SO, DECORATING THE COVERS OF THE STOIC BOOKS WE saw an *old man* holding a *baby.*

This is but a simple reminder that Seneca notes many old men (and adults of all ages) fear death, while babies do not. (Feel free to add an image of a tombstone or perhaps a skull if you want it to lock in the association with death.)

How odd that as the powers of human reason grow stronger over time, we should become more fearful than when our reasoning powers were weak or non-existent. Seneca grants that death can indeed shock and terrorize our very souls, which nature has molded with a desire for self-preservation. Still, if we can overcome the fear of death, we can overcome all manner of needless fears.

A Christian can help quell fears of death by recognizing it as the beginning of eternal life. Seneca was not a Christian, but he posits in this letter that death does not steal life away, but rather interrupts it. Considering things of the natural world like the rotation of the seasons and the cycle of night and day, Seneca concludes that death does not destroy things, but merely changes them, and that the day will come when the dead are restored to the light.

> **37** When you have made reason your ruler, you will rule over many. She will tell you what to do, and how to do it, without blundering into things. Ω

NOW FOR THAT *GOLDEN RULER* THAT SAT ON THE CHAIR on the left. This golden ruler does not symbolize the famous "golden rule," of doing unto others as we would have them do unto us (Matt. 7:12), though Seneca would be in complete agreement with it. Rather, here we refer to the rule (and the ruler) of *reason.* Indeed, it is reason through which we determine what is truly best for ourselves and for others. Stoic philosophy is reason applied to life. Seneca tells us that the wisdom sought by reason frees us from foolishness and from our passions, which can be hard task-masters. Such wisdom will render us secure, untroubled, happy, and above all (echoing Epictetus) free.

Indeed, for modern testimony to the veracity of this lesson consider reason's ruling role in modern *Rational*-Emotive Behavior Therapy and other *cognitive* psychotherapies that strive to heal those who suffer emotionally by bringing their thoughts, emotions, and behaviors under the sway of their own golden rulers.

> **38** Letters are good, but the greatest benefit comes from conversation, because it creeps into the soul, bit by bit. Philosophy is good advice. Ω

THIS IS WHY WE SAW THE TWO FEMALE PHILOSOPHERS conversing on top of the floor lamp. Why female? Why not? This is simply a reminder that women too may certainly think, talk, and live like Stoics. While Musonius Rufus addressed this most clearly among the ancient Stoics, many modern women in our time have done great work with Stoic philosophy and some have started Stoic groups specifically for women.

That important point aside, Seneca's main lesson here is that philosophy is best shared not through formal lectures, but through the dialogue and exchange of intimate conversations. He notes as well that our words need not many words, but effective words. A few simple words may act like seeds that grow over time when implanted in an attentive listener's mind.

And here I cannot help but digress with a simple story I heard in graduate school. A prison psychologist spoke to an inmate preparing for release. The inmate had reformed his behavior and done very well in academic courses while in prison. When asked what had inspired his progress, he thanked the psychologist for what he'd said to him. The psychologist was perplexed, since he had not been the man's therapist. The inmate told him that years ago when the psychologist went over some test results with him, he told the inmate, "You're a pretty smart guy." He said no one had ever said that about him before and it changed his whole way of looking at himself.

Indeed, from my own childhood years I recall a similar story that my mother used to tell. One day while the grade school principal was reviewing academic testing results with our mother, she told mom that a particular sibling of mine was a very bright young boy. Egad! Mom had been helping him do his homework for years, not realizing he had plenty of smarts to do them on his own! (Decades later he would become enthralled by the Stoics—and I would dedicate this book to him.)

Even a few simple words can truly be seeds that give rise to big things. If we would strive to think like Stoics, we would do well to consider what kinds of seeds we cast out to whomever we meet.

> **39** Pick up a list of the philosophers and that in itself will rouse you to act, once you see how many have labored on your behalf. You will yearn to become one of their number yourself. For this is the greatest quality of a noble soul, that it can be roused to honorable things. **Ω**

REMEMBER THAT BOOK OF THE *LIVES OF THE PHILOSOPHERS* sitting on the right chair? Well, in this letter Seneca exhorts us to seek the virtue of *magnanimity* (from the Latin *magnus* for great and *anima* for soul; the Greek equivalent was *megalopsychia*). Indeed, he declares, the great thing about having a great soul (or noble character, if you will), is that it is inspired by noble examples to live in a similar way. It is drawn toward greatness and repelled by the lowly and mean. The person of great soul scorns the external things exalted as great by the masses, but prefers what is ordinary and useful for living. Such a person is free from the vicissitudes of chance or fortune, and the noble goals they achieve serve to lift us up. So, if we are to take up Seneca's advice we should read and re-read of the lives and the lessons of the noble philosophers like Socrates, Epictetus, Aurelius, and others, so that their great souls will inspire us to grow great souls of our own.

**40** Philosophy should not spew out her words in a torrent, but move forward one step at a time. In short, speak slowly. 

AT OUR LAST SPOT IN THE STUDY STOOD *CICERO, TAKING his sweet time*, as he declaimed *a speech* to Atlas, holding up the globe. In this lesson Seneca advises Lucilius not to speak too quickly, for the listener's ears can only pick up so many words at a time. He advises a moderation in speech, neither too quickly or too slow, perhaps in a way reminiscent of an ancient motto made famous by Augustus Caesar: *"festina lente,"* "make haste slowly."

Yet it is actually Cicero whom Seneca cites as a great Roman example of a slower paced speaker. Though faster speech is characteristic of the Greeks, he notes that even in Homer's *Iliad* the speech of the younger man (Odysseus) flows forth like a torrent, while the speech of the older man (Nestor) flows gently, sweeter than honey. The philosopher's manner of speaking should show the same kind of moderation and order as the philosopher's manner of living.

AND THAT WRAPS IT UP FOR LETTERS 31–40, FROM THE sirens in the bookshelf to Cicero with Atlas. Do you recall the locations, the images, and the lessons? When you have them down, let's move on to our last sheaf of letters from our two famous Stoic pen pals.

# CHAPTER 11

# FROM SUCCORING THE SACRED SPIRIT TO SUFFERING THE FOOL WITHIN

## (Letters 41–50)

*"God is near you, with you, within you. A sacred spirit dwells within us, and none of us be can be good without the help of God."*

Letter 41

## MEMORY TOUR
### FOR LETTERS 41–50

AT THE FRONT STEPS **41** OF THE *STOA POIKILE*, A dove swoops into the open mouth of a Stoic student and settles in his lung. (How odd that he doesn't seem to mind. In fact, he's smiling contentedly.) Our attention moves next to the bust of Zeno **42** which has just been crowned with a laurel wreath by the philosopher Baruch Spinoza. (Can't picture Spinoza? Well, you could do a quick internet search, and if you don't, you may well have to consider this suggestion: The philosopher is *spinning* a bowl of O-shaped oat cereal in his other hand, and if you want his first name too, well he's wearing a *bear rug*.) In front of the left pillar **43** you spy a huge *cricket* in suit and tie happily chirping to a big *crowd* of people. Upon the left wall **44**, you spy *Diogenes the Cynic* shredding a show dog's *pedigree papers*. Sculpted into a relief on the left frieze **45** is a college *philosophy professor* (you can tell by his tweed sport coat with elbow patches), but instead of teaching class, he's *cutting a student's hair*.

As we gaze upon the stars over the Stoa's apex **46**, we see the constellation of Hercules, and there we see mighty *Hercules* himself

reading not Seneca's, but *Lucilius's book!* The right frieze **47** depicts a dinner party I'd certainly like to attend, for it shows our *Seneca* dining with our *Epictetus!* As we gaze upon the right wall **48**, we hear the strains of a poignant Led Zeppelin song and see a *stairway* that appears to lead *to heaven*. Out from behind the pillar on the right **49** extends two *large human palms* with huge but quite blurry *lifelines*. Finally, as we fix our glance on Epictetus **50**, we see a *goggled Seneca* right next to him, *straightening a warped board* using a modern jointer.

| LETTER/LOCATION | IMAGE | LETTERS LESSON |
|---|---|---|
| ㊶ STOA STEPS | *Dove inside student's lung* | God is in us |
| ㊷ BUST OF ZENO | *Spinoza places laurel wreath* | True excellence is rare |
| ㊸ LEFT PILLAR | *Cricket chirps to crowd* | A pure conscience for peace |
| ㊹ LEFT WALL | *Diogenes shreds dog pedigree* | Character trumps ancestry |
| ㊺ LEFT FRIEZE | *Professor working as barber* | Don't split hairs! |
| ㊻ STARS ABOVE APEX | *Hercules reads Lucilius's book* | Relish friends' achievements |
| ㊼ RIGHT FRIEZE | *Seneca dines with Epictetus!* | All humans have dignity |
| ㊽ RIGHT WALL BASE | *Stairway to heaven* | Philosophy as path to heaven |
| ㊾ RIGHT PILLAR | *Two palms with lifelines* | Quality over quantity of life |
| ㊿ EPICTETUS'S BODY | *Seneca straightens bent beam* | Philosophy can fix us all |

## THE LESSONS BEHIND THE IMAGES: FROM SUCCORING THE SACRED SPIRIT TO SUFFERING THE FOOL WITHIN (*LETTERS* 41–50)

㊶ God is near you, with you, within you. A sacred spirit dwells within us, and none of us can be good without the help of God. Ω

HOW STRANGE THAT THE STUDENT ON THE STEPS DIDN'T seem to mind when the *dove* flew straight *into his lung*. Well, we're borrowing Christian imagery here since the Holy Spirit descended "as a dove" from heaven upon Jesus at the time of his baptism as reported in all four gospels.[1] Seneca says that a sacred spirit which guides and guards us lies within each and every one of us. It is up to us whether or not we choose to follow that spirit's counsel. How interesting that Seneca quotes here a line from Virgil's *Aeneid*

---

1  Matt. 3:16, Mark 1:10, Luke 3:22, John 1:32.

that in each good person "a god dwells, but which god, we do not know." For Christian readers, this may immediately call to mind St. Paul's words to the Greek philosophers in Athens:

> Men of Athens, I perceive that in every way you are very
> religious. for as I passed along, and observed the objects
> of your worship, I found also an altar with this inscrip-
> tion, "To an unknown god." What therefore you worship
> as unknown, this I proclaim to you. (Acts 17:22–23)

Seneca describes how the great things of nature like a dense, mature forest, a great cave that holds a mountain on its back, a mighty raging river, or a hidden spring that suddenly bursts forth from the ground all point to the existence and majesty of God. Most telling, so too should the sight of a human being who remains unperturbed in the midst of adversity signal to us that God's divine power has descended upon him. God has given us a marvelous gift in our rational capacities to discern His will and live our lives in accord with it. Indeed, if we were to heed the sacred spirit within us rather than the general madness of petty human concerns, living in accord with nature would be the easiest thing in the world!

> **42**   It is not surprising that greatness comes along only at long intervals. Fortune often brings about the ordinary that serves to please the crowd, but she holds up for our admiration that which is extraordinary by the very fact that she makes it so rarely. Ω

NOW LET'S SEE WHY WE CAME ACROSS THE PHILOSOPHER *Baruch Spinoza* (or the guy in the *bear rug spinning O's*) as our image for this lesson. Probably the most quoted phrase from one of Spinoza's letters goes like this: "All things excellent are as difficult as they are rare." Spinoza was an admirer of our Stoics and he has provided a most pithy and memorable summary of one of Seneca's key lessons from this letter. Seneca calls on us to strive mightily for virtue (*arête* or "excellence" in the Greek) regardless of the hardships we may encounter. A life of virtue is the only thing worth the effort, a thing that few achieve, and sadly, a thing that few even try to attain, hence its rarity.

I should note as well that in this letter, though he does not mention Epictetus, Seneca essentially also provides his own eloquent arguments for considering the true cost to ourselves should we strive to attain external things or accomplishments, echoing with his own eloquent twists the lessons of Epictetus's *Handbook* chapters 24, 25, and 29.

> **43** A good conscience welcomes a crowd, while a bad one is troubled even in solitude. Ω

SO WHY IN FRONT OF THE LEFT PILLAR WAS A WELL-dressed *cricket* chirping to a *crowd?* It will make more sense in you are familiar with "Jiminy Cricket" in Disney's *Pinocchio* movie. Pinocchio, you'll recall, was tempted to lie, and Jiminy served as his conscience.

In this letter, Seneca specifically addresses the need for a *"bona conscientia,"* "good conscience." The Stoic does not seek to remain unruffled by his own faults. The person of truly good character is the rare individual who can live with his doors wide open, having nothing shameful to hide. A pure conscience breeds true tranquility, banishing fears that one be found out for what one truly is or has done. A bad conscience brings no peace, even while alone, always fretful of disclosure and disturbed by its own dishonorable state. To be a good Stoic is to be a good, honest person with a good conscience. Jiminy Cricket would surely chirp out his agreement.

> **44** If there is any good in philosophy, it is this—that it never looks into genealogies. A noble mind is available to all, and in this we are all nobly born. Philosophy neither rejects nor chooses anyone. It shines its light for all. Ω

NOW WE SEE WHY *DIOGENES THE CYNIC TEARS UP A DOG'S pedigree papers* at the left wall base. I threw in Diogenes the Cynic (*cynos* = dog) to shore up our dog image, since pure-bred pedigree breeds of dogs often do have such papers. Dog imagery aside, what a powerful lesson for Seneca's time and for all times is packed into this lesson. How nearly universal across time and culture have people been assigned value according to the accidents of their birth and ancestry, from the elaborate caste system in India, to the elaborate systems of nobility or peerage in Europe, to our own time when so many would value people on the degree to which their skin possesses or lacks melanin. Indeed, Seneca's passage seems prescient of Martin Luther King, Jr's. famous line: "I look to a day when people will be judged not according to the color of their skin, but by the content of their character."

Seneca lived in a Roman society with a very pronounced social hierarchy, and was himself born into the equestrian class (as was Lucilius), a rank below that of the patrician or senatorial classes, but above the common plebians, freedmen, and slaves. Still, he argued in this letter that all people are really related if we trace our ancestors back to their original source from the gods.

Indeed, in our time, there is nothing wrong with actually tracing one's genealogy as a matter of curiosity, but we might well keep in mind the line from Plato that Seneca cited here: "Every king has slaves in his background, and every slave has an ancestor who was a king."

What a noble idea it is that philosophy, the most cherished ideal of the Stoics, rejects no human being whatever, regardless of personal pedigree. Indeed, philosophy is there to help any man or woman who would care to think like a Stoic become a person of noble character. On a related note, in Musonius Rufus's eighth lecture on whether actual kings should study philosophy, he paraphrases a line from Socrates that philosophy makes every person kinglike within his own realm.

> **45** Why do you waste my time with what you call the "liar fallacy," about which many books have been written? What if my whole life is a lie? Prove that wrong, and, if you are clever enough, turn its falsehood into truth. At the present it counts as necessities things that are superfluous. 𝛺

WHY DID THAT LEFT FRIEZE DEPICT A *COLLEGE PROFESSOR* not professing, but *cutting a student's hair?* In this letter, reminiscent of the lessons of Epictetus's 52nd *Handbook* chapter, Seneca explicitly warns Lucilius (and us) not to waste time splitting hairs!

The liar fallacy to which Seneca refers goes something like this. Consider the statement: "I am lying." If the person making that statement is telling the truth, then he is lying. If he is lying, then he is telling the truth. Seneca argues that students of philosophy should not waste their time trying to unravel word riddles or paradoxes about truth, but should spend their time and energy living lives guided by truth. Indeed, if I might opine once more, it is largely because of such hair-splitting quibbling in modern times that philosophy has acquired a bad name, seen more as the love of trivial, confusing *sophistry* than the love of a sublime, life-enhancing *sophia* (wisdom).

> **46** Lucilius, I received your book that you sent me, and was so impressed with its charm that I read it in one sitting. The sunlight called, hunger gnawed, clouds gathered, but I absorbed your book from beginning to end, and it gave me not merely pleasure, but joy! Ω

SO UP IN THE STARS ABOVE THE STOA'S APEX DID *HERCULES* sit absorbed in *Lucilius's book.*

If you'll forgive yet another personal note, as an author with some young friends who spend their time crafting tomes of their own, this letter strikes a personal chord with me.[2] Those who would think like Stoics enjoy forming virtuous friendships, and find it a source of great joy when a friend attains a meaningful success. Seneca practically tells him the book had him jumping for joy. What a wonderful thing to have friends to rejoice in our accomplishments, and friends in whose accomplishments we may rejoice.

The friend's role however, is to encourage, but never merely to flatter. Seneca points out specific things he likes about Lucilius's style and subject matter. He offers no specific criticisms in this letter, but warns Lucilius he will read it again when he calms down, and will not hesitate to give him his true opinions in full after a more sober examination. Friends who think like Stoics embrace the truth, as well as each other.

> **47** I will judge them (slaves) not by their jobs, but by their characters. Each person acquires his own character, but fate assigns his duties. Invite some to share your table because they deserve it, and others, so that they may come to deserve it. Ω

NOW WE SEE WHY *SENECA DINED* SPECIFICALLY WITH *EPICtetus* in our image on the right frieze.[3] Here is another variation on

---

2 Indeed, as I type this very day (February 20, 2021) I expect any day now a copy of my friend Shane Kapler's brand new *James: Jewish Roots, Catholic Fruits,* from a publisher called, I believe, Angelico Press!

3 Epictetus was alive during the last 15 years of so Seneca's life and his teacher Musonius was also Seneca's younger contemporary by around 30 years. While Epictetus refers to Rufus several times in his writing, there survive no

Seneca's (and Dr. Martin Luther King Jr.'s) theme of the supreme importance not of a person's occupation, rank, or other accidentals, but of the character a person has built for him- or herself. Seneca, you'll recall, was a knight who rose to the court of the Roman Emperor (Nero), while Epictetus was born a slave, who never rose past the rank of a freedman and teacher. Still, judging by the contents of their *minds*, both great men achieved the highest of places in the "court" of Philosophy, and judging by the contents of their *characters,* the ex-slave would appear to have climbed far higher than the knight.

This long letter is well worth reading and pondering in its entirety. In an age when the *fact* of the *existence* of slavery had hardly been questioned anywhere in the world throughout history, Seneca strives to remind us all that slaves are human beings, just like their masters, and in a sense, every one of us is a slave to Fortune, to a myriad of things outside our control. While some Romans would be shocked by the very idea, Seneca finds it a fine thing to ask his slaves to dine with him, so that slaves of noble character are rewarded, and slaves with potential for noble souls are inspired to attain them.

Seneca provides a wealth of humane insights we'd all do well to remember and implement: "Treat persons of inferior rank just as you would be treated by those who outrank you." This variation on the Golden Rule is truly a noble precept. Indeed, how unbefitting of a Christian and/or a Stoic are those who treat their subordinates with disdain while kowtowing to their bosses.

**48** "Is this the path to the stars?" That's exactly what philosophy promises me—that I shall be made equal to God. This is what I was called for, and this is why I came. Philosophy, keep your promise! Ω

RIGHT AT THE RIGHT WALL BEGAN A *STAIRWAY* THAT looked as if it reached all the way *to heaven.* The quotation we've

references to Seneca in either man's work, and neither does Seneca reference either one of them. This is intriguing, especially since Rufus and Seneca were both of the equestrian order in Rome, and since Epaphroditus, Epictetus's one-time owner, was a secretary to Nero, whom Seneca tutored. Some have suggested that perhaps Epictetus, while a young slave, met Seneca, but as far as I know, it's merely speculation. Still, we can easily *imagine* them dining together. And what an interesting conversation they would have!

highlighted is from Virgil's *Aeneid*, 9, 641. In our summary, I followed the Graver and Long translation in ending the quotation with the word "stars." In the Gummere translation of the *Letters* he ends with the word "heaven" instead of stars, and we built upon this idea in our mnemonic image. This raises two questions: 1) which word did Seneca actually use? and 2) which word did Virgil use? Seneca used *"astra"* (stars) as did Virgil, so where does heaven come in? Well, in Virgil's original context the words were spoken by the god Apollo to the triumphant Iulus, whom he blesses, saying he and his comrades are sons of gods and sires of gods to be, so the heavenly context is there. Indeed, one English translation of Virgil reads "the starward path to dwelling place divine."[4]

Anyway, Seneca's lesson might sound quite presumptuous or even blasphemous in declaring that philosophy can make us equal to God. Gummere translates it thus, while Graver and Long use the lower-case plural "gods," in lower case. According to the Loeb editions, Seneca uses the word *deo*, the singular for "god" or "God," while Virgil used the plural *deos* "gods" in his lines from the mouth of Apollo. In any case, it is important to examine what Seneca means by philosophy making as "god-like" or "equal to God."

Earlier in this letter, Seneca expands on his warning against academic hair-splitting, focusing too much on syllogisms and too little on life. As for the possible presumption or even blasphemy, I think the point Seneca is making is that we are made in the image of God in that we are blessed with intellects that can perceive truth and that we can use such truths to live virtuous (i.e., godly) lives. The more we use our intellects to pursue virtue for our own benefit and for that of our fellow man the more closely we follow God and become godlike.[5]

Near the end of the letter, he said that we do this by becoming more honest and straightforward in our speech. This is not served by sophistic hair-splitting, but by focusing on things that are truly important. He ends by noting that with our time on earth so short,

---

4  P. Vergillius Maro, *Aeneid*, Theodore C. Williams, ed. http://www.perseus.tufts.edu/hopper/text?doc=Perseus%3Atext%3A1999.02.0054%3Abook%3D9.
5  Catholic readers might keep this Church teaching in mind as well: "For the Son of God became man so that we might become God." "The only-begotten Son of God, wanting to make us sharers in his divinity, assumed our nature, so that he, made man, might make men gods" (*Catechism of the Catholic Church*, no. 460).

it is sheer madness to waste it on the superfluous. (Indeed, if our time on earth were infinite, the study of trivial things would never provide a stairway to the starry heavens.)

> **49** Say to me when I go to bed, "You may not wake up!" Say to me when I arise, "You may not go to sleep again!" Say to me when I leave my house, "You may not return!" And when I come home: "You may never leave this house again!" Ω

REMEMBER THOSE *TWO PALMS* WITH HUGE BUT *BLURRY lifelines* that emerged from behind the right pillar? Well, here we are revisiting *memento mori* once more, a popular theme for Seneca, Epictetus, Aurelius, and virtually all of the Stoics. We all know that *one day* our lifelines will run out, but we do not know *which day—perhaps today.*

Here Seneca provides the basis of a very simple *spiritual exercise* we might consider making a habit of every morning after arising, every time we leave or return to our homes, and every night before we fall asleep. We might say those statements to ourselves, and ponder the significance of the profound truth they contain. We do not know if this is our last night or day on earth, so will we choose to make the most of each hour and live as if it were our last? Is there any good deed we would not like left undone, any kind or forgiving words to someone we would rue for never having uttered when we had the chance? Let's keep this lesson in mind every time we think of this image—or merely look at our palms.

> **50** I do not despair of even the most inveterate sinner. There is nothing that won't yield to persistent intervention, to concentrated and careful attention; no matter how bent a board may be, you can make it straight again. Ω

DO YOU RECALL THE IMAGE OF *SENECA STRAIGHTENING that warped board* with a jointer? (Not sure what a jointer is? I'll admit, I had to look it up myself.) Anyway, the jointer is not important, but straightening what's crooked is. What's warped is our *character,* and its straightener is *philosophy.*

Though Seneca wrote another seventy-four letters after this one, I've chosen to end on the fiftieth, so as not to overwhelm our memories in their first try at absorbing these lessons. How fortuitous that *Letter 50* ends on a great ray of hope for anyone who desires to reform or enhance his or her life through thinking and living like a Stoic.

One can see why Seneca was so admired by many early Church Fathers, for Christ and His Church also taught there is always hope for transformation even amongst those most mired in vice. According to Seneca "learning virtue means unlearning vice." Not only can philosophy cure from moral disease all who pursue it, it is not bitter medicine, and is sweet from the first drop, as it heals and pleases us at the same time. Indeed, a good dose of philosophy is nutritious and delicious at the same time. *"VALE."* (Farewell.)

WELL, SO ENDS OUR TOUR OF THE FIRST FIFTY OF SEN-eca's *Letters.* Do you have the locations, images, and key lessons of letters 41–50 down now? If not, please review them until your memory has them mastered. If so, please feel free to see if you know all fifty by reviewing the mastery mnemonic table at this chapter's end.

I should note as well, that perhaps some readers would like to grow further as memory masters as well as masters of Stoic lessons. First, after reading Seneca's *Letters* in their entirety, readers could feel free to add to the number of lessons they recall from each chapter. If some idea really strikes you, feel free to add a new memory image of your own that interacts in some way with our original image.

## AND ABOUT THOSE OTHER 74 LETTERS...

FOR ANY STALWART READERS WHO MIGHT LIKE TO MASTER at least one image and idea from more of Seneca's *Letters,* or even all 124 of them, *please feel free to build your own memory house,* based ideally upon your own house or apartment to add additional locations. Indeed, after my *Memorize the Faith!* came out, I was contacted by a priest who was getting ready for an assignment in China. He told me he crafted a memory house of 500 locations (fifty rooms of ten locations each) to house 500 essential Chinese vocabulary words! And speaking of foreign vocabulary words, if many of the key Stoic concepts seem "all Greek" (and perhaps "some Latin") to you, note well that in this book's chapter 14 we will work on mastering a specialized memory method that will provide the *key* to holding both the pronunciation and meanings of foreign words in mind. (In fact, it is called the *keyword method*.)

Okay, so after our review, let's move on from the emperor's adviser to the Stoic contemplations of the emperor himself!

# SENECA'S LETTERS
## MASTER MNEMONIC TABLE

| LETTER/LOCATION | IMAGE | LETTERS LESSON |
| --- | --- | --- |
| ❶ FRONT DOOR | *Clock flies out at you* | *Tempus fugit!* |
| ❷ DOOR MAT | *Illuminated book* | Reading the wisest authors |
| ❸ GLASS PANEL | *Your best friend* | Fostering true friendships |
| ❹ PORTRAIT ON BACK WALL | *Your own headstone* | Overcoming fear of death |
| ❺ GUN RACK | *Seneca embraces strangers* | *Gemeinschaftsgefühl!?* |
| ❻ CENTER OF FOYER | *Transformer gives you brain* | Joys of sharing wisdom |
| ❼ CHANDELIER | *Riot inside the Coliseum* | The dangers of crowds |
| ❽ MIRROR ON WALL | *Woman with golden chain* | Philosophy makes us free |
| ❾ CUSHIONED BENCH | *Sculptor sculpts a human* | Making new friends |
| ❿ DRAWER IN BENCH | *You, talking to yourself* | Trust your true self |
| ⓫ CENTER OF LIVING ROOM | *Your statue with red cheeks* | The limits of human nature |
| ⓬ PICTURE WINDOW | *Old man in tree house* | How to enjoy aging |
| ⓭ SOFA | *Black and blue boxer* | Challenges build strength |
| ⓮ COFFEE TABLE | *Woman walks into cave* | The solace of philosophy |
| ⓯ RIGHT SWIVEL CHAIR | *Muscleman reading book* | Good care of body and mind |
| ⓰ LEFT SWIVEL CHAIR | *Cobbler cobbles a sole* | Philosophy builds the soul |
| ⓱ PIANO | *Rich man grabs at pennies* | How to laugh greed away |
| ⓲ FIREPLACE | *Stockings begin to smoke* | Prepare for feast or famine |
| ⓳ LIVING-ROOM DOORWAY | *Spider web* | The webs of our desires |

| | | |
|---|---|---|
| **20** EXIT SIGN DOORWAY OUT | *Hobgoblin scurries away* | Consistency for big minds |
| **21** DINING-ROOM DOORWAY | *Moonlight then blinding sun* | Study will makes you shine |
| **22** HEAD OF TABLE | *Left half of a donkey* | Give your all to what matters |
| **23** THERMOMETER | *Bottle of Joy cleaner* | Learn to feel joy |
| **24** SEAT ON LEFT | *A can and a will* | The present conquers fears |
| **25** FOOT OF TABLE | *"Guardian Stoic" with wings* | Choose a noble guardian |
| **26** SEAT ON RIGHT | *Grim Reaper with sickle* | Treat each day as your last |
| **27** MIRROR ON WALL | *V key, peace symbol, Joy* | Virtue as key to peace and joy |
| **28** LIGHT OVER PORTRAIT | *Ground opens. You run!* | Our faults travel with us |
| **29** DOOR OUT | *Artist paints wisdom tooth* | How wisdom is an art |
| **30** EXIT MAT | *Socrates' death scene* | Live by welcoming death |
| **31** DESKTOP | *Sirens sing to Odysseus* | Be deaf to evil influences |
| **32** LEATHER CHAIR | *Mark Twain guides riverboat* | Stay steady in your course |
| **33** COMPUTER MONITOR | *Beautiful woman's ankle* | Wisdom in breadth and depth |
| **34** PICTURE OF PHILOSOPHERS | *Teacher pats Will on back* | Will to be good |
| **35** GREEK URN | *Seneca and Lucilius armored* | *Gemeinschaftsgefühl* 2.0! |
| **36** STOIC BOOKS | *Old man holding baby* | Neither folly nor wisdom fears death |
| **37** LEFT CHAIR | *Glowing ruler stands out* | Make reason your ruler |
| **38** FLOOR LAMP | *Two women face to face* | Cherish wise conversation |
| **39** RIGHT CHAIR | *Lives of Philosophers book* | Great souls seek excellence |
| **40** ATLAS HOLDS GLOBE | *Cicero declaims to Atlas* | Speak slowly and clearly |

| | | |
|---|---|---|
| **41 STOA STEPS** | *Dove inside student's lung* | God is in us |
| **42 BUST OF ZENO** | *Spinoza places laurel wreath* | True excellence is rare |
| **43 LEFT PILLAR** | *Cricket chirps to crowd* | A pure conscience for peace |
| **44 LEFT WALL** | *Diogenes shreds dog pedigree* | Character trumps ancestry |
| **45 LEFT FRIEZE** | *Professor working as barber* | Don't split hairs! |
| **46 STARS ABOVE APEX** | *Hercules reads Lucilius's book* | Relish friends' achievements |
| **47 RIGHT FRIEZE** | *Seneca dines with Epictetus* | All humans have dignity |
| **48 RIGHT WALL BASE** | *Stairway to heaven* | Philosophy as path to heaven |
| **49 RIGHT PILLAR** | *Two palms with lifelines* | Quality over quantity of life |
| **50 EPICTETUS'S BODY** | *Seneca straightens bent beam* | Philosophy can fix us all |

# PART III

# MEMORIZE MARCUS'S MEDITATIONS!

"So blameless was the conduct of Marcus Aurelius that neither the malignity of contemporaries nor the spirit of posthumous scandal has succeeded in discovering any flaw in the extreme integrity of his life and principles."

Rev. F. W. Farrar[1]

"It's in the nature of books about the spirit that they can be visited again and again. How often we return to books after a gap of some years and find that, with broader experience, we are able to read them in a deeper way, to see new facets that we had previously missed.

"Marcus Aurelius's book is one of these—it can't be outgrown; it does not date. It reads in a different way to someone who is twenty than to someone who is sixty yet still has something profound to tell them both about living the real good life."

Mark Forstater[2]

---

1   Seekers After God: Seneca, Epictetus, and Marcus Aurelius (Republished Classics, 2013), originally published in 1868.
2   The Spiritual Teachings of Marcus Aurelius, 12.

## CHAPTER 12

# THE MAGNIFICENT SEVEN MAXIMS OF EMPEROR MARCUS AURELIUS

*"Have also at hand some short elementary maxims, which may readily occur, and suffice to wash away all trouble, and send you back without fretting at any of the affairs to which you return."*
Marcus Aurelius, *Meditations* 4:3[1]

HOPEFULLY, WE NOW HAVE DOZENS (103 TO BE precise) of short, elementary pearls of Stoic wisdom cached in our memory banks, courtesy of the wisdom of a freed ex-slave and of a courtier to a Roman Emperor. Now it is time to collect more moral pearls from the emperor himself.

Thankfully, we have all kinds of resources addressing the life of Marcus Aurelius (AD April 26, 121–March 17, 180). I've written very briefly on Aurelius's life in *The Porch and the Cross*. An excellent, standard full-length biography is Anthony Birley's *Marcus Aurelius: A Biography*. We are fortunate to have as well a number of wonderful books expounding and analyzing the wisdom this great emperor shares in his famous *Meditations*. An excellent recent introduction to Aurelius and his thought is psychotherapist Donald Robertson's *How to Think Like a Roman Emperor: The Stoic Philosophy of Marcus Aurelius*, and a masterful analysis of the *Meditations* can be found in philosopher Pierre Hadot's *The Inner Citadel: The Meditations of Marcus Aurelius*.

Since we have so vigorously exercised our memory powers in treating Epictetus's *Handbook* and Seneca's *Letters*, I've thought

---

I  Francis Hutchenson and James Moor, trans., James Moore and Michael Silverthorne, eds., *The Meditations of the Emperor Marcus Aurelius* (Indianapolis, IN: Liberty Fund, 2008), 47–48.

it best that we rest a little bit to recuperate and recover, so this chapter's memory "workout" will be very light in comparison. While we memorized 53 key ideas from the *Handbook* and 50 of Seneca's *Letters*, we will memorize merely "*seven* magnificent maxims" from Emperor Marcus Aurelius. (Indeed, our good emperor introduces these seven maxims themselves as a leisurely retreat within one's own soul to reestablish tranquility, and to restore and refresh oneself.)

Now, psychological research has shown that the average short-term memory span for adults is seven pieces of information. In the simple memory "digit span" task, subjects are read increasingly long strings of numbers and asked to repeated them back in the same order. Most people can recall a maximum of seven. Indeed, that is why telephone numbers were made with seven numbers excluding the area code. Psychologists often employ the rule of thumb of "7 plus or minus 2" to describe the memory span capacity of the vast majority of the population. Given individual differences in natural memory power, almost every normal adult will fall within the range of 5 to 9 pieces of information that can be held at one time in their short-term memory.

Still, the memory methods we are applying in this book aim to greatly enhance our powers of recall by providing us means to store and recall far more pieces of information than "5 plus or minus 2" by moving them from the cramped spaces of our short-term memories to the almost limitless storage capacities of our long-term memories, and providing cues (locations and images) to pull them back out at will. Still, by giving our memory capacities a bit of a break in this chapter, we can focus more intently on the *meanings* and *implications* of each of the seven maxims we'll tuck away.

As for the scope of the *Meditations* themselves, they have been divided historically into 12 "books," which would be called chapters within a modern book. Marcus, like Epictetus and Seneca, addresses all kinds of Stoic themes in each of his books. In the past, when I've provided samples of key themes in each chapter, I labeled them like this:[2]

---

2  *The Porch and the Cross* (section headings referring to each of his books in chapter 11, "Lessons of Humble Grandeur").

## A SAMPLE OF GRAND THEMES IN
## THE TWELVE BOOKS OF THE *MEDITATIONS*

1. Gratitude 101
2. Preparing for Equanimity
3. Beauty
4. Perspective
5. Rising to the Work of a Human Being
6. How not to turn into a Caesar
7. Love Mankind, Follow God
8. Throw Away Bad Cucumbers[3]
9. Contentment from Womb to Tomb
10. Cultivating the Elusive Simplicity of Soul
11. Nine Rules that are Gifts of the Muses
    (and a Tenth from Apollo)
12. Fear not Death, but Failure to Live

Each book contains a collection of sayings and thoughts that vary in length from pithy one-liners to reflections as long as 60 lines per Hadot's calculations. Each meditation has been numbered, and there are between 17 and 75 of them in each of the various books. If I've done my ciphering right, there are a total of 487 of them! So again, why only seven here?

Well, Hadot has noted that in many books Marcus includes or lists *"kephalaia"* (chapter heads), which are fundamental points that he will explicate further. These *kephalaia* serve as *"aide-mémoire"* (memory aids) that help keep these key principles in mind. Indeed, "they are repeated, ruminated upon; but also explained and sometimes demonstrated. If we assemble these series of *kephalaia*...we can thus discover almost all the themes announced or developed in the Meditations."[4] Our memory tour and subsequent reflections will focus on one of the nine *kephalia* that Hadot lists, that of book 4, chapter 3.

So, perhaps you are as familiar with the *Meditations* as I am, or more so, and yet you've never heard of the "seven magnificent maxims"? Allow me to explain.

3 You'll just have to read the *Meditations* to get the full gist of this one, but perhaps a pithy summary might be "Don't sweat the small stuff!"
4 Pierre Hadot, *The Inner Citadel: The Meditations of Marcus Aurelius*, trans. Michael Chase (Cambridge, MA: Harvard University Press, 1998), 38–39.

I find the *Meditations* so worth dipping into again and again over the years that I enjoy collecting various English translations (in addition to the Loeb translation which includes the Greek text), and I like to read different translations each time I dip back into them. Well, the oldest translation I possess, translated by Francis Hutcheson and James Moor, was originally published in Scotland in 1742.[5] Now, of the six translations I use, this is the only one that sets off seven of Marcus's statements of book 4, chapter 3 within quotation marks. These caught my eye, and as a fan of the classic western "The Magnificent Seven," I decided I might as well call these the "magnificent seven maxims of Emperor Marcus Aurelius." Why not?

So, before we begin our memory tour and philosophical reflections, let me lay them out for you in Hutcheson and Moore's translation:

## SEVEN MAGNIFICENT MAXIMS OF
## EMPEROR MARCUS AURELIUS

1. "All rational beings were formed for each other."
2. "Bearing with them is a branch of justice."
3. "All mistakes are involuntary."
4. "How many of those who lived in enmity, suspicion, hatred, and quarrels, have been stretched on their funeral piles, and turned to ashes?"
5. "Either it is providence which disposes of all things, or atoms."
6. "The things themselves reach not the soul, but stand without, still and motionless."
7. "All these things presently change and shall be no more."

---

5 Francis Hutcheson and James Moor, trans., *The Meditations of the Emperor Marcus Aurelius Antoninus*, James Moore and Michael Silverthorne, eds. (Indianapolis: Liberty Fund, Inc., 2008).

## MEMORY TOUR OF MARCUS'S
## SEVEN MAGNIFICENT MAXIMS

AS WE BEGIN OUR MNEMONIC TOUR FOR AURELIUS'S MAX-ims, I am tempted to cite Monty Python again: "And now for something completely different." And yet, what follows is not *completely* different. Assuming we're all feeling at home in our memory house, I'll introduce another variation of the location system. Memory houses are easy to build, but location systems can also be built around just about anything.

The first system I ever came across in the 1970s was based on 20 parts of a car—hence the puns of both the subtitles of the aforementioned book *Your Memory: Speedway to Success in Earning, Learning, and Living* (*Featuring the Auto-Magic Memory Method*). Indeed, my memory still takes it out once in a while for a drive to this day.

For example, a few years back I was asked to give a talk about St. Martin de Porres, which I decided to do (like all of my talks) from memory. I laid out about 40 key points in order in the memory house, but I decided that by the time I completed some introductory remarks and reached the gun rack (location ❺) I wanted to digress briefly with eight key points that summarized the chronology of his life. I simply pulled the memory car up to the gun rack, placed my key ideas on the first eight locations of the car, hopped out when I was finished, and then moved right back to the center of the foyer and proceeded through the rest of the points.

Ancient orators may have set up locations in the forums or buildings where they were to speak. In the Middle Ages, as St. Albert the Great put it, some students of the art of memory would "place a church" they were familiar with. As a fan of strength training, I've even developed location systems based on common circuits of various brands of strength training machines, for example, in one system of 10 locations I might start with a Nautilus leg press and work my way through to an abdominal machine and use the same sequence through different brands, like MedX, Life Fitness, Free Motion, Hammer, Keiser, etc.

Now, the system we'll use in this chapter does not date back to Marcus Aurelius. In fact, the earliest exemplar of which I'm aware is barely over 550 years old! Still, I think we'll find it fun and effective to use.

For a little background, in 1470 a little "block book" made from woodcarvings, today known as the *Ars memoranda*, was fashioned, perhaps in a monastery, in the land of southern Bavaria. Within this ancient tome are multiple woodcut figures of four familiar seraphim (the winged man, lion, ox, and eagle). Borrowing from descriptions in the books of Revelation and Ezekiel,[6] and building upon Catholic Church tradition and sacred art, the winged man has come to symbolize St. Matthew; the lion, St. Mark; the ox, St. Luke; and the eagle, St. John.

*In the Ars Memoranda, those figures themselves served as systems of mnemonic locations,* just like the rooms of our mnemonic house or the parts of a memory car. So, an image located at the top of the eagle's head, for example, would represent an event from the *first* chapter of St. John's Gospel, with one location for each gospel chapter. We can use this system even today to build a mental outline of any of the gospels, storing in the treasuries of our memories key teachings and events in the life of Jesus Christ.[7]

Our purpose right now though is how to think and live like a Stoic and to memorize their lessons, of course, so our memory system in this book will be based on Marcus Aurelius himself, perhaps the most "statuesque" of all the Stoics! There is a famous equestrian statue of a dignified Aurelius astride a horse, bearded, without weapons, right arm raised in a gesture of clemency. The magnificent larger-than-life bronze statue stands 14-feet tall and has quite an interesting history of its own. Though it is not mentioned in ancient sources, it was most likely erected in Rome during Marcus's lifetime to celebrate victories over German tribes in AD 176. It was one of 22 *"equi magni,"* gigantic equestrian statues erected in Rome around the time. Many imperial statues were later melted down; it is the only one to survive to our day.

---

6  "And round the throne, on each side of the throne, are four living creatures, full of eyes in front and behind: the first living creature like a lion, the second living creature like an ox, the third living creature with the face of a man, and the fourth living creature like a flying eagle. And the four living creatures, each of them with six wings, are full of eyes all around and within, and day and night they never cease to sing, 'Holy, holy, holy, is the Lord God Almighty, who was and is and is to come'" (Revelation 4:6–8). They are first described in the first chapter of the Old Testament book of Ezekiel.

7  For those who might care to see this fleshed out, see my article "Memorize the Gospel of John (And Contemplate Christ)," https://catholicexchange.com/memorize-the-gospel-of-john.

It apparently stood in the Lateran section of Rome (not far from Marcus's family home and the current Basilica of St. John Lateran) as early as the late 8th century, inspiring the emperor Charlemagne to seek out something similar for his palace in Aachen. In 1538 Pope Paul II ordered the statue transferred to the Capitoline Hill. It was to be refurbished by no less a sculptor than Michelangelo. Today the statue can be seen in the Capitoline Museum and a replica in the Capitoline square.[8] It can also be seen right now, in your "mind's eye" (and in our illustration), as we begin our memory tour.

Imagine you stand in Rome looking up at the colossal equestrian statue of our philosopher-king, Marcus Aurelius himself. What a fictional, futuristic, but oddly familiar scene you spy at the horse's front flank (location ❶), for there stand *Captain Kirk* and *First Officer Spock* from the original Star Trek television series, in a warm, friendly embrace. (Indeed, even the typically, shall we say, "stoic" Spock has a big smile on his face.) Looking up at the horse's head ❷ you see balancing upon it a *bear* and it's waving a tree *branch* at your favorite *Supreme Court Justice*. Moving down to the region of Marcus's heart ❸ you spy a most disconcerting scene, for a *cardiac surgeon has just dropped his scalpel* inside of Marcus's heart, and demurely whispers *"Oops!"* On up to our philosopher's beard ❹ and you see *it's beginning to smoke*. Entangled within the beard's bronze curls is the notorious previous emperor *Nero*, beginning to roast on his funeral pyre.

Up now to Marcus's head ❺ and who should be balanced atop it but a bearded *Charlton Heston* and the mighty cartoon superhero *Atom Ant* himself! What a scene does Marcus's outstretched hand ❻ point to as the *"Thing"* from the "Fantastic Four" cartoon beats his huge stony fists upon an *impenetrable circular force-field*. (And yes, I mean Ben Grimm, the superhero who looked like he was made of red brick.) Finally, as you look at Marcus's cloak on the horse's rear flank ❼, you see *the Thing start to shrink*, and *return to the form of a human*, and then suddenly *fade away to nothingness*.

So there ends our short, and hopefully sweet, or at least memorable, memory tour of Marcus's "magnificent seven maxims." Once you have all the locations and images down pat, let's see what they really mean.

---

8 A much smaller version can also be seen on the back on the modern, Italian, half-Euro coin.

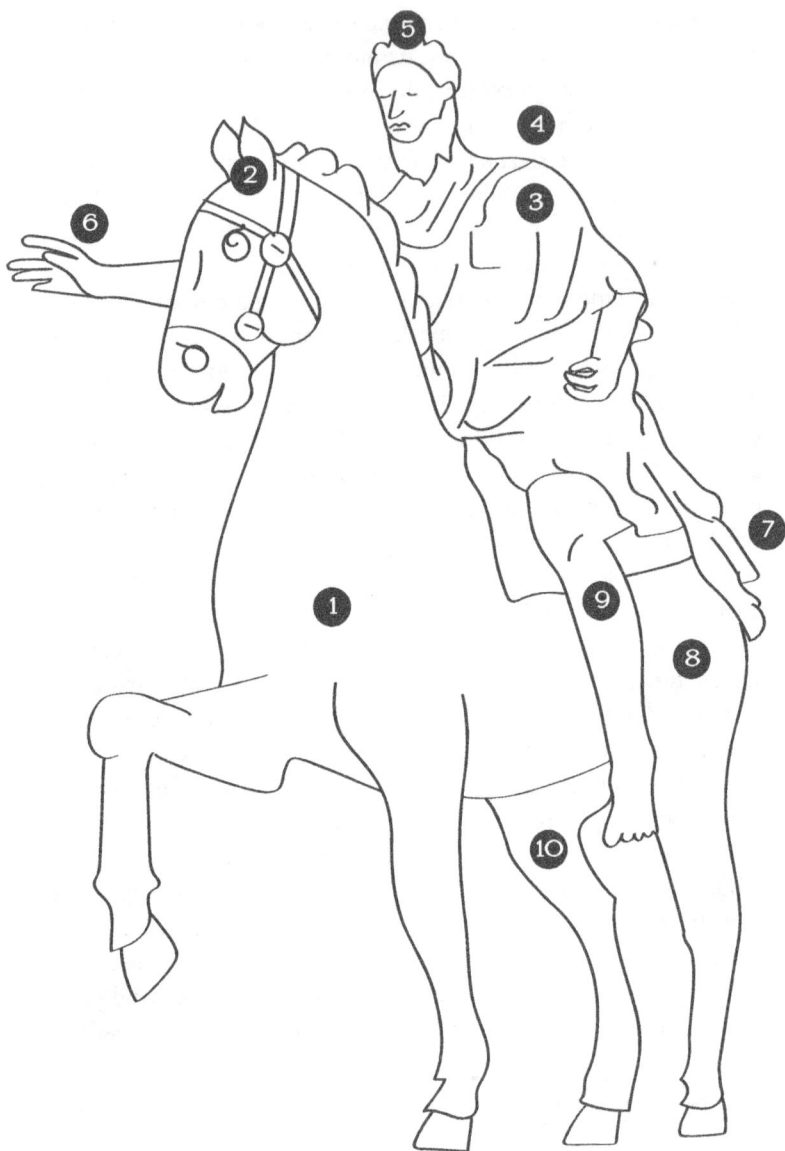

| LETTER/LOCATION | IMAGE | MEDITATIONS LESSON |
|---|---|---|
| **①** HORSE'S FRONT FLANK | *Kirk and Spock embrace* | Unity of rational beings |
| **②** HORSE'S HEAD | *Bear waves branch at justice* | Forbearance as justice |
| **③** MARCUS'S HEART | *Surgeon says "Oops!"* | Error as involuntary |
| **④** MARCUS'S BEARD | *Nero on funeral pyre* | Life too short for hate |
| **⑤** MARCUS'S HEAD | *Charlton Heston or Atom Ant* | Providence or atoms? |
| **⑥** MARCUS'S OUT-STRETCHED HAND | *Thing hits round force field* | Things can't perturb the soul |
| **⑦** CLOAK ON HORSE REAR FLANK | *Thing, Ben Grimm, nothing* | Nothing lasts as it is |

## THE LESSONS BEHIND THE IMAGES: THE MAGNIFICENT SEVEN MAXIMS OF MARCUS AURELIUS

**①** "All rational beings were formed for each other." 📖

HERE ON THE HORSE'S FRONT FLANK IS A FUNDAMENTAL theme that appears again and again throughout the *Meditations*. Sometimes the fictional *Mr. Spock* of Star Trek fame is compared to the Stoics, since Vulcans strive to guide their lives by reason and logic. *Captain Kirk*, a human, was portrayed as a man more prone to make choices through emotion and intuition. Now, as the story goes, Spock was actually half-human, courtesy of his human mother, and though he was loath to admit it, he often had to grapple with his emotional side too.

Still, though they love reason and logic, Stoics are no Vulcans, and indeed are 100% human! They recognize we are not made for reason alone—or to be alone for that matter. This theme of the universal brotherhood of man (and sisterhood of woman) is essential to Marcus Aurelius. He knows that Stoics are social beings by nature and we cannot follow nature if we do not care deeply about each other and actively cooperate in our joint welfare. (Hence the warm embrace of Kirk and Spock in our image.)

Indeed, in a quote worth memorizing verbatim (which is precisely what we'll do in our next chapter), Marcus eloquently expounds on this maxim that people "come into being for cooperation, as have the feet, the hands, the eyelids, the rows of upper and lower teeth. Therefore, to act against one another is contrary to nature; and we act against one another by showing resentment or aversion, by lashing out or turning away" (*Meditations*, bk. 2, ch. 1).

Marcus echoes lessons expounded by Epictetus (e.g., *Handbook* chs. 30, 43), and by Seneca (e.g., *Letters* 5, 35). No one can rightly claim to live like a Stoic if his or her actions are simply focused on oneself and not aimed at the benefit of all.

**2**   "Bearing with them is a branch of justice." Ω

THIS IS WHY THE *BEAR* ON THE HORSE'S HEAD WAVED A *branch* at a Supreme Court *Justice*. As we saw many times in the *Handbook* that dealt with bearing hardships including insults and injustices from others (e.g., chs. 10, 20, 22, 33, 42), we are not to respond to unjust behaviors by treating others unjustly or by trying to get even in some way. Indeed, we are to "bear and forbear" unjust treatment of ourselves, since we know that another person's actions cannot control our own emotions, judgments, and actions. Patience is a virtue the Stoics valued very highly, and indeed Marcus also gives us further advice in bearing injustices in his very next maxim.

**3**   "All mistakes are involuntary." Ω

HERE IS A MAXIM VERY DEAR TO MARCUS'S HEART. Indeed, we put our image there where the surgeon dropped his scalpel into Marcus's heart and said *"Oops!"* In Book I of the *Meditations*, Marcus's paean of gratitude to the many people who aided him throughout his life, he thanks the philosopher Rusticus for many things, including the fact that he introduced him to the *Discourses* of Epictetus from his own library. That Marcus read and digested the *Discourses* rings out quite clearly in virtually every page of the *Meditations*.

Recalling that the "repetition is the mother of memory," let's first begin with a simple pop quiz. Do you recall the subject matter of chapter 42 of the *Handbook*? (Hint: Upon the computer monitor, Zeno and Socrates sit quietly in the midst of a heated internet conference call.) Well, to flesh out and help us recall Marcus's third maxim, I believe our summary of *Handbook* Ch. 42 warrants a repetition right here:

> *If someone insults you or treats you badly, remember that he believes it is right for him to do so.* He acts according to *his* perspective and not according to *yours.* If he interprets your words or actions wrongly, it is he who is harmed and deceived. *If you keep this principle in mind, you will be gentle with those who abuse you, saying to yourself every time, "It seemed that way to him."*

The Stoic notion of the involuntary nature of people's mistakes goes back to the philosophy of Socrates, who opined that since people, by their natures, always seek what they *believe* is good for them, when they make mistakes or act unjustly, their behavior, in some mistaken way, made sense to them at the time. They believed that what they were doing was right. Indeed, don't we often apply this very rule to *our own mistakes?*

If we keep this idea in mind, we'll be much less likely to lash out at others. Still, it does not mean at all that we should not try to correct them, if possible, since the notion also holds out the hope that if people come to see the errors of their way, they may be amenable to change them. This is consonant with the Catholic understanding that appropriate fraternal correction operates through the love of our neighbor, but that it remains up to our neighbor whether or not he or she will stand corrected. We can do our best to reason with people who treat us or others badly, while keeping this advice from Epictetus's *Discourse* 1.5 in mind: "When a man who has been trapped in an argument hardens to stone, how shall one any longer deal with him by argument?"[9] Again, our beliefs and actions are up to us, but not the beliefs and actions of others.

---

9  Oldfather, v. II, 483.

> **4** "How many of those who lived in enmity, suspicion, hatred, and quarrels, have been stretched on their funeral piles, and turned to ashes?" ♎

THIS IS WHY MARCUS'S BEARD WAS STARTING TO *SMOKE* as *Nero* laid on his *funeral pyre*. Marcus employs a very powerful enhancement to the *memento mori* theme many times throughout the *Meditations*. Indeed, the theme was widely known and eloquently expressed time and again among ancient Jews and Christians, and ancient pagan Greeks as well, in these instances substituting fallen leaves for ashes:

*Like flourishing leaves on a spreading tree,*
*which sheds some and puts forth others,*
*so are the generations of flesh and blood;*
*one dies and another is born.*
Sirach 14:18

*As is the race of leaves, so is the race of men.*
*Some leaves the wind scatters upon the ground,*
*and others the budding wood produces,*
*for they come up again in the season of spring.*
*So is the race of men,*
*one springs up and another one dies.*
Homer, *Iliad*, Book VI, 145–49

*Leaves also are your children ...*
*A little time and your eyes will close;*
*and he who attends you to your grave*
*another will soon lament.*
Marcus Aurelius, *Meditations*, Book X, 34

Perhaps unique to Marcus Aurelius was his perspective as a Roman Emperor, the most powerful person on earth. Indeed, many predecessors who held his position had come to be worshipped like "gods." Marcus would have none of that. He knew he was a man, and that his predecessors were too. He speculates again and again, naming names like those of the emperors Augustus, Vespasian, and Trajan. Not only are these men gone from the earth, the same goes for all the people who lived in the time of the first two, and most who lived in the time of the last. He knows the same will apply to him, and that one day even his memory, like theirs, will be gone.

He frequently reminds himself of this sobering thought as a goad to grow in virtue and in benevolent cooperation with all those around him, who so soon would be gone. The same applies to each and every one of us as well. Think of any person right now with whom you bear a grudge. Remember that in a matter of decades you and that person will be as fallen leaves or funeral ashes. Isn't life far too short for such things?

**❺** "Either it is providence which disposes of all things, or atoms." Ω

IT'S REALLY RATHER STRAIGHTFORWARD WHY CHARLTON Heston and Atom Ant balanced on Marcus's head. *Charlton Heston* represents *Providence* (God). Indeed, he was famous for playing Moses in *The Ten Commandments* and he also played God Himself in the perhaps (well, certainly) less-well-known *Almost an Angel* with Paul Hogan. *Atom Ant* represents, well, atoms.

In any event, in maxim five we see another theme that recurs again and again in nuanced considerations throughout the *Meditations.* Here is how I summarized it in a previous book:

> We see Marcus pondering the nature of the universe, whether there is a God or gods, if He or they exist, if so, whether they intervene in the world, or whether everything is a really a matter of atoms, bouncing around by chance with no deeper meaning. He admits that such things are even hard for the Stoics to know for sure, but he has his opinion (in favor of God and purpose) and he advises a life guided by philosophy regardless of the ultimate answer.[10]

Recall, if you will, a passage from Seneca's *Letter* 16 where he addresses the possible roles of God and fate or chance in the choices and actions of our lives. He concludes as follows: "She (Philosophy) will encourage us to obey God cheerfully, but Fortune defiantly; she will teach us to follow God and endure chance."[11] In a sense, Seneca acknowledges both Providence *and* atoms!

---

10   *The Porch and the Cross,* 158.
11   Gummere, 107.

The major ancient Greco-Roman Stoics were not Christians. They applied their reason as best they could without recourse to special knowledge revealed by God. For most, their reason led them to the recognition of some kind of God, perhaps with far more pious and personal overtones in Epictetus and Seneca than in Aurelius. Still, the noble Marcus makes clear that even if the universe was ultimately a matter of chance atoms, a life guided by philosophy toward virtue is still the best choice one can make.

Perhaps this is one reason why the *Meditations* are so widely respected by Catholics,[12] by Buddhists, by Jews, by readers who adhere to all kinds of religions, as well as by agnostics and atheists too.[13] Marcus so appeals to the common ground of human rationality and decency that even those who disagree with him that such a human capacity represents "a spark of the Divine" within us acknowledge the sublime wisdom of his ethical advice.

**6** "The things themselves reach not the soul, but stand without, still and motionless." Ω

THE "*THING*" MARCUS'S HAND POINTS TO REPRESENTS ALL of the many "things themselves" we encounter in the outside world. The *invincible force field* represents the impenetrable powers of our soul, at least if we would train ourselves to turn it on. Here, of course, is a thoughtful rewording of Epictetus's key lesson from *Handbook* Ch. 5 and the cornerstone of modern cognitive psychotherapy: "People are disturbed not by things, but by the views they take of things."

Ultimately, it is up to us to choose the thoughts, beliefs, judgments, desires, and feelings we will admit into our souls. Indeed, philosopher Pierre Hadot entitled his masterful work on the

---

12 For example, many years back, while reading the diaries of Elisabeth Leseur (1866–1914), pages so poignant and powerful that after her death her atheistic husband was led to the Church and to the priesthood, I came across some lines on reason, duty, meditation, and examination of conscience that made me think "Hey, she knew the Stoics!" On the very next page, there was the name of Marcus Aurelius!—Elisabeth Leseur, *Light in the Darkness: How to Bring Christ to the Souls You Meet Each Day* (Manchester, NH: Sophia Institute Press, 1998), 44.
13 See, for example, the thorough analysis in Donald Robertson's article, *Stoicism: God or Atoms? Can you be a modern Stoic and an atheist (or agnostic)?* https://modernstoicism.com/providence-or-atoms-atoms-donald-robertson.

Meditations of Marcus Aurelius, *The Inner Citadel*, and such a citadel is exactly what Marcus calls on each one of us to build.

Constantly the focus of the wiles of sycophantic courtiers, at times threatened by usurpers from within the empire, and often literally besieged by the armies of Germanic and Central Asian Quadi, Marcomanni, and Iazyges, who had a greater need for a mighty inner citadel than Emperor Marcus Aurelius himself?

Marcus did erect a mighty citadel around his own soul through his Stoic reading and exercises, including his crafting of the *Meditations* themselves. It appears he remained a man of virtue and integrity until his dying day (March 17, 180 to be exact.) Would that we follow the Emperor's lead and build virtuous fortresses of our own to withstand the assaults of whatever things come our way, regardless of how grim (or how Grimm).

**7**   "All these things presently change and shall be no more." Ω

AND SPEAKING OF GRIM (OR GRIMM) THINGS, ON MARcus's mighty steed's flank, we saw the enormous and fantastic *Thing* transform back into *Ben Grimm*, and then fade away to *nothing*. Echoing and extending his fourth maxim that no single person, or even all persons of a particular era, last forever, Marcus reminds us that, as the saying goes, "This too shall pass." Nothing lasts forever in its present state. Marcus, like other Stoics, drew on the pre-Socratic philosopher Heraclitus here, who emphasized how change or flux characterized all things in nature. He said "No man steps in the same river twice," and that "everything flows." (Indeed, some have opined that you can't even step in the same river *once*, since it is constantly changing, even as you're stepping!)

This maxim is so obvious on its face, and it can be of great solace when we face some kind of loss or serious obstacle, knowing it cannot last forever, if we but "bear and forbear" like a Stoic whilst it lasts. The fact of change, though, can also bring us challenges of its own. We may grow to love certain things, perhaps certain friends, a particular job, the joys of physical youth, but anyone who has lived for some time on earth will know that such things will not endure forever.

Stoics, however, should not pine over lost friends, lost positions (as, perhaps, during retirement), lost youth, or lost anything, since we know that transience is built into the very nature of such things (including our very selves). On the contrary, recognition of the fleeting nature of our current life situations, of our very lives themselves, and of the lives of our loved ones should encourage us to make every minute count. (We've already seen that Epictetus and Seneca would wholeheartedly agree.)

SO HERE ENDS OUR CHAPTER ON MARCUS'S MAGNIFI-cent seven maxims, but we've not heard the last of the emperor's wisdom, as you'll see in the first chapter of Part IV.

# How to Live Like a Stoic in Heart, Mind, and Soul

*"And, coming down to practice, when we look at such treatises as the Dissertations and the Encheiridion of Epictetus and the Meditations of Marcus Aurelius, as aids to practical ethics, we see that these can never die....*

*"Nor can the philosophical writings of Seneca be other than helpful to high-toned people, eager about right living."*

William L. Davidson, *The Stoic Creed*[1]

*"Although other components of the Stoic system are important, by far the distinguishing feature of Stoicism is its practicality: it began in the guise of, and has always been understood as, a quest for a happy and meaningful life."*

Massimo Pigliucci, *How to Be a Stoic*[2]

---

1   *The Stoic Creed* (Edinburgh: T. & T. Clark, 1907), 252–53.
2   *How to Be a Stoic: Using Ancient Philosophy to Live a Modern Life* (New York, NY: Basic Books, 2017), 6.

## CHAPTER 13

# HOW TO LEARN STOIC
# SAYINGS BY HEART

*"[A]n arrangement of images succeeds only if we use
our notation to stimulate the natural memory, so that
we first go over a given verse twice or three times to
ourselves and then represent the words by means of
images. In this way art will supplement nature. For
neither by itself will be strong enough..."*

Cicero, Ad Herennium, III, xxi, 34[1]

### MEMORIA RERUM VERSUS MEMORIA VERBORUM

F OR THOSE WHO WOULD STRIVE TO LIVE LIKE A
Stoic in heart, mind, and soul, it might do well to learn at
least a few Stoic sayings and quotable quotes word-for-word,
that is—by heart. The ancient memory masters long distinguished
two kinds of potential uses of these ancient artificial memory techniques. The first, and most prominent, was known as *memoria rerum,*
from *"res,"* being Latin for "thing," while the second was known as
*memoria verborum,* from *"verbum,"* being Latin for "word."

Thus far in this book, we have certainly memorized a great deal
of information that can be expressed in words, but our task was
primarily one of *memoria rerum,* memory for things. The "things"
we have memorized have been key Stoic concepts, principles, and
lessons. We memorized the gist of the *Handbook* chapters, the *Letters,*
and maxims from the *Meditations* without particular attention to
any specific wording. Indeed, since the originals were in Greek or
Latin, the vast majority of us use translations anyway, and as you
all know, since the specific words translators use can vary widely,
the most important "things" are the ideas behind the words. After

---

I  [Cicero] *Ad Herennium,* Harry Caplan, trans. (Cambridge, MA: Harvard
University Press, 2004), 225. Cicero had been traditionally considered the
author for many centuries, but modern scholars disagree and its authorship
remains a mystery at this time.

all, we are not striving merely to be able to parrot back Stoic ideas like, well, parrots, but to come to ponder, digest, and understand them as befits rational animals.

Still, there may well be times when we would like to be able to reproduce specific quotable quotes from the Stoics as presented in some eloquent translation or even in our own words. To know such quotations by heart might prove useful and inspiring, especially since, once memorized, we can recall and rehearse them any time we want, perhaps as an alternative to staring vacantly at a TV screen in an airport or a celebrity magazine in the doctor's office.

*Memoria verborum*, memory for words, has quite a history within the Christian world. This may call to mind how some devout Protestants have mastered the exact wording of many Bible verses. Centuries before the Reformation, many monks were memory masters. Indeed, per a modern expert on the history of memory methods:

> The Rule of Ferreolus observed, "anyone who wishes
> to be worthy of the name of monk is forbidden to be
> ignorant of letters; he must also hold all of the Psalms
> in his memory"—"totus psalmos," in their entirety.[2]

Memory for words for most modern Catholics comes in the form of memorizing the words of various prayers: the Our Father, Hail Mary, Glory Be, Prayer to St. Michael the Archangel, and others, as well as the Nicene Creed. Typically, this memorization is accomplished without specialized memory methods, relying instead on rote repetition. Indeed, many who pray these prayers at home and hear them prayed at Mass may repeat them countless thousands of times throughout a lifetime. Our goal here though is not to spend *a lifetime* mastering key Stoic passages verbatim, but to cut to the chase so we can do so perhaps well within *one-half hour* or so each!

Now, it has long been recognized that the kinds of artificial visual imagery-based memory techniques we are employing here are far more readily applied to memorizing key ideas, rather than long passages verbatim. (Just look at our opening quotation from the oldest extant book on the art of memory, dating to

---

2  Mary Carruthers, *The Book of Memory: A Study of Memory in Medieval Culture* (Cambridge, UK: Cambridge University Press, 1990), 88. She elaborates that this usually took 2–3 years, though some mnemonically gifted individuals could memorize all 150 of them in about six months.

approximately 84 BC.) Too many images can indeed become cumbersome. Still, our memory methods can successfully supplement natural memory and help us more quickly and more completely master verbatim passages of our choosing.

I'm going to provide two examples to show how this can be done. The first, from Marcus Aurelius, is one I've actually memorized myself so I could reproduce it verbatim during live talks.[3] I also find it personally helpful to recall and recite it from time to time as a Stoic spiritual exercise.

So, let's begin by following the advice of the author of the ancient *Ad Herennium*. Please begin by going over it two, no *three* times, reading it to yourself, even out loud if you prefer, trying to get a sense of the cadence and rhythm, as well as the words. Here it is:

## MARCUS'S MORNING MEDITATION:
### *Premediatio Malorum,* Negative Visualization, Stress Inoculation
### *MEDITATIONS,* BOOK 2, CH. I

Say to yourself every morning: Today I will encounter the busybody, the thankless, the overbearing, the treacherous, the envious, and the unneighborly. All this has befallen them because they do not know good from evil. But I who have seen the nature of the good that it is beautiful, and the nature of evil that it is ugly, and the nature of the wrong-doer that it is akin to me, not as partaker of the same blood or seed, but of intelligence and of a portion of the Divine, can neither be harmed by any of them, for no one can involve me in what is debasing. Nor can I be angry with my kinsman and hate him. For we have come into being for cooperation, as have the feet, the hands, the eyelids, the rows of upper and lower teeth. Therefore, to act against one another is contrary to nature; and we act against one another by showing resentment or aversion, by lashing out or turning away. Ω

DID YOU RECITE IT THRICE? (IF SO, THAT'S VERY NICE.) Now, I recall in high school having to memorize Abraham Lincoln's Gettysburg address for a class on the American Presidency. My

---

3 Here is one of them captured on video, if you'd care to check it out sometime. It starts at around 29 minutes in: https://www.youtube.com/watch?v=o3wv7Hy5BHY&t=2321s

computer tells me it contains 272 words. I got the job done. Now, I was quite young at the time, but I had not yet become aware of the ancient arts of memory. I don't know how old you are, but the passage from Marcus in only 168 words long and you are growing in your mastery of the art of memory. So, let's see if we can supplement your powers of natural memory with a little help from the art of memory, specifically the method of loci.

Here is one way you can do it. Assuming you have read the passage at least three times and are beginning to get a sense of its rhythm and wording, I suggest you form a memory image for the first word of each of ten phrases, the idea being that this will then serve to trigger the few words that immediately follow upon it. Now, as I've presented it below, I've *italicized* each of the words to which I chose to give special emphasis during my live talks. (Perhaps you would choose different words?) As for the images, I have suggested some, as you'll see in just a page or two. I have also used our house's foyer to house this passage (so to speak) since I imagine you've become quite familiar with it by now.

So first, let's look at Marcus's morning exercise in the form of ten discrete phrases:

1. **Say** to yourself *every morning*:
2. *Today* I will encounter the busy-body, the thankless, the over-bearing, the treacherous, the envious, and the *unneighborly*. (BTOTEU—see below)
3. **All** this has befallen *them* because they do not know *good* from *evil*.
4. **But** *I* who have seen the *nature* of the *good* that it is *beautiful*, and the *nature* of *evil* that it is ugly, and the nature of the *wrong-doer* that it is akin to *me*,
5. *not* as partaker of the same *blood* or seed, but of *intelligence* and of a portion of the *Divine*,
6. **can** neither be *harmed* by any of them, for no one can involve *me* in what is debasing.
7. **Nor** can I be *angry* with my kinsman and hate him.
8. **For** we have come into being for *cooperation*, as have the *feet*, the hands, the *eyelids*, the rows of upper and lower *teeth*.
9. *Therefore,* to act against one another *is contrary to nature*;
10. **and** we act against one another by showing *resentment* or *aversion*, by *lashing out* or *turning away*.

I won't go through a complete memory tour narrative at this point, because I'm pretty confident that by now you know how they work. Oh, and as for the "BTOTEU" after the second phrase on the doormat, I've found that for lists of things, sometimes acronym-based mnemonics deriving from the first letter of each word can be helpful. In the translation I prefer, the six kinds of people Marcus says to tell ourselves we'll meet are the busybody, the thankless, the overbearing, the treacherous, the envious, and the unneighborly. This is where the "BTOTEU" came from. I remember it as "Bachmann Turner Overdrive," a popular Canadian rock band from the 1970s, also known as "BTO." As for the "TEU," I imagine the phrase, "Tell everyone 'U' know!" coming after it. So, for me anyway, after repeated practice "BTO, tell everyone U know" triggers busybody, thankless, overbearing, treacherous, envious, and unneighborly. Regardless of the translation you might prefer (and if you prefer the original Greek, you have my *kudos*), you could craft an acronym based on those particular words that would trigger them for you.

At any rate, here's a table summarizing the suggested memory tour. Practice this for a while, and then see how you do. (If you find I've expected too much of you, just remember that Marcus warned you'd encounter the overbearing!)

| LETTER/LOCATION | IMAGE | STARTING WORDS |
|---|---|---|
| I. FRONT DOOR | *You speaking to yourself* | Say to self *every morning* |
| 2. ENTRANCE MAT | *Calendar page shows TODAY* | Today I will meet (BTO-TEU) |
| 3. GLASS PANEL | *"All" detergent or an "awl"* | All of this has befallen *them* |
| 4. PORTRAIT ON WALL | *Butting rams hit eyes* | But *I* who have seen |
| 5. GUN RACK | *Knot (bloody with seeds)* | not as partaker of same blood |
| 6. CENTER OF FOYER | *Can of soup* | Can neither be harmed |
| 7. CHANDELIER | *Nora or NORAD* | Nor can I be *angry* |
| 8. MIRROR ON WALL | *"Fore" yelled by golfer* | For we have come into being |
| 9. CUSHIONED BENCH | *"There's four!" boy yells* | Therefore, to act against |
| I0. DRAWER IN BENCH | *Ampersand brand (&)* | And we act against one |

Now let's examine a touch of commentary on Marcus's morning meditation. Please note the distinction he makes between things outside our control (others' behaviors) and within our control (our own thoughts, emotions, and actions), and how through our capacity to control our judgments, we can remain undisturbed by things outside our control. Through regularly rehearsing and practicing this idea early in the day, *we can inoculate ourselves*, building up our intellectual defenses and shoring up our emotions against all kinds of stressors we'll face in a day. It will also help us get along better with even the orneriest of others, if at the instant we begin to allow them to get on our nerves, we recall our morning exercise.

When I've presented possible adaptations of Marcus's passage to modern audiences, I often start with something like this:

> Today I will encounter the nosey, the ungrateful, those
> on a power trip (some things never change), and indeed,
> before I reach them, someone is likely to cut me off on the
> highway, or drive so ridiculously slowly that I get stuck
> at a red light while they saunter their way through it.

When I presented it in 2019 to a conference of the Catholic Medical Association focused on physician burnout, I elaborated on it like this:

> Today I will encounter a nosey patient's family member
> seeking information protected by HIPAA (Health Insur-
> ance Portability and Accountability Act), the ungrateful
> patient who complains about his wait time (though
> the clinic manager had overbooked me), the person
> who saw a television commercial and will tell me what
> medication I should give her, the government agency
> that expects me to spend hours completing forms, the
> pesky disability adjudicator (I personally used to work
> as one!) trying to call and speak to me when I've already
> released all of that patient's records.

My practical suggestion to *you* in an effort to inoculate against emotional exhaustion is to construct a similar stress inoculation script addressing the likely stressful scenarios you face each day, and in language that resonates with you. What might your own morning exercise look like?

## SECOND REHEARSE, DIFFERENT FROM THE FIRST

IF YOU'D CARE TO PRACTICE SOME MEMORY FOR WORDS with another Stoic passage worth remembering, I suggest we try our mnemonic wiles on the concluding chapter (53) of Epictetus's *Handbook.*

### EPICTETUS'S EPILOGUE

> *Lead me thou on, O Zeus, and Destiny,*
> *To whatever goal you assign me.*
> *I will follow and not falter,*
> *But even if my will proves weak and craven,*
> *I'll follow anyway.*
>
> *Whoever has rightly complied with necessity*
> *Is counted wise and skilled in things divine.*
>
> *Well, O Crito, if it is pleasing to the gods, then let it be so.*
>
> *Anytus and Meletus can kill me, but they cannot harm me.*

Now here it is with first words emphasized:

### EPICTETUS'S EPILOGUE

> **LEAD** *me thou on, O Zeus, and Destiny,*
> **TO** *that whatever goal you assign me.*
> **I** *will follow and not falter,*
> **BUT** *even if my will proves weak and craven,*
> **I'LL** *follow anyway.*
>
> **WHOEVER** *has rightly complied with necessity*
> **IS** *counted wise and skilled in things divine.*
>
> **WELL,** *O Crito, if it is pleasing to the gods, then let it be so.*
>
> **ANYTUS** *and Meletus can kill me, but they cannot harm me.*

If I've counted right, there are only 9 key starting words to memorize through images. This passage would easily fit within our foyer, but allowed me to suggest something completely different (as Monty Python was wont to say). *Please construct a 10-location room* based on a room in your own house or apartment. After all, what rooms are more familiar to you? Remember too, that once you build such a location system, you can use it time and time again with any information of your choosing. Further, you could even build your own entire memory house if you might find it useful. I'll provide the starting words, but leave the locations and the images to you.

| LOCATIONS (YOUR HOME) | IMAGE | STARTING WORDS |
|---|---|---|
| 1. | | LEAD me on.. |
| 2. | | TO whatever goal.. |
| 3. | | I will follow.. |
| 4. | | BUT even if.. |
| 5. | | I'll follow anyway |
| 6. | | WHOEVER has rightly.. |
| 7. | | IS counted wise.. |
| 8. | | WELL, O Crito.. |
| 9. | | ANYTUS and Meletus.. |
| 10. | | |

# CHAPTER 14
# HOW TO KEEP KEY STOIC CONCEPTS IN MIND

*"The artificial memory is that memory which is strength-*
*ened by a kind of training and system of discipline."*
Cicero, *Ad Herennium*, III, xvi, 28[1]

P ERHAPS MANY OF THE ORIGINAL WORDS FOR KEY STOIC
concepts are "all Greek" to you. That is certainly appropriate,
since most were indeed expressed in the Greek language. A
few of the later key concepts are better known in Latin, thanks to
good Romans like Cicero and Seneca. Still, if you are not fluent in
classical Greek or classical Latin the ancient art of memory has one
more trick up its sleeve that might come in handy to help you keep
some key Greek and Latin terms ready at hand, and always in mind.

This is the last mnemonic technique in the house (although we
won't need the memory house to use it). I first saw the technique
referred to as the "keyword method" in the psychological research of
the 1970s, but some variant has surely been around as long as people
have sought to learn and remember new words.

Memory historian Frances Yates provides an interesting excerpt
on memory methods from a Greek fragment known as the *Dialexis*
that dates around 400 BC. It runs as follows:

> A great and beautiful invention is memory, always useful
> both for learning and for life. This is the first thing: if
> you pay attention (direct your mind), the judgment will
> better perceive the things going through it (the mind).
> Secondly, repeat again what you hear; for by often hear-
> ing and saying the same things, what you have learned
> comes complete into your memory. Thirdly, what you
> hear, place on what you know. For example, Χρύσιππος
> (Chrysippus) is to be remembered; we place it on χρυσός
> (gold) and ἵππος (horse)...[2]

---

1   Caplan trans., 207.
2   Yates, 29–30.

Now, the first two recommendations on focused attention and repetition should sound quite familiar to readers of this book (or to anyone with a sense of how memory naturally works). It is in the third "thing" that we come across a visual imagery memory technique that suggests the modern "keyword method."

How interesting for Stoic readers that the first example is Chrysippus. Alas, if this fragment was dated correctly, it does not refer to our Chrysippus, the third leader of the Stoic school, since he was born over 100 years later in 279 BC. Still, if you would care to remember what our Chrysippus's name means literally, just picture him riding a great *golden horse* and that should get the job done. This might call to the minds of some Christian readers the great Eastern Church Father, St. John Chrysostom (3rd–4th century), so eloquent in his preaching that he was called the χρυσός (golden) στομα (mouth)!

Now, as for the modern keyword method itself, it is used to aid primarily in the recall of new, unfamiliar vocabulary words within one's own or any foreign language. I'll never forget an example for one of the studies in which students were taught how to better recall archaic English words. To remember *both* the *pronunciation* and *meaning* of the word "carlin" the students were advise to imagine an *old woman* in a *car* whose name was *Lynn*. "Car" and "Lynn" provide the pronunciation, but what does carlin mean? Well, an old woman, of course! (There's a Carlinville, Illinois not far from my home. I'll have to check sometime to see if old women founded it—or perhaps conquered it at some later date.)

The pioneering psychological studies used this method for all kinds of foreign language learning too, including Spanish and French. A simple example in Spanish is to picture a *duck* with a *pot* on its head to recall that the Spanish word for duck is *pato*. The *pot* sounds like *pato* and the *duck* provides the meaning. Want to remember the French word for *books* is *livres?* Just picture a tree with branches loaded with *books* instead of *leaves*. The *leaves* will remind you of the word *livres* and the *books* will remind you of exactly what *livres* means.

The method is very simple and straightforward. No wonder it often led to the kind of improved retention I mentioned in the introduction where middle school students outperformed high school students and where students who were taught the method often outperformed same-age peers by 100%, doubling their natural recall abilities.

So, let's get down to business and come up with some key words for some key Stoic concepts. I've pulled out some Stoic *livres* (βιβλος if you prefer the Greek or *libris* if you prefer the Latin) and come up with a list of *vingt-et-un*, είκοσι ένα, *vicesimum*, or to keep it simple, *twenty-one* of them.

| GREEK OR LATIN WORD(S) | POSSIBLE KEY-WORD IMAGES | MEANING |
|---|---|---|
| **ANDREIA** | Your friend *Andrea* acting very *courageously* | Manliness or courage. One of the four cardinal virtues, along with *phronesis*, *dikaiosyne*, and *sophrosyne* (all defined below) |
| **APATHEIA** | You come across *a path* and *feel completely at peace* | Freedom from disturbing passions (a Stoic goal) |
| **ARÊTE** | You are surprised to hear that the letter *R ate* A, because R is known to be so *virtuous* | Excellence or virtue |
| **DIKAIOSYNE** | You say to yourself that a Supreme Court *Justice* named "Deekio" saw your knee (i.e., *"Deekio seen knee!"*) | Justice. One of the four cardinal virtues. Giving each person his rightful due |
| **EUDAIMONIA** | Accented person is *completely happy* when she sees her friend Damon and calls him over: *"You, Damon, (come) ee-ya!"* | Literally being of good spirit, a happiness that comes, according to the Stoics, through living according to nature |
| **EUPATHIA** | You *feel quite content* when you come to the *path* marked with a *U* | The state of good feelings and healthy passions that all Stoics seek |
| **FORTUNA** | You remain calm while *four tuna* fish tell you that *you won the lottery* (or that *your car was just stolen*) | Fortune, or chance events (as you may have surmised). Seneca often writes about remaining tranquil despite good or ill fortune |
| **HEGEMONIKON** | You call out to the *ruler* (head) of your college's *faculty,* "Look in that *hedge*, it's *a manikin!*" | The human intellect or the ruling faculty of the mind |

| GREEK OR LATIN WORD(S) | POSSIBLE KEY-WORD IMAGES | MEANING |
|---|---|---|
| **HORMÊ** | You can't resist *the urge* to open up and wolf down a can of *Hormel* chili (for some reason) | An impulse that motivates us to action. Epictetus advises us to monitor and control our impulses. Its opposite is *aphormê* (repulsion) |
| **HUPEXHAIRESIS** | You decide you will *hold back* and *not expect to win* the hula hoop championship with that odd looking hoop with an X on it, since something appears to be growing from it. As you explain to your sister, *"Hoop X is hairy, sis!"* | This is the "reserve clause" Marcus Aurelius so often reminds us about. We can control our intentions, but not necessarily outcomes |
| **HYPO-MNEMATA** | Oddly enough, someone *writing in his journal*, suddenly sticks a *hypo*dermic needle into a *nematode* | Written notes or journaling as an aid to memory and immersion in Stoic concepts, as in the *Meditations* |
| **KATHEKONTA** | An Italian says to his friend Kathy, "*Katha counta* these for me," as he shows her a list of his *virtuous actions* | Appropriate virtuous actions or duties |
| **LOGOS** | You consider buying your child a product labeled as the world's most *rational* building toy, capable of building a universe: no mere *Legos*, but *Logos!* | Reason, word, or ordering principle of the cosmos |
| **MEMENTO MORI** | The *memento* your friend *Morey* just gave you is a *skull!* | This one is most familiar in the Latin. "Remember you must die." (Indeed, a classic representation is precisely that of our image—a human skull.) |
| **OREXIS** | "Give me those *Oreos with X'es!*" you demand (already beginning to salivate like a Pavlovian dog) | Desire for things that we want. Epictetus's second discipline is the discipline of *orexis* or desire. Its opposite is *ekklisis* (aversion) |

| GREEK OR LATIN WORD(S) | POSSIBLE KEY-WORD IMAGES | MEANING |
|---|---|---|
| **PHRONESIS** | You tell your sister that a man she knows just pretends to be *wise.* In fact, "He's a *phony sis!*" | Practical wisdom or prudence—another cardinal virtue |
| **PHUSIS (or PHYSIS)** | You accidentally stumble and bump a *physicist* at a museum of *Natural* History and say to your sister, "*Foo, sis!*" | Nature, from which we get the word "physics." Along with logic and ethics, one of the three key fields of study for the Stoics. A fundamental Stoic ethical principle is to live *kata phusin* (according to nature) |
| **PREMEDITATIO MALORUM** | You try to decide before you *meditate on some bad event that may happen soon* whether you'll nibble on a marsh*mallow or* chug a shot of *rum.* (I'd advise the rum.) | To meditate in advance on the evils that may befall us as a means of inoculating ourselves and avoiding anxiety |
| **PROHAIRESIS** | Yoda declares, "*Pro hairy, he is!*" (Sound familiar?) Yet this time he also commends him for his high *moral character* | Perhaps Epictetus's most fundamental concept, our capacity to make reasonable, virtuous choices, to choose whether or not to give assent to impressions, and to guide our own actions |
| **PROKOPTÔN** | A *pro cop* who weighs a *ton* makes true *progress in philosophy* | A person making progress in the Stoic art of living, not yet a *sophros* (sage), but moving that way. (Hopefully we are all *prokoptôns*, to some extent, by now!) |
| **SOPHROSYNE** | Noticing that a certified nursing assistant of your acquaintance has stopped pacing about and *acting out immoderately and desiring inappropriate things,* you say, "Why do you stop going so and *fro CNA?* (And she answers, "*sophrosyne*"!) | A moderation or soundness of mind conducive to virtue. In its role of reining in appetites or desires the Stoics equated it with *temperance* as one of the cardinal virtues |

Of course, the twenty-one words I provided are a somewhat arbitrary and very incomplete sample of key Stoic concepts in Greek or Latin. Further, since Greek philosophical terms are often unfamiliar, long, and rather polysyllabic, they may test the key-word method more than words in modern European languages. Hopefully, they will still give you a start and some practice in the method so you can construct keywords of your own for any key Stoic concepts of your choosing.

# CHAPTER 15

# HOW TO FEED
# OUR SOULS UPON
# STOIC TABLES

*"One should always read a text from the same codex, so
that the features of the page on which the particular
segment of text appears become part of one's mnemonic
apparatus. 'Indeed I consider nothing is so useful for
stimulating the memory as these,' Hugh writes."*[1]
Mary Carruthers, *The Book of Memory*

## THE NINE CELLS OF
## YOUR INNER CITADEL

ONE MEMORY METHOD ESPECIALLY POPULAR during the Middle Ages, and still useful today, is to memorize information obtained from books by mentally picturing the actual page of text. This might be one reason some medieval texts were so carefully laid out and so artfully illustrated and decorated, like the beautiful *Book of Kells* mentioned earlier in this book. It also argues for the value of attractive, carefully crafted books today.

And yet there is another very simple way we can tap into the natural powers of visual memory to make written material more memorable, the use of *summary tables* and *charts*, a favorite technique employed in good textbooks. They allow us to condense a lot of information into a relatively small space. I'll provide two such Stoic (and Stoic-inspired) tables in this chapter, the first adapted from the writings of Pierre Hadot, a great historical philosopher of the Stoics, and the second from Albert Ellis, the seminal psychologist who helped found and build cognitive psychotherapy (Rational Emotive Behavior Therapy to be exact) upon the firm foundations of the *Stoa Poikile*.

---

1 Carruthers, 93 (citing a memory treatise of Hugh of St. Victor [1096–1141]).

This first table, adapted from Hadot, illustrates the relationship between the three great Stoic disciplines that correspond to the fundamental powers of the human soul found in Epictetus and expounded in Marcus Aurelius, the disciplines of *judgment, desire,* and *impulse,* and "the three domains of reality: our individual faculty of judgment, universal Nature, and human nature."[2]

| DISCIPLINE OR ACTIVITY | DOMAIN OF REALITY | INNER ATTITUDE |
|---|---|---|
| (1) JUDGMENT | Faculty of Judgment | Objectivity |
| (2) DESIRE | Universal Nature | Consent to Destiny |
| (3) IMPULSE TOWARD ACTION | Human Nature | Justice and altruism |

1. When we exercise our *hegemonikon* to test and *judge* appearances we must seek out the objective truths about our experiences so that our opinions, beliefs, and *judgments* about things and events match up with *external reality.*

2. As we determine what we ought to *desire,* as Epictetus so often advises, we must always ask ourselves the true nature of that thing. Do you desire that things you enjoy should last forever? If so, you are ignoring the very *nature of the universe.* Do you weep or complain when some kind of material loss or hardship comes your way? If so, you have failed to *consent to destiny* and needlessly disturbed yourself.

3. So how are we to live? What kinds of actions are *kathekonta* (as you may recall from our last chapter, appropriate, virtuous ones) for us? If we strive for fleeting externals that we cannot control we forget our human nature, including the fact, which Seneca and Marcus are so fond of repeating, that humans are literally made for each other, to cooperate in the spirit of justice and love.

Hopefully that small table has given us a little bit to chew on. Sometime please sit down with Hadot's *Inner Citadel,* pages 43–47 to enjoy the full feast with him.

Here is one more table to feast your eyes (and memories) upon. I first found versions of this table when I studied Ellis's

---

2 Hadot, 44. (Our table is slightly adapted from the table Hadot presents on that same page. The numbered comments that follow are mine.)

Rational Emotive Therapy (as it was then called) as a psychology undergraduate.

Now, we've briefly mentioned before that acronyms can be a helpful aid to memory. Hopefully you'll recall how we employed "Bachman Turner Overdrive, Tell Everyone U know" (BTOTEU) to help us remember the busybodies, the thankless, the overbearing, the treacherous, the envious, and the unneighborly folk Marcus warned us about. Well, Ellis crafted an acronym that fleshes out Epictetus's fundamental insight of *Handbook* Ch. 5: "People are disturbed not by things, but by the views they take of things," and makes it as easy to understand and remember as ABC (as well as D & E). Let's look at this in terms of a very simple example of emotional upset.

## SEEING SALLY, YOU SELL YOURSELF
## SHORT BY THE SIDEWALK

LET'S SAY YOU SEE YOUR FRIEND SALLY STROLLING BY on the other side of the street. She looks your way, you wave exuberantly, and she continues on her way without a wave or even a smile. What do you do? Perhaps your wave has been deftly transformed to look like you were just patting down your hair as you hope that no one else noticed the slight.[3] How do you feel? Embarrassed perhaps and saddened that you have been shunned? There is nothing unusual here and it would seem to clearly illustrate that old "S-R" psychology. The stimulus (Sally's snub) has triggered your emotional response (embarrassment, sadness, perhaps even anger at Sally, and perhaps a sense of rejection and loneliness as well).

Still, was it really as simple as that? While the 20th-century behavioral psychologists had a good deal of success explaining, predicting, and controlling animals' behaviors with their stimulus-response models, their method often did not work out so well with humans. Something seemed to get in the way.

---

3  Ever done such a thing yourself? These almost reflexive kinds of transformations of movements to avoid embarrassment are called "modifiers" in the language of body language studies.

## EPICTETUS IGNITES
## A COGNITIVE REVOLUTION
## (OVER 1800 YEARS AFTER HIS DEATH)

IN THE 1960S A "COGNITIVE REVOLUTION" TOOK PLACE in psychology when through a series of insights an "O" was added to the old S-R model, yielding S-O-R, where O stands for the organism, the living being, in our case, the human being. Seems we are not really black boxes as the behaviorists had supposed. *Important things go on inside an organism between a stimulus and a response.* In animals this would be *instinct.* Sometimes certain animals could not be trained to consistently display certain behaviors that contradicted their instincts, regardless of stimulus or reward.[4] In humans the intervening factor would be our abilities to *think,* to *evaluate* and to *talk to ourselves* about the various stimuli we encounter through events in the world. After all, not every person reacts the same way to the same events.

In the world of psychotherapy, the greater awareness of the power of human thought or cognition gave rise to "cognitive therapy" in the 1960s, pioneered by psychiatrist Aaron Beck and laid out in his book *Depression: Causes and Treatment* in 1967 followed by his very popular and influential *Cognitive Therapy of Depression* in 1979. He argued that a key component of depression is the way depressed people bring and keep themselves down by consistently thinking in negative ways about *one's self, the world,* and *the future,* what he called the *"cognitive triad of depression."* Further, he argued that by ferreting out and changing such patterns of thinking, depression can sometimes be quite successfully treated.

Shortly before Beck, in the mid-1950s, psychologist Albert Ellis had pioneered his Rational Therapy, later to be called Rational-Emotive Therapy, and finally and quite comprehensively, Rational-Emotive Behavior Therapy (REBT). His most popular and influential early books on the subject included *A Guide to Rational Living,* first

---

4   In an important and humorous example from the early 1960s, after animal trainers used tasty rewards to train a pig to deposit wooden coins in, most appropriately, a piggy bank, it began to drop the coin on the ground, pushing it around with its snout, and flipping it up into the air, never quite making it to the piggy bank. This instinctual porcine behavior called *rooting* became the crucial element of the "O" that got between the trainer's stimulus and the desired response.

published in 1961, and *Reason and Emotion in Psychotherapy* in 1962. Ellis took the new S-O-R model and ran with it for all kinds of mental disorders and also for the kinds of emotional distress those of us without a formal psychiatric diagnosis are still prone to in our daily lives. In fact, I have adapted our Sally example from Ellis.[5] He went further, as well, and boiled down this scenario (and countless others like it) to their simple ABCs. Here's how:

## WHEN I KNOW MY ABCS, IT WON'T MATTER SO MUCH WHAT YOU THINK OF ME

LET "S" (THE STIMULUS) BE "A" (AN *ACTIVATING EVENT*), and let "R" (the response) be "C" (the emotional/behavioral *Consequence*). Getting back now to Sally by the sidewalk, when she passes by (A) and we are embarrassed or sad or angry (C), we tend to act as if "A" caused "C"—but Ellis points out the often-neglected but most important true causal factor. Let the activities of the organism (O) be represented here by "B" (our *Beliefs*). *Sally did not cause us to feel a certain way. We actually did it to ourselves!*

How can we show this? Let's say, for example, that while you walk on all disgruntled, you soon see Sally getting out of her car on your side of the street, and she beams you a smile and calls you over. Oops! That wasn't Sally after all. Are you still sad or mad at her? Or let's say it was Sally. You see her later and she tells you that she just got back from the eye doctor and her eyes were dilated, or she wasn't wearing her contacts, or she just heard some tragic news and was lost in thought. Are you still sad or mad? Hopefully, not!

This is one simple way we can see how our beliefs or cognitive evaluations play a crucial role in determining our emotional reactions. Methods that Ellis, Beck, and other cognitive therapists employ train us to examine the accuracy of our thinking in social situations, since we tend to have habitual initial reactions in the form of "automatic thoughts" that serve to distress us without our full conscious awareness. Adapting such methods to question our first impressions of potentially distressing situations we encounter can go a long way toward alleviating all kinds of emotional

---

5 From his *How to Keep People From Pushing Your Buttons*, if I recall correctly.

distress. (Detect any echoes yet of Epictetus's *Handbook* chapter 1 advice to test and question harsh appearances or impressions [i.e., discipline #1]?)

All right, but Ellis's ABC system of psychotherapy goes much deeper even than this. He goes beyond merely advising us to make sure that our beliefs (B's) accurately reflect activating events (A's). *What if Sally really did snub us?* Must we still become embarrassed, sad, angry, or lonely? More accurately stated, must we still *make ourselves* embarrassed, sad, angry, or lonely? Ellis answers with an emphatic "No!" (Epictetus, of course, would wholeheartedly agree!)

If we became embarrassed, sad, or angry only when we suffered true injustices of various sorts—well, as fallible and imperfect as we all are, we would still go around embarrassed, sad, angry, or lonely a good deal of the time! Further, Ellis notes that when we suffer various slights or ills, insults or injuries, we tend to ruminate and keep thinking about the incidents, stacking one irrational belief upon the other as we talk to ourselves about it. If we feel slighted, we might start questioning our own worth: *Hmmm, didn't so and so also slight me last week?* If we feel angry, we might start cataloging Sally's other faults and work ourselves up against her. We might even realize at some point that we are being a bit unreasonable, but then start to bash ourselves for it: *Oh, I always overreact! What a sad specimen am I!*

So how can we employ this "ABC model" to help ourselves cope with snubbing and with all kinds of situations that might lead to all varieties of emotional distress? Well, this is where "D" and "E" come into play. When we experience some kind of slight or insult that leads us to feeling upset, we need to become aware of our "B's," our beliefs—the kinds of things we are thinking and repeating to ourselves to make ourselves upset. Then we need to bring in the "D," that is, to *dispute* those beliefs, to make ourselves aware of their irrationality and replace them with saner ways of looking at the situation. When we have done so successfully, then "E," the new emotional consequence, will take its place as we become less distressed and better able to get on with our lives. Let's lay this out succinctly for the worst of the two Sally scenarios, the one in which she has really snubbed us:

## THE ABCS OF EMOTIONAL DISTURBANCE
## (AND HEALING)

| A | B | C | D | E |
|---|---|---|---|---|
| **ACTIVAT-ING EVENT** | **BELIEFS** (irrational) | **CONSE-QUENCE** (emotional) | **DISPUTA-TION OF BELIEFS** | **EMOTIONAL CONSE-QUENCE** (new one) |
| Sally actually snubs us | "Other people saw her snub me. They think I must not be important to her" | Embarrassment | "This can happen to anyone and others don't really under-stand the sit-uation. I won't sweat it" | At most very mild chagrin |
| | "I don't rate with her How terrible!" | Sad | "That's her opinion! So what!" | Mild disappoint-ment |
| | "How dare she! How wicked!" | Angry | "That's her problem! I'll pray for her!" | Mild irritation, and concern for Sally |

Now, this understanding of human mental distress and how to alleviate it blossomed in the 1960s and grew into various modes of cognitive-behavioral therapies, among the most successful for treating a variety of mental problems including depression, anxiety, anger, loneliness.

I hope you will forgive this second long, discursive rift on *Hand-book* chapter 5, but it has had such a powerful influence in our modern times, and both Ellis and Beck explicitly acknowledged their debt to our own Epictetus in providing the foundation of their systems of psychotherapy.

In sum, twentieth century psychoanalysts and behaviorists decreed: *"You are disturbed by things!"* The first-century Stoic, Epic-tetus, got it right nearly twenty centuries before when he declared to the contrary: *"You are not disturbed by things, but by your judgments about things!"* A myriad of modern cognitive-behavioral therapy techniques grew from such fundamental insights into how we can rein in disturbing *emotions* by *thinking* more like a Stoic. I hope you will memorize Ellis's ABCs and practice his Stoic alphabet with the *erstwhile* "disturbing things" in your life.

# OUT FROM THE PORCH AND INTO THE WORLD

*"In every discipline artistic theory is of little avail without unremitting exercise, but especially in mnemonics theory is almost valueless unless made good by industry, devotion, toil, and care... In placing images you should exercise every day... So, since a ready memory is a useful thing, you see clearly with what great pains we must strive to acquire so useful a faculty. Once you know its uses you will be able to appreciate this advice."*
Cicero, *Ad Herennium* III, xxiv, 40[1]

*"In ancient philosophical sources the idea of an 'art of living' is primarily associated with the Stoics."*
John Sellars[2]

## NEVER FORGET THE ANCIENT ART OF MEMORY

Y OU'VE HAD PRACTICE APLENTY OF THE ANCIENT art of memory within these pages. Hopefully you've found the experience both useful and memorable. I would like to conclude by making clear that artificial memory prowess, like all virtues, grow easier over time with repeated practice. Aristotle wrote that we become builders by building and harpists by playing the harp. So too do we become memory masters by repeatedly mastering memorization. Further, you may recall that the medieval philosophers and theologians, building on the writings of Cicero, a "fellow traveler" of the Stoics,[3] considered memory an essential,

---

1   Caplan, trans., 225.
2   *The Art of Living: The Stoics on the Nature and Function of Philosophy* (London, UK: Bristol Classical Press, 2009), 55.
3   "Cicero the Fellow Traveler" is the title of his chapter in Ryan Holiday and Stephen Hanselman's *Lives of the Stoics: The Art of Living from Zeno to Marcus Aurelius* (New York, NY: Portfolio/Penguin, 2020).

if not the most important, element of the virtue of prudence or practical wisdom.

We saw too that virtues are *habits* that perfect our powers. If you regularly practice these artificial memory methods, as suggested by the author of the *Ad Herennium* in our opening quotation, they will become second nature to you—and the Stoics, of course, also advise us to live *kata phusin* (according to nature)! With repeated practice, you will find you can easily recall all the specifics of the locations of the memory rooms (and statue) provided in this book, backward, forward, or in any order. And once the locations are mastered, you can fill their contents with any kind of information that is important to you, be it your academic coursework, facts or procedures relevant to your profession, or any area of interest. Indeed, you may find that the powers of your own memory are far more "up to you," and "under your control" than you had ever realized.

Since the publication of *Memorize the Faith!* in 2006, many people have told me or written in reviews that the methods helped them, their children, or their students learn all kinds of things including English, Spanish, Latin, and Chinese vocabulary, and preparation for successful completion of the GRE (Graduate Record Exams), and indeed, even trumpet playing. To date, three people have told me they used the methods to pass their legal bar exams. This could not be more fitting, since the very first example of these methods in the very oldest extant memory book (yes, the *Ad Herennium* again) showed how to use memory images to memorize all the essential details of a prosecutor's summation of a particular murder trial!

In 2012 I was pleasantly surprised to see *Memorize the Faith!* listed among the references in a journal of economics and finances of all places. The article presented an empirical study that demonstrated the power of the mnemonic technique of the method of loci among college students. Among their conclusions: "An advantage of the method of loci technique is its applicability to any discipline, and students who discover the technique in an economics course likely will find it useful in any other course that requires some amount of memorization" (p. 137)—to which I say, "Amen."[4]

---

4  M. Shaughnessy and Mary L. White, "Making Macro Memorable: The Method of Loci Mnemonic Technique in the Economics Classroom," *Journal of Economics and Finance Education* 11, no. 2 (Winter 2012): 131–41.

The Stoics (especially Epictetus and Marcus) never tire of reminding us that we all have our own unique work to do and roles to play in this life. Memory methods like these might help you better act out whatever parts the Playwright has assigned you. So, hopefully you will never forget these memory methods, keeping them always ready at hand, and ever in mind.

## IT'S ALWAYS TIME FOR THE TIMELESS ART OF LIVING

Of course, Stoic lessons are not principles to merely *read about,* or even *memorize,* but things to strive to *live* every day of our lives, never knowing for sure if today should be our last. Hopefully, we've all been inspired to keep developing our knowledge base of Stoic wisdom as a base from which to bring those lessons out from the porch and into the world, as we aspired to a noble happiness through virtuous living, showing God gratitude for the great gift, not only of memory, but of our *prohairesis* by exercising it daily in all matters in accordance with His will, and in loving cooperation with all who share this planet with us during our fast-fleeting time upon earth.

*Χαιρε, Vale,* Farewell.

KEVIN VOST holds a Doctor of Clinical Psychology (Psy.D.) degree from Adler University in Chicago and has taught at schools including the University of Illinois at Springfield and Aquinas College in Nashville, Tennessee. He is the author of over twenty books, including *The Porch and the Cross: Ancient Stoic Wisdom for Modern Christian Living* and *Memorize the Faith! (And Most Anything Else) Using the Methods of the Great Catholic Medieval Memory Masters.*

www.ingramcontent.com/pod-product-compliance
Lightning Source LLC
Chambersburg PA
CBHW031249090426
42742CB00007B/376